# TWENTIETH CENTURY VIEWS

The aim of this series is to present the best in contemporary critical opinion on major authors, providing a twentieth century perspective on their changing status in an era of profound revaluation.

Maynard Mack, *Series Editor*
Yale University

# KATHERINE ANNE PORTER

# KATHERINE ANNE
# PORTER

## A COLLECTION OF CRITICAL ESSAYS

*Edited by*

Robert Penn Warren

Prentice-Hall, Inc.  A SPECTRUM BOOK *Englewood Cliffs, N.J.*

Bib: 40776

*Library of Congress Cataloging in Publication Data*
Main entry under title:

KATHERINE ANNE PORTER: a collection of critical essays.

   (Twentieth century views)   (A Spectrum Book)
   Bibliography: p.
   1.   Porter, Katherine Anne, 1894-      —Criticism
and interpretation—Addresses, essays, lectures.
I.   Warren, Robert Penn (date)
PS3531.0752Z715          813'.5'2          78-21453
   ISBN 0-13-514679-8
   ISBN 0-13-514661-5 pbk.

          10   9   8   7   6   5   4   3   2   1

          PRENTICE-HALL INTERNATIONAL, INC. *(London)*
          PRENTICE-HALL OF AUSTRALIA PTY. LIMITED *(Sydney)*
          PRENTICE-HALL OF CANADA, LTD. *(Toronto)*
          PRENTICE-HALL OF INDIA PRIVATE LIMITED *(New Delhi)*
          PRENTICE-HALL OF JAPAN, INC. *(Tokyo)*
          PRENTICE-HALL OF SOUTHEAST ASIA PTE. LTD. *(Singapore)*
          WHITEHALL BOOKS LIMITED *(Wellington, New Zealand)*

For Eudora Welty

# Contents

# Acknowledgments

The quotation from *The Ship of Fools* (New York: Columbia University Press, 1944), translated by Dr. Edwin H. Zeydel from Sebastian Brant's 15th century *Narrenschiff*, is used by kind permission of Edwina Zeydel Worsley.

Quotation from a Critique of *Ship of Fools* by Wayne Booth, *The Yale Review* (Summer 1962) is used by kind permission of *The Yale Review*. Copyright © 1962 Yale University.

Quotations from "Notes on a Criticism of Thomas Hardy" by Katherine Anne Porter, *Southern Review* VI (1940), are reprinted by permission of William Morris Agency, Inc. on behalf of the author. Copyright © 1940 (renewed) by Katherine Anne Porter.

The quotation from "Gerontion" by T. S. Eliot from *Collected Poems 1909-1962* is used by kind permission of Harcourt Brace Jovanovich, Inc. and Faber and Faber Ltd.

Excerpts from Katherine Anne Porter's "Pale Horse, Pale Rider," "Noon Wine," "The Cracked Looking Glass," "Old Mortality," "The Grave," and "Flowering Judas" are reprinted from *The Collected Stories of Katherine Anne Porter* by permission of Harcourt Brace Jovanovich, Inc. and Jonathan Cape Ltd. Copyright, 1930, 1935, 1936, 1937, 1958, 1963, 1964, 1965 by Katherine Anne Porter.

Excerpts from "Holiday" by Katherine Anne Porter are reprinted by permission of William Morris Agency, Inc. on behalf of the author. Copyright © 1960 by Katherine Anne Porter.

Excerpts from "The Days Before" from the book *The Collected Essays and Occasional Writings of Katherine Anne Porter* by Katherine Anne Porter are reprinted by permission of Delacorte Press/ Seymour Lawrence and Joan Daves. Copyright © 1943, 1952 by Katherine Anne Porter. They were originally published in *Kenyon Review*.

Excerpts from *Ship of Fools* by Katherine Anne Porter are used by permission of Little, Brown and Co. and Martin Secker & Warburg Limited. Copyright © 1962 by Katherine Anne Porter.

*xi*

Excerpts from the Introduction and Preface of the Modern Library Edition of *Flowering Judas and Other Stories* by Katherine Anne Porter are used by kind permission of Random House, Inc.

Quotations from *This Is My Best* by Whit Burnett are used by kind permission of The Dial Press.

# Introduction

*by Robert Penn Warren*

In an essay about Katherine Mansfield, written in 1937, Katherine Anne Porter remarks that the greatest misfortune that can happen to an author is to have interest in the work overwhelmed by interest in the life. Indeed, some writers have apparently disagreed so violently with this view that they have exploited an interest in their lives to the point of frenetic headline grabbing, or even by acts little, or not at all, short of suicidal—when they might better have been meditating their art. But many others, among them some of the most eminent, have agreed wholeheartedly with Miss Porter. Auden has tried to recover and destroy all his letters and has declared that a writer's work should be his only biography. And Faulkner, writing to Malcolm Cowley, once said: "It is my ambition to be, as a private individual, abolished and voided from history, leaving it markless, no refuse save the printed books." And added that his epitaph should be: "He made the books and he died."

The writer may well feel that his true self, without the rag-tag-and-bob-tail of his ordinary life, his follies and his errors, appears, directly or indirectly, only in his works—and certainly many writers Shelley for one, seem most incongruous in that Sunday best of their work when we investigate the day-to-day actualities in contrast. Or to take another paradox, it is odd that the wastrel Robert Greene, who spent more time in the evil company of taverns than by the fireside of the gentlewoman he married and ruined, should have written one of the most beautiful lullabies in the language: "Weep not, my wanton." But man is, in any case, a mixed bag, and literature is written neither by spooks nor pure spirits, and the reader, even the common reader, nourishes an interest in the person who wrote as well as in the thing written, and, naively or professionally, an interest in the connection between the work and the world it arose from. And even Katherine Anne Porter once said that the person who sits down to be a writer must give up hope of privacy. In other

*1*

words, in a deep sense, as well as in any shallow one, writing is self-revelatory. But there is a difference between the inevitable revelation of "personality" in its broadest sense, and the revelation of autobiography.

There was something prophetic in the remark about Katherine Mansfield made long before the accretion of Katherine Anne Porter's own fame and an atmosphere of legend—that of a beautiful woman, wanderer in many lands, witty, restless, fanatically devoted to her art, a charming and accomplished conversationalist, and in the end, after all sorts of poverty, rich and famous. In addition to conversation there were, as she grew more famous, the perennial interviews. But if she was talkative, and sometimes even revelatory, especially on attitudes and points of view, she generally managed to be enigmatic in the end. There are few hard facts available. Some day the people whose business it is to dig for hard facts will have more handy. Meanwhile, Katherine Anne Porter's fiction remains, perhaps, the best source of biography in its deeper sense. In an interview about Mexico called "A Country and Some People I Love," she said that "everything I ever wrote in the way of fiction is based very securely on something in real life," and then proceeded to analyze the story "Flowering Judas" in this respect. Elsewhere—in her journal of 1936 —she declared that all her "experience seems to be simply memory, with continuity, marginal notes, constant revision and comparison of one thing with another. Now and again thousands of memories converge, harmonize, arrange themselves around a central idea in a coherent form, and I write a story." There are thousands of hard facts. We know only a few.

The few hard facts—some not so "hard"—that we do know give us something like this. Though the first Porter came to Pennsylvania in 1720, the founders of the maternal line settled in Virginia in 1648. Somewhere along the way Daniel Boone's brother Jonathan entered the picture, to become one of the writer's great-great-grandfathers. In the Civil War, the family was Confederate to the bone, with the paternal grandparents, Asbury and Catherine Anne Porter, after the defeat, moving to Kyle, Texas, where a few ex-slaves lived with them after the long trek, and where the grandfather died in 1879. The writer's father, Harrison Porter, settled, after marriage, in Indian Creek, where Katherine Anne Porter was born in 1890. A couple of years later, after the death of the mother, the family was back in Kyle, under the domination of the grandmother, whose image looms so large in the stories, and who had a house in town and a farm not too far off, where the family spent the summer. Here in Kyle and on the farm, what, we are told in "Portrait: Old South," had once "been a good old family of solid wealth and property" found haven, long on land and short on cash, but with a room called "the library" containing a collection of wide range and serious cultivation from which the writer got her passion for literature and her education—a writer already at the age of six who had written, illustrated, and sewed together the sheets of a "nobbel" about the "hermit of Halifax Cave." So the child grew up in the shadow of memories, "precocious, nervous, rebellious, unteachable," as she was later to describe herself.

After the death of the grandmother, when the "unteachable" child was eleven, there was moving about, with the child spending some time in convent schools. Few facts are hard here. It is not even known how and why the child was in a Catholic school, the family being, it is reported by some researchers, Methodist. And certainly it is not clear when, and in precisely what sense, Katherine Anne Porter became a Catholic—or even if she formally did. But when she was sixteen the convent walls (of the Ursulines in New Orleans?) did not detain her; she eloped (like the Miranda of "Old Mortality") and after three years got a divorce. A little later she was in Chicago, with a job on a newspaper and carrying on her long, arduous, silent, and greatly fruitful apprenticeship as a writer to the climactic moment when she opened Joyce's *Dubliners.* But, after a period in which she did small parts in the burgeoning movies (this in Chicago), poverty, a breakdown (presumably from tuberculosis), and a hitch on *The Critic* at Fort Worth, she was by 1918 in Denver on the *Rocky Mountain News,* where she fell in love, had the flu, and nearly died (her soldier sweetheart did die), but recovered to find herself with white hair to set off the youthful face and brilliant dark-violet eyes. Denver, with war, disease, and love, is the scene, of course, of "Pale Horse, Pale Rider," which was not to be written until more than twenty years of the characteristic marination in the mix of memory.

During all these years so poor in "hard" facts, there is one hard fact: her sense of vocation as an artist. This she was to call "the basic and absorbing occupation, the line intact of my life, which directs my actions, determines my point of view, profoundly affects my character and personality, my social beliefs and economic status, and the kind of friendships I form." She has, however, pointed out a doubleness in her conception of the role of the artist, holding that the artist is a person who must live with other persons and in society, and cannot escape the consequences of this fact, even though the personal and private role, if necessary to the point of violent dissent, must be preciously guarded. For the arts, she could say long after she had dissented from orthodox Christianity (not merely Catholicism), "do live continuously and they do live by faith...they represent the substance of faith and the only reality. They are what we find when the ruins are cleared away."*

But to return to our meager chronology. During a brief period in New York City, she supported herself by ghost writing, and made the acquaintance of Mexican artists, who persuaded her that their country was where exciting things were to happen. She arrived in Mexico in time for the Obregon revolution. But soon back in Texas, she was writing about Mexico, one product being the story "María Concepción," which ended the long apprenticeship by being published in *Century Magazine*[1] Again in Mexico, she participated in organizing an exhibit of Mexican art and crafts to be sent to the United States (where it was still-born). In New York, still writing stories but publishing few, doing reviews and articles, deeply involving herself in the defense of Sacco and Vanzetti, she finally selected a few stories and published the first little book, *Flowering Judas*, the title story of which is, again, drawn from the Mexican experience. This story, one of the most famous of our time, has its germ in an episode in Mexico, a germ which the author has preserved for us:

> "Flowering Judas" was written between seven o'clock and midnight of a very cold December, 1929, in Brooklyn. The experiences from which it was made occurred several years before, in Mexico, just after the Obregon Revolution.
>
> All the characters and episodes are based on real persons and events, but naturally, as my memory worked upon them and time passed, all assumed different shapes and colors, formed gradually around a central idea, that of self-delusion, the order and meaning of the episodes changed, and became in a word fiction.
>
> The idea first came to me one evening when going to visit the girl I call Laura in the story. I passed the open window of her living room on my way to the door, through the small patio which is one of the scenes in the story. I had a brief glimpse of her sitting with an open book in her lap, but not reading, with a fixed look of pained melancholy and confusion in her face. The fat man I call Braggioni was playing the guitar and singing to her.

*Introduction to *Flowering Judas* (New York: Random House, Inc., Modern Library, 1940.)

[1]For years after this debut into the world of writers published in large national magazines (1922), Katherine Anne Porter offered her work only in "little magazines, such *transition, Hound and Horn,* and *The Southern Review.*

In that glimpse, no more than a flash, I thought I understood, or perceived, for the first time, the desperate complications of her mind and feelings, and I knew a story; perhaps not her true story, not even the real story of the whole situation, but all the same a story that seemed symbolic truth to me. If I had not seen her face at that very moment, I should never have written just this story because I should not have known it to write.[2]

The new volume made a reputation among the discriminating and gained a Guggenheim Fellowship for the author, who immediately returned to Mexico, the country she "loved." But this time, the romance was wearing somewhat thin (partly because of the proximity of Hart Crane and the intrusion of his drunken and homosexual riotousness on her life),[3] and in August of 1931 she found herself on a German ship, bound for Bremerhaven, observing the fellow passengers, and keeping a journal-letter for the novelist Caroline Gordon, which was to be the germ of *Ship of Fools,* published more than thirty years later, meanwhile going through a series of provisional titles. After visiting Germany, and having encounters with some of the boastful monsters who were shortly to aim at seizing Europe, she married a member of the U.S. Foreign Service. In the late middle thirties, she returned alone to America, living in New Orleans, then, after a third marriage, in Baton Rouge. The marriage ended in divorce a few years later and she moved again East.

Despite movement and confusion, to this decade belong some of her most splendid work, "The Circus," *The Old Order,* "Hacienda," "Old Mortality," "Noon Wine" and "Pale Horse, Pale Rider." The next period produced the long story "The Leaning Tower," a creation of indisputable merit, but not in the first rank of her achievement. And in this period, too, work was going on, by fits and starts, on the novel that, known earlier as *Promised Land* and then *No Safe Harbor,* was to become *Ship of Fools.* But in spite of this brooding progression of the novel, and the completion of "Hacienda" and "Pale Horse, Pale Rider" perhaps the most marked achievements of the general period are the results of memories of the early years in the South and Southern Texas. The childhood experiences, the Grandmother, the temper and aura of the Old Order and its inner tensions, as in "Old Mortality," "Noon Wine," and some of the short pieces, are nothing short of masterly, and Miranda, in addition to

---

[2]Whit Burnett, *This is My Best* (New York: Dial Press, 1942).
[3]Returning from Mexico in 1932, Crane committed suicide by jumping overboard.

her personal story of growing up, provides a perfect strategic point from which to command the field, a strategic point that appears again in "Pale Horse, Pale Rider," in which we see the Miranda of the Old Order now emerged into the New and trying to come to grips with it. It is hard to read "Pale Horse, Pale Rider" without thinking of the last lines of "Old Mortality." There, Miranda, returning home to a family funeral, feels herself cut off from the past, from family, from all affections, and promises herself that she will detach herself from the family legend and self-deception, and will find her own "truth." She promises herself this "in her hopefulness, her ignorance."

After the period in Baton Rouge, the collection of three novelettes under the title *Pale Horse, Pale Rider,* appeared, and it was clear that a writer of a high order had to be reckoned with. Soon, in 1944, the reputation of the writer was reinforced by the volume *The Leaning Tower,* containing such pieces as "The Source," "The Circus," "The Old Order," and "The Grave." By this time, too, the rumor was afloat that a novel was in progress, one based on material originally intended for a novelette for the *Pale Horse, Pale Rider* volume. Work had been going on in a fragmentary way from the time of the letter-journal to Caroline Gordon, but the process now was more and more of an obsession. And here it is important to remember that the author, in spite of the scattered appearance of much of her work, has declared that she thought of it all as a unit, and a unit concerned with the down-hill drag of Western civilization.

She worked on the novel in dozens of places—the Yaddo colony for writers and artists at Saratoga Springs near Albany, New York, Colorado, a house she bought in upper New York State, in Manhattan, in this and that university—a page here and a page there, until the middle fifties, when she sought seclusion in the country in Connecticut, near the village of Roxbury, seeing only a few friends and rarely emerging into the world. There momentum gathered, the marination process was drawing to an end, and in a surge of energy the last phase of *Ship of Fools* was soon to be completed.

It was published in the spring of 1961, one of the publishing events of all time, with a $50,000 advertising campaign announced by Little Brown & Company, a great swatch of reviews of lyrical praise, enormous sales and a movie in a high financial bracket. This spectacular success was accompanied, quite naturally, by a sometimes rabid reaction of critical distaste, some samples of which appear in later pages of this collection, along with the record of critical praise. And the debate about *Ship of Fools* still continues.

Meanwhile, as early as 1952, dated from the Rue Jacob in Paris, under the title *The Days Before,* appeared a collection of critical essays, including some personal essays such as "Portrait: Old South" and two pieces on life, "The Necessary Enemy" and "Marriage is Belonging," both of which have bearing on her fiction in general and contradict some of the clichés about it, especially about *Ship of Fools.*

After *Ship of Fools* come *The Collected Stories,* with some additions, including the masterpiece "Holiday, A Christmas Story," and *The Collected Essays and Occasional Writings.* In the fall of 1977 appeared a personal memoir, a small book, an account of the author's involvement in the Sacco-Vanzetti defense—which brings me a recollection that I think merits record. In Boston she was arrested and photographed being escorted by a burley Boston cop to the paddy wagon. A day or two later, after her return to New York from jail and Boston, I remarked to her that I had seen her advertisement in the *Globe* or whatever it was. She said, "Yes, I started out to give 'em a tussle, the best I could." Then musingly, "But one was such a nice young fellow and nice-looking, and then he said to me, 'Aw lady, please come peaceable, I been doing this all day and my feet are killing me.'"

She paused again, then: "What can you do with a nice young fellow like that whose feet hurt? Well—I just went peaceable."

But that book about the Sacco-Vanzetti case will not be the literary end. The massive journals and correspondence remain unpublished. It is, however, saddening to think of the time when they will be published, however much they may enrich the record and broaden our knowledge, sympathies, and understanding.

Since *Ship of Fools,* our subject has lived for a long period in Washington, and more lately on the top floor of a massive but rural apartment complex in College Park, Maryland, the seat of the University to which she has given her literary collection. From this eyrie, until a recent illness, she could look over miles in any direction outward, or into the great depth of memory, where, no doubt, some significant marination proceeds. Or before the illness, she might— famous cook that she is—entertain a few guests with a *cordon bleu* dinner, a memorable wine, and more memorable conversation.

Until lately she still might venture down to give a reading, or visit a university, or attend a meeting of the American Academy and National Institute of Arts and Letters. But for long periods she has cultivated her solitude.

It is a peculiar fact that Katherine Anne Porter has been for generations luminously present, but never, not even with *Ship of Fools,* really at the height of fashion. The work, in general, has had from the beginning distinguished appreciation but that appreciation has never been based on the accidents of the moment, on social or political views, or literary innovation, or newly fashionable liberations of life. If we look back at the first collection, *Flowering Judas,* published at the end of the twenties (a period for which she had never found much good to say, certainly not of Fitzgerald and his school or Gertrude Stein and hers) we find little to remind us of the textbook tags of that time, and as little to place us in the opening grimness of the Depression. If we turn to the triumphant novelettes of the thirties, how little reminds us of the virulent polemics or stylish posturings or self-deceivings or fanatic virtues of that time? It is true that the title story of the volume *The Leaning Tower* has an air of topicality in the attitude toward Germany, but that is certainly one of the weakest items in a volume which contains some masterpieces of the Old Order.

There is a peculiar similarity, among all the dissimilarities, between Porter and Faulkner. They both turned to the past for a significant part of their material, but turned to an informed and moralized, not romanticized, past; and both in the end tell a story of the passing of the Old Order and the birth of a New Order. Both regarded the present as a product of the past, to be understood in that perspective, and both, though repudiating the romance of the past, saw in it certain human values now in jeopardy, most of all in jeopardy the sense of the responsible individual, and at the same time man's loss of his sense of community and sense of basic relation to nature. To return to our beginning, both lived through the twenties and the thirties unreverent before, even inimical to, the shiboleths of the age.

We have referred to the contrast between the Old Order and the New as a theme in Katherine Anne Porter's work, but that is only one aspect of a deeper, more inclusive theme which springs from the candor, the willingness to confront and explore inner tensions, the conviction that reality, the "truth," is never two-dimensional, is found in process not in stasis. All this gives the peculiar vibrance and the peculiar sense of a complex but severely balanced form to all the stories, even those not concerned with the generations or with an over-all society, but with more strictly personal issues. In a story like "Theft" the drama develops from the tension between "world-as-thief" and "self-as-thief," in a rigorous balance of argument subtly unfolding beneath the circumstantial surface of the narrative. In "He," and in "Holiday," the drama develops from the tension between love and compassion, on the one hand, and the gross force of need and life-will on the other. In "María Concepción" the drama lies in a contrast between the code of civilization and the logic of natural impulses. In "Noon Wine" it revolves about the nature of motive and guilt. Did Mr. Thompson really see a knife in the hand of Mr. Hatch? Did he brain the monstrous Hatch to save Mr. Helton's life or to defend the prosperity which Helton had brought him? Or had some other, more mysterious force guided his hand? Poor Mr. Thompson—he can never know and, not being able to live in this nest of ambiguities, must put the shotgun muzzle under his chin.

The dark pit where motives twine and twist is a place well known, of course, to our modernity; it is the milieu of much modern fiction. It is the milieu deeply pondered and scrupulously reported by Katherine Anne Porter. But it is important to see the difference between her treatment of such ideas and that found in writers whom we think of as specifically "modern." For one thing, Katherine Anne Porter never confounds the shadowy and flickering shapes of the psychological situation with vagueness of structure in the fiction itself, or permits the difficulty of making an ethical analysis to justify a confusion of form.

In fact, it may be plausibly argued that the most powerful tension in her work is between the emotional involvements and the detachment, the will to shape and assess relations in experience; and the effect of this is sometimes to make a story look and feel strangely different, unanalyzably different, from the ordinary practice. But there is a more significant difference. A great deal of the current handling of the psychology of motive is a kind of clinical reportage. In two respects the work of Katherine Anne Porter is to be distinguished from this. First, she presumably believes that there is not merely pathology in the world, but evil—Evil with a capital *E*, if you will. Along with the pity and humor of her fiction, there is the rigorous, almost puritanical attempt to make an assessment of experience. Second, she presumably believes in the sanctity of what used to be called the individual soul. She may even go as far as Hawthorne in "Ethan Brand," and elsewhere, in regarding the violation of this sanctity of the soul as the Unpardonable Sin. But those characters who are more than touched (who is not touched?) with evil or fatuity are not deprived of a vital rendering; the ethical judgment is not a judgment abstractly passed on a robot, and the difficulty of judging any human being is not blinked.

If neither the ethical bias in the fiction of our author nor the notion of the sanctity of the individual soul seems, at first glance, modern, let us recall that both are related to an issue which undercuts the clinical and reportorial concerns often passing for modernity. The issue is this: given the modern world of the Technetronic Age and the great power state, on what terms, if any, can the individual survive? The abstractions that eat up the sense of the individual—and have been doing so since before the time of Kierkegaard and his mordant analyses of the modern "public"—call forth her most bitter ironies. Of Braggioni, the "professional lover of humanity" who cannot love a person, she says: "He has the malice, the cleverness, the wickedness, the sharpness of wit, the hardness of heart, stipulated for loving the world profitably." And oh, the beauty here of the word *stipulated!*

The chic phrase is the "crisis of identity," and a consideration of that crisis lies at the heart of this fiction. It lies so near the informing heart, so deep in fact, that it can be missed; for Katherine Anne Porter sees the question in radical terms: ethical responsibility and the sanctity of the individual souls. Without that much, she might argue what would identity mean? It is chic to discuss the crisis of identity, but it is not chic to explore it in terms that could—that, in fact, undercut the chic. One might conceivably state the issue here in theological terms. But there is no need to do so, and it might be irrelevant to the author's view. The logical terms are enough.

To take another approach to the question, there is a more personal aspect to the tension underlying these stories, and, in a sense, *Ship of Fools,* too. The story of Miranda is that of a child, then of a young woman, trying, in the face of the Old Order, and then of a New, to find her own values, to create her own identity. The exact ratio of fact and fiction in Miranda's story, and of autobiography and fiction in the portrait, is something we cannot—and in one sense, the author could not—know. It is not even important for us, or for the author, to know. Clearly, there is a degree of overlap and projection, but, clearly again, there is one important difference between Miranda and her creator. The creator is an artist, and her own rebellions, re-jections, and seekings, as shadowed forth however imperfectly and with whatever distortions, inevitably have some relation to this role in real life. No doubt, the artist, in all periods, is stuck with some sense of difference, of even alienation, no matter how stoutly, or cynically, he may insist on identifying himself with the world around him; and in our world, this alienation of the artist—even the "path-ology" of the artist—is not only an element in his experience but often a basic theme. It is, in one perspective, a theme often implicit in our author's work, in much the same sense that it is a theme of Hawthorne, James, Kafka, or Mann. It is implicit, over and over, and in "Holiday" it finds something close to an explicit statement in this little poem celebrating the artist's doom:

> I loved that silence which means freedom from the constant pressure of other minds and other opinions and other feelings, that freedom to fold up in quiet and go back to my own center, to find out again, for it is always a rediscovery, what kind of creature it is that rules me finally, makes all the decisions no matter who thinks they make them, even I; who little by little takes everything away except the one thing I cannot live without, and who will one day say, "Now I am all you have left—take me." I paused there a good while listening to this muted language which was silence with music in it; I could be moved and touched but not troubled by it, as by the crying of frogs or wind in the trees.

The artist must find the right distance from life, put the right shape or frame on life, and at the same time must render, to a greater or lesser degree, its quality, its urgency.

The tension between involvement and apartness has, in this fic-tion, been peculiarly fruitful, for one reason because of its special presence in the author's consciousness, and for another, because it provides the tension underlying the various individual dramas re-counted. With a simple candor the artist has accepted her role. She knows the deep ambivalences in that role: *the world—life—is a be-loved enemy.*

If, on the one hand, life must be mastered in the dialectic of her forming, on the other, life must be plunged into—or realized as though one had plunged into it and were totally immersed. In all the stories, the dialectic is severe, and in what, at first glance, as in "He," seems casually devised will be found to be the fruit of a deep-set logic. But always, there is the vivid circumstantiality—vivid without being decorative. Braggioni, the fat revolutionist in

"Flowering Judas," "sighs and his leather belt creaks like a saddle girth." When Granny Weatherall lighted the lamps, the "children huddled up to her and breathed like little calves waiting at the bars in the twilight." In "The Old Order," at the annual arrival of the grandmother and family, the "horses jogged in, their bellies jolting and churning, and Grandmother calling out greetings in her feast-day voice."

This is a poetry that shows a deep attachment to the world's body. But it is not a self-indulgent poetry, and its richness is derived from precision—precision of observation and precision of phrase. From, shall we say, the hard intellectuality that veins that love, and that manifests itself elsewhere, and more fundamentally, in the dialectic of form.

As the love of the texture of the world is set against this intellectuality, so the world of feeling is set against the dialectic. Gaiety, humor, and good humor abound here; for instance, the whole first section of "Old Mortality" spills over with it, and even in the last section, as we approach the climax, there are flashes of humor in the encounter with the formidable Cousin Eva.

But gaiety, humor, and good humor represent only one segment of the spectrum of feeling found in this body of work. Think of the heart-wrenching moment, for instance, at the end of "He," when all the tortured complexities of Mrs. Whipple's attitude toward her son are absorbed into a sudden purity of focus. Or the moment in "The Old Order" when Nannie, after the words of the judge who had sold her years ago as "crowbait," make her burst out to her mistress with a sudden awareness of her lifelong condition of being regarded as subhuman. Or in "Holiday," when the mute cripple, who works as a servant in the house of her own parents, shows the narrator the blurred photograph of a fat, smiling baby, and then turns it over to point to the name—her own name—written carefully on the back. Whether it is the bleak purity of emotion in "He," or the name on the back of the blurred photograph, Katherine Anne Porter has the gift of touching the key of feeling. She never exploits this gift, can even disinfect with rigorous observation the most pitiful scene of feeling (as with the crippled beggar in Vera Cruz). Certainly, she never indulges in random emotionality; she knows that the gift must never be abused or it will vanish like fairy gold.

She knows, too, that shifts in feeling are essential if we are to sense the movement of life. A feeling suddenly explodes against the counterpoint of other feelings, other tones, as the pathos of the scene at the hotel room, in the second part of "Old Mortality" bursts against the humor associated with the little girls upon their return to the convent. And always feeling appears against a backdrop of two other factors, the strain of irony that infuses the work (even though the writer knows that the exploitation of irony is as dangerous as that of feeling) and the rigor of form. The writer has some austerity of imagination that gives her a secret access to the spot whence feeling springs. She can deny herself, and her own feelings, and patiently repudiate the temptation to exploit the feeling of the reader, and therefore can, when the moment comes, truly enter into the heart of a character. One hesitates to think what price may have been paid for this priceless gift.

The tensions we find here spring from the author's will to see "all" of a thing. She must try to explore, as it were, the inner resonances and paradoxes of her own situation and her own sensibility. She is willing to try to keep uncorrupted her own consciousness. One feels that for her the act of composition is an act of knowing, and that, for her, knowledge, imaginatively achieved, is, in the end, life. Without it, all the bright texture of the world and experience would be only illusion.

She knows, too, that if one is to try to see "all," one must be willing to see the dark side of the moon. She has a will to face, and face in its full context, what Herman Melville called the great "NO" of life. If a deep stoicism is the underlying attitude of this fiction, it is a stoicism without grimness or arrogance, and though shot through with irony and aware of a merciless evil in the world, yet capable of gaiety, tenderness, and sympathy, and its ethical center is found in those characters who, like Granny Weatherall, have the toughness to survive, but who survive by a loving sense of obligation to others, this sense being in the end, only a full affirmation of the life-sense, a joy in strength. And we should not forget the penniless woodcarver who drowns trying to save a peculiarly pampered and idiotic bull dog.

Like all strong art, this work is, paradoxically, both a question asked of life and a celebration of life; and the author knows in her bones that the more corrosive the question asked, the more powerful may be the celebration.

To return to Faulkner, there is another point of similarity that demands remark, and that helps us to determine a relation between

*Ship of Fools* and the main body of Katherine Anne Porter's work. The works of Faulkner, with a few exceptions, are parts of a single saga—a saga, in many ways, closely related to that of Leatherstocking of Cooper, especially in the variations on the theme of civilization and nature and civilization and individual integrity. In Faulkner, as in Cooper, certain books come clear in their structure only when seen as part of the saga, or of the *oeuvre*. At first glance, the work of Katherine Anne Porter seems more scattered, the individual items more self-contained. We see the stories of the Old Order, those of the New (including "Pale Horse, Pale Rider," and the recent book on the Sacco-Vanzetti case). Then there are the Mexican stories and sketches, the odd stories (sometimes of the highest quality, like "Holiday" and "The Downward Path"), then the European fictions, including the novel *Ship of Fools*.

It has been said that the work of a major poet, in contrast to that of a minor poet, possesses, among other things, a centrality of coherence —or even obsession. The more we steadily inspect the work of Katherine Anne Porter, the more we see the inner coherence—the work as a deeply imaginative confrontation of a sensibility of genius with the *chiaroscuro* of modern civilization, in which it is often hard to tell light from dark. It becomes clearer and clearer what she meant when she said that she had been working on one central plan "to understand the logic of this majestic and terrible failure of the life of man in the Western World."

And this theme, or a central aspect of it, is the dissident individual facing the modern world with all its depersonalizing forces—not in terms of virtues of the past (although such are recognized), but in terms of human possibility. Thus, if the work looks back on moral awareness and social achievement in the past, and sees less than automatic progress in the present, it still recognizes a ground, however shadowy, of human reality and therefore happiness, even in the face of the disaster toward which Western civilization often seems to be plunging. But if such a ground exists it will not be automatic— not arranged by sociological schemes, but by the cultivation of integrity and clear sight in individuals, one by one. And here we face the question put long back by many philosophers and historians, but more recently by Zbigniew Brzezinski: "Can the institutions of political democracy be adapted to the new conditions [what Brzezinski calls the Technetronic Age] sufficiently quickly to meet the crises, yet without debasing their democratic character?" That is, he continues: "Can the individual and science co-exist?" Here Brzezinski asks the question in general and abstract terms, but it is the same question that concerns our author in terms of imagination and ethics. Both ask on what terms the responsible individual can exist in the world now promised us.

What we find in the fiction is a hatred of all things that would prize anything above the awareness of human virtue: that is the essence of the author's dissent and the core of the despair that sometimes appears for our future—a future in which the responsible individual disappears into a "nothing," a mere member of what Kierkegaard called a "public," a "kind of gigantic something, an abstract and deserted void which is everything but nothing."

Before turning to *Ship of Fools,* let us remind ourselves that the work was originally conceived as a novellette to be published with "Old Mortality," "Noon Wine," and "Pale Horse, Pale Rider," and try to see how, as a fourth, it would have had thematic relation with the previous three. The first is about the dialectic of history and the slipperiness of truth. "Noon Wine," among other things, shows us, in Hatch, Evil masked as law, and, in Mr. Thompson, a man torn to death between truth and a lie, doomed in his incorrigible habit of day dreaming (pulling the cord of the churn when we first see him, he has the attitude of a man driving a fine spanking horse) and self-delusion which can no longer support him. "Pale Horse, Pale Rider" shows a child of the Old Order, who had promised herself to know the truth about herself, caught in personal grief and the social horror (including the self-deceptions) of the New Order. It may be only a step from the New Order to totalitarianism, the total de-humanization which Nazism and Communism shared, and which we may eventually share, in one way or another.

I have not been trying here to give thematic tags to these pieces, but to indicate some line of psychological continuity that might help us see our author's novel as part of an *oeuvre* instead of a separate thing, a kind of "sport." To give another indication of the interpenetration of the novel and other work, we may remember that the thirty-year period between the letter-diary of the voyage to the publication date, the work on the novel had been deeply interwoven with almost the entire body of work on which Katherine Anne Porter's reputation is based. The novel is not a summarizing footnote. It is part of a long process.

If *Ship of Fools* has a relation to the stories of the volume *Pale Horse, Pale Rider,* it has in structure and tone a much more obvious relation to the earlier novelette "Hacienda" (1934), which in her general disillusionment with the land she had loved and had held such revolutionary hopes for, and in the sardonic and ironic portrayals of the Soviet film-makers, the aristocratic master of the hacienda and his lesbian wife, the corrupt American business man, the homosexual director, and the drunken musician, might be termed "Hacienda of Fools." But this was a work which admirers of Katherine Anne Porter had generously accepted, or ignored, just as some, bemused by charm of style or moments of warmth and sympathy, had chosen to ignore the iron substructure of many of the stories.

I have dwelt on these earlier works (to which I might have added a number of the stories) merely to express my surprise that certain critics and readers who had accepted these earlier works were shocked by *Ship of Fools,* which continued themes consistently developed in earlier pieces. We can find a provisional answer, perhaps, in the sweeping claim to truth made in the new title, and the author's note —it claims universality[4] while earlier work merely offered her "Misanthropism" (to use the word often applied to *Ship of Fools*) and her stoicism piecemeal.

More than one critic has complained that there are not enough nonfools on the Ship, not realizing that Brant (like Katherine Anne Porter) denies true wisdom to men, and in a sense, saw all men struggling in their foolishness. To put it in contemporary terms, there are not enough "good" people on the Ship to give a true picture to the modern optimistic and progressive mind—which is a little bit like attacking Thoreau for saying that most men live lives of quiet desperation, ignoring divorce statistics, dodging war news in the papers, or denying the existence of Harlem. The complaint may be

---

[4]In Sebastian Brant's *Narrenshiff* (Ship of Fools) of 1494, the original work in a tradition of which Katherine Anne Porter's novel is the latest, Brant says that even Plato, Pythagoras, and Socrates had their "foolishness," and

> "...could not picture bright and clear
> The real wonders dwelling here,
> Wherefore the Lord did say,
> 'Their knowledge, skill, I'll toss away
> And wisdom too, who here are wise.
> Let children have it—this their prize.'"

(*The Ship of Fools,* translated by Edwin H. Zeydel [New York; Columbia University Press, 1944] ).

And of the fools, Brant himself says, "I'm number one" on the ship. If Katherine Anne Porter does not claim to be "number one," she at least describes herself as a passenger.

made, to use Solotaroff's word, that the novel is "saturnine." There are, indeed, good people and good deeds on the *Vera,* but they are admittedly few—the ship's doctor is a good man and the death of the poor artist-peasant Echegaray in trying to save the bulldog from drowning is a good deed. But many a masterpiece has survived "saturnine" doctrine, without even such meagre exceptions offered —*Troilus and Cressida, Measure for Measure, Jude the Obscure, Madame Bovary,* and *Vanity Fair,* not to mention numerous works by Celine, Dostoevski, Balzac, Maupassant, Zola, and Evelyn Waugh, to reach out for a few examples. And we may remember that Mrs. Hawthorne took to her bed for three days after being subjected to *The Scarlet Letter* and that Emerson, after reading the book, could only exclaim "Ghastly, Ghastly!"

Another objection offered to *Ship of Fools* is that love comes in for a shabby deal. Love does, indeed, come in for a shabby deal in the cases analyzed, but it is not denied. It can be argued that the Mexican bride and groom who float ghostlike in their bliss across the general scene will come to the same end as the rest. But it is equally possible that theirs is "the kind of love that makes real marriage," to quote from our author's essay "Marriage is Belonging," in which she adds "there is more of it in the world than you might think" even if "it demands of all who enter into it the two most difficult achievements possible: that each must be honest with himself, and faithful to another." Not that we see much of this. We see only the present self-contained bliss against which failures are measured, or, as with the ship's doctor, the discovery too late of the nature of love. The snake-pit writhing and frog-coldness of sexuality elsewhere in *Ship of Fools* is in contrast to the concept of love and to the figures of true love who, wordlessly, appear on deck. There is another example of love that seems "true," that of Herr Freytag, who, in spite of his perfect Aryan handsomeness, has a Jewish wife back home, a beautiful and cultivated young woman to whom he appears devoted, but whom he, caught in the tangle of antisemitism and drunkenness of the fiesta, would have betrayed had not excessive alcohol intervened. Which is not to say that his love has not been wounded. All depends on what he makes of his experience. Which we never know.

This leads to another objection to the novel, one best put by Solotaroff: that Herr Lowenthal, the only Jewish passenger, who naturally sits alone and not at the Captain's table with all the good Germans, is presented as a most antipathetic character, "the stage Jew of the modern literary tradition whom other writers of sensibility (among them T.S. Eliot) have dragged out of the ghetto to represent the vulgar and menacing dislocation of the traditional order." Lowenthal is unattractive enough, God knows, and bigoted enough; but let us suppose that the only Jew aboard had been a learned and holy man or a charming and cultivated lady (as Frau Freytag is described as being), what would be the effect? If the isolated one is attractive the growing shadow of the gas oven takes on a special pathos; but I should submit that such a pathos would be spurious. The question is not that an *attractive* person may be gassed, but that a person, however *unattractive,* may be gassed. Nor is it a question of the ratio of attractive and unattractive persons. The question is not one of attractiveness at all—but, of justice or humanity—a factor which Herr Lowenthal's characteristics, as he moves toward his fate, may be taken to underscore.

All of this is not to say that *Ship of Fools* is flawless, even if I, personally, find no fault with its general scheme, and even if, by and large, the writing is of an excellence not admitted by all readers. There is, indeed, a thematic blur, not fatal but disturbing, between the idea of the decay of Western civilization (a very complex idea indeed) and the distastefulness of the German portraits, even those that point most directly toward Nazism. And one reason is that *Nazism is as much a symptom as a cause.* What about Russia—and even some aspects of our country? Furthermore, the idea of the "collusion" of decent people with evil, on which the author has commented in talking about her book, is sometimes quite overwhelmed by what I regard as her irrelevant anti-Germanism. The Germans were not the only people willing to give a downward push to the Western world— even some Americans who pass for liberals, equating liberalism with lack of standards and lack of individuality, have quite unconsciously given a healthy heave-ho downward. But to return to our Germans. In fact, from the self-righteousness and self-satisfaction of the Captain's table or even from some species of our "liberal" one may turn with relief to the complete amorality of the Spanish contingent.

But one last comment on the credit side of the ledger. Approaching the end of the book, for the first time one wonders how it can end. The episodic structure of action seems to imply that it may simply have to stop quite arbitrarily when the ship docks. But it doesn't simply stop. Or if it stops, in terms of action, it does so with a last little scene which alters and humanizes the book. Among the ship's band, now putting their instruments away after "Tannenbaum", amid the rattle of the landing-gear, is "a gangling boy, who looked as if he had never had enough to eat in his life, nor a kind word from anybody, and did not know what he was going to do next." He stands there staring with blinded eyes, "his mouth quivering while he shook the spit out of his trumpet, repeating to himself, just above a whisper, 'Gruss Gott, Gruss Gott,' as if the town were a human being, a good and dear trusted friend who had come a long way to welcome him."

And we see this poor little derelict of the Master Race caught in his nameless and grateful emotion, and knowing, as we do, something of the fate that hangs over him, poor victim of history, the emotional center of gravity of the book shifts, and we are keenly aware, for the first time, of the general human lot.

For what it is worth, I'll submit the fact that the first time I picked up a copy of *Ship of Fools*, I expected to read through breakfast and then go to work. I did not lay the book aside until after midnight, and not once did I worry about method, point of view, thematic concerns, or the relation of this or that episode to the entire work. I was simply caught in its toils. And so with my last reading. Of how many books since World War II can one say that?

# A Country
# and Some People I Love

*An Interview by Hank Lopez with*
*Katherine Anne Porter*

Katherine Anne Porter, whose *Ship of Fools* and many other stories have ensured her place as one of the great American writers of this century, talked with Mr. Lopez in Mexico City last December. This summer, at home in Washington, she reviewed and filled in the text of their tape-recorded conversation. Mr. Lopez, director of the Inter-American Cultural Institute, describes Miss Porter as a "fascinating conversationalist—volatile, pensive, profoundly humorous, and almost disturbingly speculative."

INTERVIEWER: Miss Porter, since our magazine, *Dialogos,* is based here in Mexico, we're especially interested in your Mexican experiences. You once stated that "I went to Mexico because I felt I had business there, and there I found friends and ideas that were sympathetic to me. That was my milieu." Could you expand on that?

KATHERINE ANNE PORTER: Yes, of course. But let me approach it this way: I've had a great deal of difficulty persuading young people who want a beginning in what they call a literary career, that we don't begin it as a literary career. We begin as a vocation, and you don't go looking for material. They're always looking for material. And that was the reason why at this time in my generation all the young people were heading off for Europe. It was all this going into exile and being so romantic about it and turning their backs on this "crass American civilization" and so on. Well, I am an old North American. My people came to Virginia in 1648, so we have had time to become acclimatized. I can leave it when I please and go back when I please. Everybody was hastening off for Europe, at that time, and going into exile. It seemed so provincial and so ignorant, and they were ignorant and provincial.

INTERVIEWER: You're talking about those young writers that went to Europe?

KAP: I'm talking about that whole gang that headed out and made Jimmy's Bar famous, you remember. The so-called Hemingway period in Paris. Well, I had no business in Paris. I was born in Texas, brought up there partly, and my father brought me to Mexico when I was ten years old. We were not rich people, we were Southern people who had many losses in that famous war and we didn't travel to Europe because we weren't able to. Our foreign travel was Mexico, which we loved, and so when the time came for me to travel and get out in the great world a bit, I just came back to Mexico.

INTERVIEWER: Had you met some Mexicans in New York? Were they your entrée?

KAP: I was brought up in San Antonio, which was always full of Mexicans really in exile — since Diaz was overthrown. It was a revolutionary city, so, we kind of kept up with things in Mexico. But in New York almost the first people I ran into were all these charming young Mexican artists, and Adolfo Best-Maugard was among them. He died a few days ago; was a lifelong friend of mine from that day to this. And there was a wonderful lad — he called himself Tata Nacho. He's still living — he was at Adolfo's funeral the other day. He was playing the piano in a Greenwich Village cabaret to make his living, and he was a great revolutionary. I was living in Greenwich Village, too, and we got to be friends. I was thinking of going to Spain. But they told me, "Don't go to Spain. Nothing has happened there for four hundred years. In Mexico something wonderful is going to happen. Why don't you go to Mexico?" We talked it over and I finally decided I would. I headed down for Mexico in December 1920.

INTERVIEWER: Just about the time of the Obregon Revolution.

KAP: Yes, just a few days, just a little while after he came into the City.

INTERVIEWER: How did you come down here then? Train? Boat?

KAP: Very simple. Train. I went out all by myself, and this crowd of Obregon revolutionists stayed in Greenwich Village.

INTERVIEWER: I call that courage.

KAP: When you're young you don't know that you have courage. It never occurred to me I was doing anything unusual at all. When I got on the Mexican train, the whole roof was covered with soldiers and rifles and young women with charcoal braziers and babies, you know. So I said to this man who spoke to me, "What's going on, what's happening?" And he said, "Well, we're having a little revolution down here." I thought this was interesting, kind of exhilarating, you know.

INTERVIEWER: Were there many other Americans on the train with you?

KAP: Two others, two men. They didn't seem to think it was so strange for a young American girl to be traveling by herself. The worst thing was that the coffee gave out. But we did get to Mexico City perfectly safely.

INTERVIEWER: Did you have trouble adjusting to the revolutionary turbulence of Mexico?

KAP: Not at all. I went and looked for a room, and I got a very nice one on 20 Calle Eliseo. I had the ballroom on the third floor, absolutely open, no glass in the windows, no furniture, and I went to the National Pawnshop and bought furniture, an old desk, a bed, and a couple of chairs. I was absolutely comfortable with that. Then Adolfo Best-Maugard sent me to Manuel Gamio and Jorge Enciso, who were then young, extremely learned, attractive young men.

INTERVIEWER: Were they engaged in the Revolution?

KAP: No, they were sympathetic, but they were not active. They were, after all, already in the National Museum, in archaeology and that sort of thing. They were altogether pleasant to me, gave me all kinds of advice, introduced me to a few revolutionaries, and sort of handed me around.

### The Dissenting Party

INTERVIEWER: When one reads "Flowering Judas" one can't escape the conclusion that you yourself were rather actively engaged in the Revolution.

KAP: Yes, I was.

INTERVIEWER: Can you tell us about that?

KAP: I didn't do it on purpose. I just got drawn in because I was interested, I always used to say that if I were English I would be the Loyal Opposition. I am always the Loyal Opposition. *I'm the dissenting party, by nature.* My father was a real old-fashioned conservative stubborn Jeffersonian Democrat in the most absolute tradition that you can imagine, and he rejoiced when the Russian Empire fell because he said that nothing could be worse — it must be a change for the better. Well, that's the way he felt about Mexico at that time.

INTERVIEWER: So you had a predisposition yourself in favor of the Revolution?

KAP: Yes, I did. I was involved in that atmosphere. I was drawn into it like the girl who took messages to people living in dark alleys. I was really like that girl.

INTERVIEWER: I rather suspected.

KAP: But I'm not the girl entirely. I'm not the girl the young Zapata captain tried to take off of the horse one day. That was Mary Doherty. She's still here.

INTERVIEWER: Now that you mention some specific characters, was "María Concepcion" based on some actual event or some specific person?

KAP: I would tell you as an absolute rule that has never been broken yet, that *everything I ever wrote in the way of fiction is based very securely on something real in life.* In the case of "Flowering Judas" it was just exactly this: There was a man (you would know his name if I mentioned it, but I rolled four or five objectionable characters into that one man) who was showing Mary a little attention. Now Mary was one of those virtuous, intact, straitlaced Irish Catholic girls. Paul Rosenfeld once said that the Irish were born with the fear of sex even before Christianity. Well, this fat revolutionist got in the habit of dropping by with his guitar and singing to Mary. Goodness knows, nothing could be more innocent. But you know, she wasn't sure of him; so one day she asked me to come over and sit with her because so-and-so was going to come in the evening and sing a little bit and talk. She lived alone in a small apartment. The way I described the place was exactly as it was. There was the little round fountain, and what we call a flowering judas tree in full bloom over it. As I passed the open window, I saw this girl sitting like this, you see, and a man over there singing. Well, all of a sudden, I thought, "That girl doesn't know how to take care of herself."

INTERVIEWER: And so you undertook to help her.

KAP: I decided I could stand guard or something. Baby-sit, you might say. As I came in this fellow gave me kind of a sidelong look, but I sat down and sat and sat and finally outsat him. I think that's a universal international situation, don't you? But it just had its special flavor and color for being where it was and the time it was and the kind of man he was. You know this thing stuck in my mind and stuck in my mind, the whole situation. So that story is made of a great complex of things that really happened. But not all at once or to the same people. I had come in all fresh and wide-eyed and taking in everything, and suddenly I began separating the villains from the heroes, don't you see.

INTERVIEWER: I gather from the story that there were some presumed heroes who weren't all that heroic.

KAP: They certainly were not. The fighting heroes nearly all went out when their war was won. You know the trouble with every movement, every revolution, is that the people who do the work and do the fighting and bloodshedding and the dying, quite simply are not the people who run the thing afterwards. It's a phenomenon that exists everywhere. And it was happening here in Mexico, but you know they didn't quite get away with it. I never heard of a revolution more successful than this one was.

INTERVIEWER: The Mexicans would say is...

KAP: Yes, *is, is.* But I saw things as they were, *then,* and everybody said, "You mustn't say this, you mustn't say that because, you know, it's..." And I said, "It's absurd to pretend that all these people are good and brave, when this man is distinctly trying to undercut his own people." This wicked sort of man had got his own intrigues, and I couldn't see where I was obliged to say that he was a hero when he wasn't. Even as "propaganda" this was no good. You know it's not true that wickedness is more interesting than goodness. I don't find it so, but I do find it compelling because it is so often unrecognized, it so often gets away with its murder for the reason that no one has had the courage to oppose it; or perhaps they sympathize with it secretly.

## Dug Out of the Earth

INTERVIEWER: I am just wondering if the Mexico of that time offered a more authentic reason for writing than Europe?

KAP: In retrospect? Why yes, of course. But it would depend so much on the person. It certainly offered more to *me* because I was not running from anything. I wasn't living in exile. I just came to Mexico because it seemed the natural place for me to come after meeting my young friends in New York. When I got here, a little *chamaco* (is that a nice word now?)—named Covarrubias, Miguel Covarrubias—was a great favorite of mine. I have caricatures he made of me when he was fifteen. I took his first caricatures to New York and showed them to Frank Crowninshield and editors on *Vanity Fair* and places like that. And they brought him to New York and he had a tremendous career there. By the time he was nineteen years old he was the most famous caricaturist in the United States.

INTERVIEWER: Now that you've mentioned Covarrubias, you said the other day at the North American-Mexican Institute that you had some role in arranging for that Mexican exhibit that first went to the United States. Would you tell us about that?

KAP: We, myself and the Mexican artists and archaeologists in Mexico, were all passionately interested in the Indian and Mexican popular arts, not the bourgeois arts of the mid-ninteenth century which I find very interesting now. Of course, the Pre-Columbian things hadn't been discovered—what we were interested in was the whole history of the Indian art from the beginning, things they had dug out of the earth in buried cities. It was Adolfo Best-Maugard who headed the whole thing. He was in a way the intellect of the crowd, the really conscious person who had a plan. It was he who suggested to the President that he needed me as the North American representative and organizer and subsequently appointed me formally. I was to go back to the United States and get the galleries lined up for the show. The plan was to have an enormous traveling show, the first that had ever been sent out of Mexico.

INTERVIEWER: What went into this Exhibit?

KAP: It was a grand idea. It had eighty thousand objects of the most beautiful work that was ever made in Mexico. We had the most beautiful statues. We even hauled this enormous Chac Mool around—then known as the Mayan Bacchus. It was a tremendous idea and the whole thing was done by very young people—I was almost the oldest person in the crowd. I was twenty-seven. Adolfo Best-Maugard was twenty-eight. But Covarrubias, who developed into a perfect genius of discrimination and selection, was about fifteen; and Lozano and Merida, the young painters, they ran around twenty-one or twenty-two. All of us taking advice from Jorge Enciso and Manuel Gamio in the National Museum. We collected it in about six months, and I did the monograph in about the same time.

Then I went on back to the United States to see if I couldn't get galleries, and I couldn't get any. I tried the Corcoran in Washington, the Anderson in New York, and in St. Louis and Chicago, and in all cases they wouldn't let us have the gallery—because the political pressure had been put on. The U.S. government did not allow the show to come into the country because it was "political propaganda" and the government hadn't recognized Obregon's government. I could tell you one of the most appalling stories about our active enemies who really stopped us.

You can't imagine the number of powerful men who were determined that the government was not going to be recognized. And they attacked that show, they wouldn't let us take it into the country. Finally somebody said if we'd bring it to California they would see that we got it going. So we took it up there, a great trainload of specimens, but we were stopped at the border. They said we couldn't go through unless we declared it as a commercial enterprise and paid duty.

INTERVIEWER: That must have been heartbreaking.

KAP: Yes, this is what we were up against. It was the hardest thing that ever happened to us. They kept us on a siding for nearly two months. We tried everything in the world. But you know you can't fight international politics, at least we couldn't. So there was a dealer who came and said that he would buy the whole show.

INTERVIEWER: A Los Angeles merchant?

KAP: Yes, he bought it. And so we had this great show that made the most enormous hit. All the tremendous interest in Mexican art in the United States stemmed from that. People poured into that place from all over the country and they bought all of these beautiful things. It was scattered all over the world. And so we were all in simple despair. I just threw up my hands and quit. Xavier Guerrero, Covarrubias, Best-Maugard, Tito Turnbull the photographer (the working team), we were all separated and scattered by that time, off in different places, trying to salvage the pieces. All of us really heartbroken. Honestly we were emotional about it.

INTERVIEWER: Did you ever write about this incident?

KAP: Not immediately. I just put it aside, and thought, "That's a defeat if ever I saw one."

INTERVIEWER: You saw parts of the Exhibition later?

KAP: Yes, in 1952, which was exactly thirty years after our disaster in Los Angeles. I was one of the representatives of North American literature to the International Festival of the Arts in Paris in 1952. Just after the exhibit began, my good friend and French translator, Marcelle Sibon, said to me, "Do you know that the Mexican exhibit here is the best thing in the show? Why don't you go to see it?" And I said, "I've seen a Mexican show, Marcelle, I don't want to see another." I was still as bitter as gall that politicians could have been allowed to do so much destruction, so much damage; that internal politics, and oil and finance could ruin art... was just to me horrible. Then she said to me one day, "I never saw you behave like this before; I don't understand it. You're just missing something."

I did finally go by myself; and oh, they had it laid out in the most marvelous way. I walked into that great hall with the great dome over it, and there was our show. Re-collected from all over the world. It's incredible, isn't it? And this is the strange thing— everybody on the committee was still alive then and everybody had worked on it again except me. They hadn't invited me again because I had gone into such a rampage the first time.

INTERVIEWER: Had anything been added?

KAP: Yes, they had gone into the Pre-Columbian things, brought us right up to the Diego Rivera thing which happened immediately after. And I must say it was the least interesting of all the things there, because I never (after sort of being hoodwinked by that particular school of art) appraised Diego quite the same way. Before I was finished I didn't like his character—he was a treacherous man and a dishonest artist. When I was there I used to go and grind paints for Rivera over at his place. Everybody did—it was the thing to do—go and grind paint for Rivera. I knew all of the people around Rivera—Siquieros, Tina Modotti, and Dr. Atl—all the young artists and would-be artists.

### Haunted and Bedeviled

INTERVIEWER: You have visited Mexico many times since your first visit here in the twenties. How do you feel about the intellectual and cultural climate of Mexico today?

KAP: I always thought it was good and do now. You know I am an artist and I am really not an intellectual, but I feel the atmosphere of the living arts, and I think I know intellect when I meet it; I've always had a very comfortable feeling here. I like the way people talk, the way they are not afraid of talking about the serious things of life, at least the things that appear serious to me. There are certain atmospheres in the United States where there seem to be airless little ghettos, full of people who live in tight knots trying to run things, making a cartel of the arts. There doesn't seem to be that kind of competition here in Mexico, as if the arts and literature were an arena or a gladiatorial contest or something of the sort.

INTERVIEWER: Recently here in Mexico there was a conference at Chichén Itźa of writers and artists. What do you think of that kind of conference?

KAP: I think it's just nonsense.

INTERVIEWER: For what reason?

KAP: Because—when I left to go to Europe in 1931 they had established in the United States a dreadful thing called writers' conferences, in which they were trying to teach young people to write. They'd have these cut-and-dried sessions, and I just think they are death-dealing. The French writers used to have a summer session in the abbey of Pontigny, in Burgundy, where they used to meet once a year—the men of letters. They would simply spend a season together in which they talked, discussed, associated, reminisced...

INTERVIEWER: Without any formal structure?

KAP: Without much formal structure, just enough to hold the thing together. I think that artists and such people associate by nature, they're birds of a feather. But these conferences to "teach" writers to write—absurd.

INTERVIEWER: You know, we haven't had a chance yet to talk about *Ship of Fools* at any great length. I've wondered how you decided upon the structure.

KAP: I didn't, really. Do you remember the little set of three short novels, "Noon Wine," "Old Mortality," and "Pale Horse, Pale Rider"? When I signed a contract for those stories I had had them in mind for years. Then all of a sudden, it's like an egg forming, they were ready to go. So I went to see my publisher and said I'm ready now to make those stories that we were talking about. They gave me a contract for four short novels and so I took my little notes and papers and went up to the country and sat down in a little inn and wrote the first one in seven days—"Old Mortality." I wrote the second one, "Noon Wine," in another seven days. And then I was interrupted, as usual, you know. People came and caught up with me and I had to jump up and run to another place. I went to New Orleans and sat down and wrote "Pale Horse, Pale Rider" in nine days. It was nearly six months later.

And then I came to the really tough one, which I called *Ship of Fools,* based on my voyage from Veracruz to Bremerhaven, my first voyage to Europe. Would you believe it wouldn't accommodate itself. I couldn't do it in 25,000 words. And I said I'm not going to do anything more. This is my limit. I'm a short-story writer, and if I can't say what I've got to say in 25,000 words, I won't begin. And this kept haunting me and bedeviled me and I kept writing and taking notes and thinking about it—how to get this into 25,000 words. And it would not. It just obstinately would not. I finally just kept writing and writing. Years passed and I'd go back and add some more and then I'd worry about this thing. I couldn't get rid of it. It had to be written and I had to find a way to write it. And I couldn't, because I was obstinate, you see. I would not write a novel. They'd been after me to write a novel for years. I kept telling them, "I will not—you have to leave me alone. This is my way of working and I am not going to do anything to change it." It was partly obstinacy, partly professional pride, partly the fact that I thought I knew what I could do and what I couldn't do. And I had to work it out. It took me years and years. I'd go back and add again, and I'd go back over it, and little by little it shaped itself in my mind. But I was doing so many things, you see, I was teaching and lecturing and I published three other books. I also did some translating and was very tired most of my time. And finally I thought I must begin and it's going to be maybe not a novel, but a long, long story. I simply sat down in the middle of July or August. I think it was 1942.

I recall writing "Flowering Judas" in that same frame of mind. It was a cold January evening about seven o'clock when I started. And I was out on the corner just after midnight dropping it in the mailbox to send it to Lincoln Kirstein, who was running the *Hound and Horn.* And he published it.

INTERVIEWER: You wrote that story in five hours, then.

KAP: Five hours. And just corrected a little with a pen. And that's the way with this novel. I just sat down and started it. And all of a sudden my mind cleared. In about six weeks I wrote the first forty-eight pages of that novel. And then I was interrupted. A terrible domestic crisis—I had something practical in my life I had to do, and I stopped writing for a little while. From then on, and for years and years, I was separated from that book sometimes as much as five years. And sometimes I was interrupted in the middle of a paragraph with all kinds of things. You know how life is. I've never had any protection or margin, nor any buffer between me and the economic grimness of life. So I would leave it in the middle of a paragraph and maybe not get back to it for months. I said once upon a time, "This story has been cracked and mended in a hundred places. And does it show?" And someone said, "If you hadn't told me I wouldn't have known it wasn't one piece." Well, it was one piece in my mind. But getting it down on paper was the hardest thing I ever did in my life.

## Ship of Fools: *The Finish*

KAP: Finally I said I'm going to finish this if I die for it. And I did finish. I took three months off and went up to Cape Ann and sat there just the way I sat in the inn when I was doing the short novels. I said to the people, "Now, don't let anybody come near that door. Give me my breakfast at eight o'clock in the morning. I will leave the room for an hour for the maid to do it up, and otherwise I'll come out when I get hungry." Well, they left me

alone, and I finished it. It took me three months. It took me another month to do the proofreading, but it was over. I think it was
from '42 to '62, just twenty years almost to the month. They keep
saying, "Why did you take so long?" They stand over you in the
United States, and breathe down your collar while you are working. They say, "Why don't you finish that book," as if you had
promised to turn one out every year. And I just say to them,
"Look here, this is my life and my work and you keep out of it.
When I have a book I will be glad to have it published." You
know, they don't understand anything. They invade. They have
as much right to do that as they have to break into other peoples'
houses, but they don't understand that either.

INTERVIEWER: There's talk of the movie version they are going to
do. Have they started on this?

KAP: Oh, they've done it. They're going to bring it out, I think in
January or February. And they tell me they've absolutely changed
it; you couldn't recognize it to save your life. Everything I did—
the whole point of my book—has been completely put aside, I
am told by friends who saw a preview.

INTERVIEWER: Speaking about movies, you had a movie experience
yourself, didn't you?

KAP: Oh, dear Lord, do you know about that? It's the funniest
thing—the most curious thing. Oh, dear, I cannot say it. Well,
they used to think I had good legs and feet! I never could see it
myself, but I couldn't help but be pleased. There was a little man
here. His name was Roberto Turnbull, and he came and asked me
if I would pose for the legs and feet in a little comedy he was going
to make about a young man who was working in a half-cellar and
fell in love with the legs and feet of a girl passing by the narrow
window above. The whole story was his pursuit of the upper part
of this girl.

It was just about as silly as anything could get, I expect. But,
you know, it was fun. They made me seventeen pairs of the most
beautiful shoes you ever saw, everything from red and gold bro-
cade to the most exquisite black satins and colored shoes and
beautiful suede—oh, lovely shoes. And these beautiful thin stock-
ings. I said, "Oh, I'll settle for that." Of course, I wore them in
the picture, you see. That was what they were made for. I went to
see it later. It was really very funny. From the knees up was played
by an extremely beautiful girl and I felt that her feet and legs

were quite as good as mine and certainly her hands were just perfect, exquisite. I never had good hands. And so they finally got us together. But there was some embarrassment. The camera wasn't quite good enough at that time and they never did get my legs matched to that Mexican actress. But where did you hear of it?

INTERVIEWER: I don't remember, I heard this years ago.

KAP: Yes, and do you know something? Several years later I met a Mexican artist who gave me that dead-fish-eye look in the face and then his gaze wandered on down past my knees to my feet and he said, "Oh, I know you, I know you, I remember you now." I never did ask him why.

### All Ages, Sorts, and Sizes

INTERVIEWER: You make those Revolutionary days sound amusing as well as exciting.

KAP: Yes, they were lovely. But we also knew what the tragedies were. Many of my friends died in that time, and some of them just threw their lives away as if they were throwing off an old hat. They did it so well though. After all, Felipe Carillo was lined up against a cemetery wall with fifteen of his cabinet members, three of his brothers, I believe. Death was there among us all the time. Every kind of tragedy, and the most incredible criminality, international criminality. But the young can't be crushed by it. They have to live. Even with all those problems, it was a very good time. I remember saying this to poor Hart Crane. He came down here a long time after, and I tried to take care of him. He said once he wished he had come to Mexico in the first place, when I first told him about it, that he would have done better than to go to Paris. "Here I feel that life is real, people really live and die here. In Paris," he said, "they were just cutting paper dollies."

INTERVIEWER: I believe you yourself said that you felt Scott Fitzgerald was writing about people who were of no importance.

KAP: I did. And I still think so. Somebody said I shouldn't feel like that, that everybody was important. Well, that's just one of the fallacies of the world. That's one of the things we say when we think we're being democratic. Eighty per cent of the people of this world, as Ford Madox Ford said, are stuff to fill graves with. The rest are the ones that make it go round. We might as well face that. I was in New York at the time they were having those tea dances and Scott Fitzgerald's romantic dreams about all the collegiate boys and girls dancing in the afternoons of false romance and luxury, and the low sweet fever of love. That sort of thing. And I simply couldn't stand it because I couldn't stand the society of those people. I ran like a deer every time I got near them. And poor Hart, he came here and said they were just cutting paper dollies. Poor man, what a terrible time we had with him. He was doomed I think. His parasites let him commit suicide. He made such a good show and they had no lives of their own, so they lived vicariously by his, you know. And that of course is the unpardonable sin.

INTERVIEWER: Who of this newer generation of writers do you like most?

KAP: I never got the habit of thinking in generations of writers: my living favorites are of all ages, and degrees of reputation. We have always with us the professional promoters of the trade of writing, who appear to choose their candidates by lot, who drum up a new school of writing every five years or so, and while raising their new group they try to destroy the older ones. This is not necessary at all, there is room for all, but just the same I too have my choices, every one very dear to me—all ages, sorts, and sizes. I leave out the spectacularly famous (except Eudora Welty), but here are the names of writers whom I found for myself and chose from the first work of theirs I read, with no advice from anybody, and disregarding then as I do now the commercial reviewers. I want to tell you there are some good ones in this list, and I'll bet you never heard of some of them; we have some big-time rotters who are getting all the foreign and most of the national publicity.

Peter Taylor is one of the best writers we have—do you know him? He has published three books, and the latest one, *Miss Leonora When Last Seen*, is a collection of splendid short stories. Then Eudora...

INTERVIEWER: I remember *The Ponder Heart*...

KAP: Yes, but *A Curtain of Green*, *The Wide Net*, and *The Golden Apples* have her finest stories. Do you know J. F. Powers, a great short-story writer whose latest book is a fine novel, *Morte d'Urban*? He has been for a good while a superb artist, so at last one of our prize-giving organizations got round to giving Mr. Powers an award, and high time, too. Flannery O'Connor, who died lately, was greatly gifted, a dreadful loss to us all. Glenway Wescott and Caroline Gordon are two such different kinds of writers it seems strange to put their names in one sentence. But they are both quietly geniuses, good working artists who have yet to publish a bad piece of work; as with all the writers I admire so much, I read everything they publish with pleasure, and I have my favorite works, too. Wescott's *The Pilgrim Hawk,* a masterpiece; and Caroline Gordon's *None Shall Look Back*—the best novel I know set in the South during the Civil War. It is a grand book, and I am amazed to learn that it has been allowed to go out of print. ...

It's that kind of neglect that sometimes disheartens me about—not American writing, that is safe and sound in some good hands—but American publishing and debasement of American taste. I don't suppose I could like an artist—not only writers, any kind of artist—if I didn't like and respect his work. In fact, I can't separate anybody from his words and acts, but especially this is true with artists.

INTERVIEWER: You know, when I read "Noon Wine" I had a feeling that Flannery O'Connor was very heavily influenced by you.

KAP: She said she was. But I cannot see it. William Humphrey, who has just published a brilliant novel, *The Ordways,* is the only writer I know who ever said in print that his writing and his style and his feeling about writing have been influenced by me. I have read carefully everything he has published, and I cannot see a trace of my influence to save my neck. But if he wants to say I influenced him, I'm very flattered, for I do so like what he writes. There is young Walter Clemons, who has a first book of short stories, *The Poison Tree*—he is not well known, but he will be. You watch him. Another good beginner is George Garrett.

It is probably my own personal preference in forms, but every one of these writers are also first-rate short-story writers; in fact, with one or two exceptions, I prefer their short stories to their novels, but their novels are among the best being written too. We are being sluiced at present with a plague of filth in words and in acts, almost unbelievable abominations, a love of foulness for its own sake, with not a trace of wit or low comedy to clear the fetid air. There is a crowd with headquarters in New York that is gulping down the wretched stuff spilled by William Burroughs and Norman Mailer and John Hawkes—the sort of revolting upchuck that makes the old or Paris-days Henry Miller's work look like plain, rather tepid, but clean and well-boiled tripe. There is a stylish sort of mob promoting these writers, a clique apparently determined to have an Establishment such as their colleagues run in London. It's perfect nonsense, but it can be sinister nonsense, too.

## The Unclobbered

KAP: Also it is very hostile to the West and, above all, to the South. They read us out of the party ever so often; they never tire of trying to prove that we don't really exist, but they haven't been able to make it stick, so far. New, gifted, unclobbered heads keep bobbling up from all points of the distant horizons, and they can never know from what direction they may come. Truly, the South and the West and other faraway places have made and are making American literature. We are in the direct, legitimate line; we are people based in English as our mother tongue, and we do not abuse it or misuse it, and when we speak a word, we know what it means. These others haven fallen into a curious kind of argot, more or less originating in New York, a deadly mixture of academic, guttersnipe, gangster, fake-Yiddish, and dull old worn-out dirty words—an appalling bankruptcy in language, as if they hate English and are trying to destroy it along with all other living things they touch.

But I have named my candidates for a living American literature, only a prime few of many whose work I love and treasure; they cannot be destroyed and they will keep coming on, decade by decade, one at a time—never in a group, never with a school, never the fashionable pet of a little cartel, never in fact anyone but himself, an artist—no two alike.

We can afford to be patient.

# Katherine Anne Porter
# Personally

## by Glenway Wescott

The only real voyage is not an approach to landscapes
but a viewing of the universe with the eyes of a hundred
other people.

MARCEL PROUST

Having had the pleasure of lifelong friendship with Miss Porter,
I find it irksome to call her "Miss Porter." It has been mainly a
comradeship of the literary life, and on that account perhaps, in conversation and in correspondence, I often address her as "Porter." A
host of her fellow writers and others speak of her and to her as
"Katherine Anne," with or without a basis of intimacy. Somewhat
like Jane Austen, or like Colette, she has an unassuming sort of
celebrity that invites or at least inspires friendliness. Let me now
also take the fond informal tone, to celebrate the publication of her
novel *Ship of Fools,* twenty years in the making.

First, some facts: She was born on May 15, 1890, in Texas, in "soft
backland farming country, full of fruits and flowers and birds," on
the banks of a branch of the Colorado River denominated Indian
Creek, small and clear, unimportant but unforgettable. She went to
a convent school, perhaps more than one, and was an uneven student: A in history and composition and other subjects having to do
with literature, but, she admits, "D in everything else, including
deportment, which sometimes went down to E and stopped there."

She spent an important part of her girlhood in New Orleans, and
afterward lived in New York City and in Mexico City and in Paris
and in Baton Rouge, Louisiana, and in more recent years, in upper

New York State and in southern California and in Connecticut and in Washington, D.C. Prior to *Ship of Fools,* she published five short novels or nouvelles, and approximately twenty short stories (my count), and several dozen essays and criticisms and historical studies; quality always instead of quantity. She is an incomparable letter writer, sparkling, poignant, and abundant, and a famous conversationalist.

Now let me try to describe her, as to her physical presence and personality. Like many women accustomed to being loved, she dreads and disapproves of photographers, although in fact usually she has lent herself well to their techniques, and they have been on her side. I remember one of her diatribes, some years ago, against a photographer and an interviewer sent by one of the news weeklies, who, she said, had caught her unawares and committed a misrepresentation of her. In the photograph in question when it appeared she looked (to me) like Marie Antoinette young, her hair perfectly coifed and powdered-looking, playing her typewriter as though it were a spinet. And it amazed me to note how skillfully she had been able to simplify the record of her life for the interviewer also.

She has in fact a lovely face, of the utmost distinction in the Southern way; moonflower-pale, never sunburned, perhaps not burnable. She is a small woman, with a fine figure still; sometimes very slender, sometimes not. Her eyes are large, dark, and lustrous, and they are apt to give one fond glances, or teasing merry looks, or occasionally great flashes of conviction or indignation. Her voice is sweet, a little velvety or husky. In recent years she has familiarized a great number of appreciative fellow Americans with it, by means of reading and speaking engagements, and phonograph recordings.

I remember hearing her read her finest nouvelle, "Noon Wine," one summer afternoon in 1940, at a time of cruel setbacks in her personal life, in a little auditorium on the campus of Olivet College planted with oak trees. It was hot and the windows stood open. The oak trees were full of bluejays, and they were trying to shout her down. Were they muses in bird form, I remember humorously asking myself, inspiring her to cease publicly performing old work, to start writing something new? (In fact it was later that year that she began *Ship of Fools,* then temporarily entitled *No Safe Harbor.*)

She must have had a bout of bronchitis that spring or summer; she almost whispered the great tale, breathing a little hollowly, with an uneasy frayed sound now and then. Certainly there were not as many decibels in her voice as in the outcry of the jays. Nevertheless, her every tone carried; her every syllable was full of meaning and easy to understand, just as it is in print.

Certainly not muses, she protested years later, when I had written her a reminiscent letter about our brief sojourn together on that campus: "Jays are the furies, never trust them, never be deceived by them."

They congregated on the hilltop in Connecticut where she then lived, "thieving and raiding and gluttonizing everything in sight," depriving even the squirrels of their peanuts, and of course driving away from the seed table "all the little sweet birds" that she especially wanted to feed and save.

Characteristically, she had in mind a certain hierarchy of the bird world, poetical but perhaps not just. One day she looked up and discovered hawks hovering over the wooded-lot and the meadow, closer and closer, and it came over her with dismay that by drawing the small birds together she was simply facilitating matters for the predators. That was the underlying theme of "Flowering Judas," the story that made her reputation in 1930, a theme of intense concern to her all her life: involuntary or at least unintentional betrayal.

But, she wrote, the songbirds of Connecticut "were skilled and quick, and we know that they can make common cause and chase a hawk away; we have seen that together, have we not? And in some way, I cannot hate a hawk; it is a noble kind of bird who has to hunt for living food in order to live; his risks and privations are great. But the jay! there is no excuse for his existence, there should be a bounty on every ugly hammerhead of that species!"

Throughout human history hawks have been thought godlike, or at least comparable to the greatest men of action, our heroes, our lords and masters. In this letter Katherine Anne seemed to make some identification of the small birds with men and women of letters and of the arts, a somewhat more modern fancy. In a later letter she referred once more to *Cyanocitta cristata*, the middle-sized hammerhead ones, as emblematic of certain intrusive parasitic persons who devote themselves to writers, perhaps to her more than the average. "They are as rapacious and hard to fight off as the bluejays," but, she boasted, "I have developed a great severity of rejection that I did not know I was capable of. We were all brought up on the Christian and noble idea that we have no right to deny our lives and substance to anyone who seems to need either or both. Never was a fonder delusion." And then with characteristic love of justice, even in the midst of irritation, she reminded herself that, to some extent, life and substance had been contributed to her by certain persons in her day; how had those persons known that she was a songbird? Are there, for human beings also, what ornithologists call "field marks"?

One of her "field marks," I think, is a profound, inward, hidden way of working; not just thoughtfully, methodically, as perhaps prose writers ought to be able to work, as indeed in her case the finished product suggests that she may have done. "I spend my life thinking about technique, method, style," she once told me. "The only time I do not think of them at all is when I am writing."

...Literary critics and historians have often remarked the mighty contributions of the female sex to literature, far and wide and always. For the most part those who have done the contributing have been spinsters, nuns, courtesans, invalids, a little exempt from the more distracting, exhausting aspects of womanhood as such. Katherine Anne, throughout her youth and middle age, led a maximum life, concomitantly with her perfect, even perfectionist story writing. As I have remarked, she seems to like to simplify a part of the record of her existence for any sort of questioner. In fact, except for essentially private matters of love and marriage and ill-health and economics, it really has been simple. And therefore I (and other friends), instead of concentrating on ascertaining all the realities, the dates and the names and the locations and so on, have always interested ourselves in what might be called story material about her, somehow more characteristic than her mere biography.

For example, when she was a girl somewhere in the South, she had to spend months and months in a sanitarium with a grave pulmonary illness, diagnosed as one of the baffling, uncommon forms of tuberculosis. She was too ill to have visitors. Letters also evidently were over-stimulating and exhausting. Even books seemed not good for her; her reading had to be rationed, just a few pages at a time. Then it was discovered that the intense restlessness of her bright eyes gazing at the ceiling, examining and re-examining the furniture, staring at the solitude, gave her a temperature. Her doctor therefore prescribed that a restful green baize cloth be placed over her face for an hour or two every morning and every afternoon, as one covers the cage of a canary when one doesn't want it to sing. I feel convinced that if anything of the sort were done to me I should give up the ghost, on account of the auto-suggestion and the discouragement. Not Katherine Anne! That was only the beginning of a lifetime of delicate health and indomitable strength.

All this balance of physiology in her case, strong constitution, poor health, has mystified those who care for her. Perhaps the physicians whom she happened on here and there—"the pulse-takers, the stethoscope-wielders, the order-givers," as she has called them— have been mystifiers in some measure. One of them, in upstate New York, told her that her trouble was all a matter of allergies, and when she inquired, "What allergies?" his answer was, "You're allergic to the air you breathe."

Another, in California, she wrote me, "set out to change my chemistry, which made him say tst, tst, after a very thorough going-over, and he aims to supply all my lacks and to suppress all my internal enemies. There is about the whole project something so blithely Californian that I cannot but fall in with it."

Still another, a young one in Connecticut, pleased her by practicing "real materia medica," and not saying anything at all about her state of mind or her nervous condition. She has always objected to having strangers, even specialists, fussing around in her psychology, comparing them to the most disrespectful, disrupting type of cleaning woman. "They mess the place up; they don't know where things belong, or what goes with what."

One year at Christmastime, when she had been felled for ten days by some form of influenza and had been taking one of the sulfa drugs, she got up out of bed, though in mortal weakness; took a look at herself: prettily dressed, with "her hair in a curl or two," with an expression on her face which she could not quite make out, "distinctly remote, disengaged, full of mental reservations"; and then in a longish letter undertook to make clear to me her whole view of life. But it was unclarifiable, inexplicable, she had to admit, even to herself as she was living it, "because its truth or falseness cannot be known until the end."

Therefore, instead, she concluded that letter with an account of the medicines she had been taking: "a fantastic row of apothecary's powders, pills, and potions, all of them in the most poisonously brilliant colors, amethyst and sapphire and emerald and purple, each with its own mission of soothing or elevating the spirits, calming the heart or stimulating it, loosening the phlegm and tightening the nerves, stopping the cough and lowering the fever.

"As for the sulfa, I have had to take a tablet every four hours for two nights and two days, and never once did my mind fail to wake me at the right hour, on the hour, like a little radio station. Once I slept stubbornly, and was waked finally by a sharp rapping at my door. It was four in the morning; the whole house was asleep and quiet. I sat up in bed, knowing Who had done it."

It is hard to read this slight incident rightly, with its capitalized Who, suggestive of the commissioning of Mozart's never-finished Requiem by Whoever that was, a being never seen again, and of other such myths. But, stop and think, if that rapper at Katherine Anne's door at four in the morning had been Death, He would have stayed his hand and let her sleep and skip the sulfa. That was in 1943; it is pleasant to think that the greater part of *Ship of Fools* was written on time borrowed from Him.

No doubt about it, there are warring forces in Katherine Anne. Is it that her physique wearies of having to house a spirit so strenuous and emotional, and now and then tries to expel it or to snuff it out? Or is it instinctive in her soul to keep punishing her body for not being superhuman, for not being ideal, for not being immortal? Neither has ever exactly prevailed over the other; both have been invincible. Nothing has come of the great dichotomy; or, to be exact, literature has come of it.

"Every force of instinct and every psychic evil in us," she once wrote, "fight the mind as their mortal enemy; but in this as in everything else I have known from the beginning which side I am on, and I am perfectly willing to abide by my first choice until death; indeed I can't do otherwise. For death it must be in the end, so far as the flesh is concerned; but what lives on afterward can be honorable." To wit, twenty-six works of fiction of different lengths, honorable and (I am sure) durable; and more to come.

She lived in Mexico for a good while when she was young, and a number of the men who revolutionized that intense and artistic though primitive nation were her friends. In 1922 she brought the first exhibition of Mexican-Indian folk art north of the border, but only as far north as Los Angeles. One of the revolutionaries wrote a song about her, "La Nortena," which, I have heard tell, has become a folk song; little companies of young singers, mariachis, like boy scouts in a dream, sing it in the streets. I understand that another lady also lays claim to it. Be that as it may, "Flowering Judas" softly resounds with music of that kind, strummingly accompanied and perhaps mortally seductive.

Some years later in Paris she wrote another Mexican tale, a nouvelle in memoir form, "Hacienda." It is a rarity in her lifework in that it is all a clef; mainly a portrait of the great Russian film maker, Eisenstein, with others of note, helpers and hinderers of his work in

Mexico, clustered around. It has a singularity of style also, somehow an outdoor style, leafy and tendrilous, seeming to weave itself into a fabric without her usual touch; soft breeze sentences, with a warmth and animation unlike her earlier writing.

Certainly it points toward *Ship of Fools.* For some mysterious reason, perhaps nothing but the timing in her life, her recollection of Mexico evidently has lapsed less for her, subsided less, than that of other places she has lived. "Flowering Judas" had an odd, almost painful dreaminess, with only present-time verbs; and in the first twenty pages of *Ship of Fools,* when the passengers are assembling and waiting to sail, as in "a little purgatory between land and sea," the half-Indian world seems to reach out after them, overstimu-latingly, and it haunts the entire volume, across the ocean, though its subject matter is mainly German and American.

In another way the latest of her nouvelles, "The Leaning Tower," must also have served as a study for the future greater undertaking; a tale of Berlin on the eve of the Nazi revolution, when in fact Kathe-rine Anne spent a winter there, and saw the dangerousness of the Germans, and understood how risky it was to fear them or, on the other hand, to be too simply prejudiced against them. Doubtless also, while writing it, during World War II, she was aware of the aesthetic pitfall of propagandizing in any sense, with the excitement of the time. She holds her breath in it.

Now to turn to another area of the legendry of Katherine Anne's life, which she has not perpetuated in any of her fiction.—Someone, years ago, used to say that at an early age she had been in the movies as a Mack Sennett bathing girl, along with Gloria Swanson and Mabel Normand et al. Certainly she was as good-looking as they, whether or not she could have performed as funnily. For some rea-son I never quite like to question or cross-question her about things; but I once ventured to do so about this. It was a matter of journalism, she explained, not show business. Commissioned to write an article for some newspaper or magazine she pretended briefly to be a comedienne for the sake of the realistic detail and local color.

Not so long ago she had a try at earning her living by script writ-ing. Her first Hollywood assignment was not so much to write as to be attached in an Egeria-like or muse-like capacity to a famous producer, now dead. For a while this amused her; at least she sent back to the Eastern seaboard amusing reports of it. "One or the other of us," she reported—he had another salaried writer also at his beck and call, perhaps more than one—"tosses a tiny shred of an idea at him. He seizes it out of the air and without stopping for breath constructs a whole scene. He then asks us what we think of it, and as we open our mouths to answer, he says, 'It's a wonderful scene. Now what else have you got in mind?' And the thing is repeated; sometimes we just sit there for two hours." What he had in mind, or perhaps I should say, in the works, was a film about Queen Elizabeth I.

Presently she began to feel like "a fox with his leg in a trap," gnawing away at it; and by the end of the thirteen-week stint contracted for in the first place she had persuaded her famous man that she was not the inspirer he needed. A part of their maladjustment, she sensed, was the fact that he was a Christian Scientist, whereas she had been brought up a Roman Catholic. During the thirteen weeks he had seemed deeply disapproving of the large salary that he or his studio had been paying her; but suddenly, she wrote, when she was on her way, he "began to worry about my future. What on earth was I going to do now? where was I going? did I have any money? I was happy to be able to tell him that I was relatively rich and wasn't going anywhere."

In fact she was relatively poor; apparently they had been paying her in Confederate money or fool's gold or something. Not seeing any other solution for her practical problems just then, she transferred her talents to another studio, where she was put to work on a film about Madame Sans-Gene.

All her life Katherine Anne has been bewitched by the hope of ceasing to be homeless, of settling somewhere and getting her books and manuscripts and notebooks out of storage and within reach somehow, on shelves and in filing cabinets and in ring-binders. With the evanescent Western money she bought a small segment of mountain for a building site, but could not keep it. One day as she sat peacefully writing in a rented ranch cabin in the Mojave Desert a Western wind arose and tore out a window frame over her desk and slightly fractured her skull; once more, the Furies! But, never forget, the Furies sometimes are on the side of the angels. She did not properly belong out West, at least not then.

In subsequent years, a good deal of the time, at intervals, she has had to depend on the universities and colleges for her livelihood. As a rule, at the beginning of her various stints or bouts on campuses, she has been persuaded by the literature-loving educators who have arranged things, or she has persuaded herself, that not much actual pedagogy would be required of her. Usually, however, they seem to have got the harness on her in some way. I remember a letter from a very great university indeed, in the Middle West, specifying her teaching schedule: only five hours a week actually behind the microphone in the classroom (so specified in her contract) and only about eighty term papers to be read and graded. But she also had to examine the manuscripts of the more creative young persons on campus and to advise them in hour-long sessions; about fourteen of these a week. Also once a week she had to give a spontaneous hour-long lecture to some special class or group or club. It may be that no trained and experienced professional would find this schedule at all onerous or unfair. To Katherine Anne, as a mature woman of genius in delicate health, perhaps somewhat proud and euphoric, with so much creative work of her own not only in mind but partly on paper, and covered by publishers' contracts, it seemed hard; and all too often her university engagements were terminated by illness.

As the quantity of my quotations will have suggested to you, I have been rereading my precious file of long letters from her, and another set addressed to Monroe Wheeler, about two hundred in all. She and I made friends in Paris in 1932 and began our correspondence upon my return to this country in the autumn of 1933, and it has been continuous ever since. Yes, yes, probably she should have repressed or restrained this long-distance friendliness somewhat, in order to produce more for publication. But as I peruse her letters, now that much of the circumstantial detail in them has ceased to be of interest, and therefore the main elements and outlines of her mind and her life appear more impressively, as it were a range of hills which the autumn has stripped of leaves, I am struck by something about them that may have conditioned her, even benefited her, in her art of fiction.

It is that they are extraordinarily, uniquely subjective: self-judging and explanatory and disciplinary, and self-defending, with matchless detail and finesse in all these mirrorings of the heart and the mind, shifting and shining, and, in a way, hypnotizing. Whereas in fiction she has been free from herself. In fiction she has maintained a maximum impersonality, a disengagement from any sort of autobiographical point of view, a distinctness between her own ego, her sensitiveness and compulsions and illusions, and those of all the alter egos that she writes about, and an abstention from fantasy and lyricism and rhetoric, of which most novelists, indeed even many journalists and historians, are incapable.

It is almost startling to compare her with other famous twentieth-century women in this respect: Virginia Woolf! Colette! Even reticent and rather cold writers such as Maugham have made use of their shyness, exercised their self-consciousness, almost as a convention or a technique. As for the writing of our more extreme, compendious, sociological novelists, it is a sort of concavity, which almost teases one to deduce what they themselves are, convexly; rather like the shapes of ancient Pompeians in the awful layers of ashes from Vesuvius.

Katherine Anne is not like that at all. The objectivity of her narrative art, if I may apply to her Coleridge's famous formula (only Shakespeare really filled the bill, *he* thought), is a matter of sending herself out of herself; of thinking herself into "the thoughts and feelings of beings in circumstances wholly and strangely different" from her own: *hic labor, hoc opus.*

I believe that her vast self-expressive and confidential first-person communication to her friends, freshly inspired or provoked each time, swiftly produced on the typewriter, and not rewritten, scarcely reread, has served to purify her mind of a good deal of that pride and willfulness and narcissism and excitability by which the life-work of most modern fiction writers has often been beclouded, enfeebled, blemished. Of course her letter writing must have shortened her working days and used up incalculable energy, thus reducing the amount of her production of the more public forms of literature.

In the earliest of her nouvelles, "Old Mortality," a Northerner may mind the extremely regional feeling, the patriotism of the South, which is a group subjectivity. But even this is so much less soft and heady and spicy than the accounts that other fiction writers have given us of that important part of the world, its premises, its problems, that it seems almost bitter, like a medicine, like a lesson. At the end of it the protagonist, Miranda, realizes how much of her girlhood she has spent "peering in wonder" at other people's notions of the past, "like a child at a magic-lantern show," and resolves to close her mind stubbornly to all such secondhand remembrance, spiritual predigestion.

In "Pale Horse, Pale Rider," and in later stories featuring that same somewhat autobiographical Miranda—the best of which is perhaps "The Grave," an episode of almost mystical childhood, having to do with the closeness and connectedness of life and death, womb and tomb (as in medieval religious imagery)—all is self-possessed and responsible, thoughtful and indeed philosophical. What I call her impersonality applies even to the painting of her own portrait, when it is fictitious. And apparently the saving thoughtfulness, the mastery of her mind over every sort of old ideal and dark prejudice and grievance and self-flattery, takes place at the time that she stores things away in her memory, for future use; not just according to her formal intellect and her sense of story pattern when she begins to work. Again, we may see in this something of her classic practical womanly temperament, housewifeliness! Subject matter that she deems worth keeping she simply folds up a little, scales down a little, and deflates and dehydrates, with applications of sense of humor, sense of proportion, sense of justice, as it were against moth and worm and mildew and dust.

It pleases me to recall a conversation that I had with Katherine Anne while she was writing "Pale Horse, Pale Rider" and was having trouble with a passage in it toward the end in which Miranda, desperately ill, almost dead, was to see heaven. She told me that she herself, at the end of World War I, had experienced this part of what she had created this heroine to experience and to make manifest; and because, no doubt, it really was heaven, she found herself unable to re-see it with her lively, healthy eyes.

This conversation took place in a valley in New Jersey where I used to live, which has been turned into a water reservoir, gone forever! It was springtime; the sward or sod was moss green, strewn with little blue shadows under the trees half in leaf; the vistas upstream and downstream were dim, Bavarian-looking; and there were some soprano voices within earshot, I have forgotten whose voices. With characteristic, somewhat superficial helpfulness I proposed to my dear friend and rival, "Why not at that point just write a page about your inability to recede, your impotence to write? Eternal curtain, blinding, effulgence! Let each one of your readers fill in the kind of heaven that his particular life has prepared him to go to, when his turn comes.

"What else is heaven, anyway?" I went on, where angels fear to tread. "What can it be, empirically, but the indescribable; the defeat of literature; the end of empiricism?"

To my amusement and perhaps regret, mingled with a little vanity, Katherine Anne did not take to this suggestion. She let "Pale Horse" go for another year, and turned to other work. She said au revoir to her New York and New Jersey friends and went to live for a while in Louisiana, perhaps waiting all that time to re-see Miranda's heaven.

In due course, *Pale Horse, Pale Rider* appeared in book form, in 1939, with the vision worth a year's waiting: "thinned to a fine radiance, spread like a great fan, and curved out into a curved rainbow." What comes before this also is extraordinary: Miranda at death's door with the influenza of 1918, afraid of her doctor just because he is her doctor, in charge of her death, and because he is a German doctor, and because it is 1918. Even in Denver, Colorado, where that story is set, a world war does not let one even die at peace. I think that, if the years to come winnow literary wheat from chaff as the past has done, this story may be valued as a unique record of that modern curse and ailment, horror of the German, which lapsed during the twenties, then began again; also as a prelude to *Ship of Fools.*

Miranda's beginning to recover from influenza is another extraordinary page; just less and less bitterness of pus in the naturally sweet flesh, up and up toward life, with a wink of consciousness more and more often. The strangest return, the way of the solitary ego, the opposite of the great legend—the Orpheus in Miranda keeping the Eurydice in her alive not by looking away but precisely by contemplating what was happening every instant.

Of the three nouvelles in that volume, indeed, of the five that she has published thus far, "Noon Wine" is the one that I love best. I may say, parenthetically, that Katherine Anne herself objects to my use of the borrowed French word and its several cognates, also European in origin, novella, novelle, and novelette. I see her point. As to vocabulary, whatever the problem, she is a purist, and it is vulgar to trick out one's writing about writing with this and that imported feather (though Poe did so a good deal). Also, as the author, to date, of only one large-scale work of fiction in an era when "novel," is the word to conjure with, and when most of the praise as well as the pay goes to bulky productions, she must be glad of any nuance of one's criticism which will remind the reader that "Pale Horse, Pale Rider" and "Old Mortality" and "Noon Wine" and "Hacienda" and "The Leaning Tower" are major works. They are, indeed; and doubtless it took more skill, more time, and more creative strength to keep them to the length that, as it seemed to her (and as it seems to me), inspiration and subject matter in those five cases called for than it would have taken to amplify them, to swell them up with self-generating detail, to spin them out with extra passages of introductoriness and didacticism and suspense and consequences, as large-scale novelists ordinarily do.

But for my part, I cannot wean myself from the use of the term "nouvelle," because it designates not just a certain length, let us say, twenty or thirty thousand words, but a scope and particular inspiration fundamentally differing from the several types of short story and the several variations of the novel. The nouvelle is an account of a limited number of characters in close connection, or in consequential or interesting contrast; and of their situation as a whole and their state of being in some detail and in depth, not just an incident or episode in their lives. It is a mode of narration in which the narrated time serves as a window to illuminate a remoter past and to reveal something of a foreseeable future; multum in parvo, but very multum and not too parvo. It often shows as many faces of meaning as a novel, but it does not apply to as many levels of experience and observation and significance. Along with Goethe's nouvelle which is called *Die Novelle* and Mann's *Death in Venice* and Benjamin Constant's *Adolphe* and Merimee's *Carmen* and Colette's *Gigi* and Melville's *Billy Budd* and Forster's *The Eternal Moment,* Katherine Anne's "Noon Wine" is a model of the form, an example for the textbooks.

It has an epic quality despite its small scale and modern dress, with only two heroes, one heroine, and one significant villain, expressing themselves commonly, and in natural pitiful circumstances. The epic that it makes me think of, I may say, humorously but not insincerely, is *Paradise Lost,* because it has Lucifer in it, a very modern and American Lucifer named Mr. Hatch. Hatch, not exactly fat, "more like a man who has been fat recently"; Hatch, who goes to and fro "telling other people what kind of tobacco to chew"; Hatch, with the discovery and roundup of "twenty-odd escaped loonatics" to his credit. His prey this time is Olaf Helton, whose brother years before took away his harmonica, who therefore stabbed said brother with a pitchfork. He escaped, and since then has been working for lazy Mr. Thompson and his dear sickly wife. He has somewhat lightened their burden and much restored their prosperity. They have got in the havit of hearing what you might call his theme song, a drinking song, rendered over and over on a series of new harmonicas.

When Hatch appears on the scene it all goes like a charm, like a curse. To save Helton, as he thinks, Thompson kills Hatch. He is tried and acquitted; but the breach of the great taboo is too much for him to forgive himself. The Eumenides are in him, nagging, arguing; soon his state of mind is such that he frightens even his beloved wife. Therefore he condemns himself to death and executes himself. There is a most touching page toward the close which is like a song or an aria: Mrs. Thompson weeping to have Helton back, saying a sort of prayer against the violence of menfolk, kneeling before her icebox as if it were an alter; the icebox Helton had helped her to buy. This perfectly womanly woman, eternal bystander and born widow; and the typical hired man, the type of wrong-doer whom even the Eumenides might spare because there was no idea or idealism behind his wrong, whom everyone except the Hatches of this world must forgive; and the Thompson's fine little boys, by the evolution of whose characters we are subtly made to feel time passing and humanity incessant: all these are exemplary, human and arch-human, in the grandest manner. Grand also, the way in which the murder of Hatch is made to epitomize our lesser losses of temper also, even the wielding of the jackknife of wit and of the little hatchet of righteous criticism, by which the psyche of the stupid man may be somewhat murdered and the heart of the murderous-minded man himself broken. Also it is a reminder of how evil may come of resistance to evil, of which the worldly man in this half-Germanized world needs to be reminded.

There is no end to the kinds of evil which Hatch typifies. You belittle him unfairly and unwisely if you assume that he has gone hunting his twenty-odd madmen just for the cash compensation. It has been chiefly to satisfy his clear sense of right and wrong; and to exercise the power to which he is entitled as a democratic citizen. There is some repression of the ego in our comfortable country, and therefore some perversion of it, therefore cruelty. Hatch has the legal mind, particularly what you might call the blue-legal mind.

Behold in him also political genius, which is psychopathic unless it is psychiatric, and in either case more oratorical than honest. At the start he positively woos Thompson, like a candidate for public office: Hatch "For Law and Order." And you might think that this hell-bent bullying technique would not get one vote; but you learn that it gets millions. In him also may be seen some evils of journalism, and some evils of the police, so worrisome and intimidating that one scarcely cares to comment on them.

Look at him as you like: he signifies always a little more than you have seen and seems larger than life-size; and you think that he must have more lives than a cat; and with facets like a diamond he throws bright, instructive flashes, on one thing and another. Thus I feel justified in having used that moot, incongruous word "epic." He is not only a man hunter, he is mankind as man hunter, semipiternal. He is not only a busybody, he is the great American busybody; godlike as only a devil can be. Lucifer! No wonder that Thompson at first is reminded of someone he has seen before, somewhere. Katherine Anne just mentions this, without explanation. It is perhaps the only signal she gives that she meant Hatch to be a personification as well as a person. Thompson hates him long before there has been a peep out of him about his man hunt; and so does the reader, surely, upon instinct. Hatch-malevolence can often be felt previous to, and lies deeper than, Hatch-activity. It lies so deep indeed that one is half afraid to say simply that it is evil. I always particularly resent the fact that he has kept, as you might say, virtuous, in order to accumulate a good conscience, as one might pinch pennies half one's life to invest a big business; and his air of friendliness without affection, curiosity without imagination, and the detached manner of his invasion of the others' privacy. Of course it is scarcely detachment to get chopped open by one's host's ax; but I feel that this is the least that could be expected to happen to him in the circumstances, an occupational hazard. I resent the fact that he manages—Katherine Anne lets him manage—not to deserve it.

A specific and unabashed (though somewhat mysterious) morality works through and through this whole tale, like a fat, like a yeast, like an antidote. Katherine Anne does not pity Hatch, but seemingly she would like to; she abstains from despising him. Perhaps suspicious of the very clarity of her hatred of hatchism, she compensates the individual Hatch for it by a kind of demi-deification and enlargment. She is as careful about him as if she were wearing his face as a mask for her face, and this were confession of a misdeed of hers. Do not forget that both Helton and Thompson commit murder; and the latter's plea of self-defense is specious or erroneous, if not dishonest. Hatch is not to blame for anything except his being, and his happening to be just there, in juxtaposition with these others. For many years he has been doing what he attempts that day; no one has ever objected before; what reason had he to suppose there was any law against it? The written law is a makeshift, and the unwritten law all double meaning. In entire civilization, every one of us is partly responsible for this darkness. Katherine Anne, mild even as she contemplates murder, assumes responsibility.

Let me say finally that it is a great factor in my admiration of this story that she has not pointed out any one of the significances I have seen in it and tried to list. There was no need to, I admiringly think. As critic, pro tem, it is my pleasure to point. The feeling of the good and evil in question doubtless accumulated in her heart in the abstract, for years; and the contrast of the two, no three kinds of humanity, and eternal warfare of the two equally sincere schools of morality, must have come to her mind one day with such energy that there was no resisting the impulse to show them in action, in an ideal bout. Then, because of her humane and womanly humility, abstraction blushed; abstraction bowed to fate, the truest fate of all, that of circumstance and coincidence and dialogue; abstraction stooped to human nature, and dressed itself and embodied itself in this episode, whether fact or fancy or a mixture.

One could not ask for a more objective work of fiction that "Noon Wine." Everything that it tells is a question of its time and its place and its conjunction of characters, only four principals, with nothing of that darkling presence and involvement and purpose of the author behind the scenes, between the lines, which may be said to give a poetical quality or a fourth dimension to narrative. It is freestanding, with little or no pedestal, little or no matrix; and her important essay about the writing of it in the *Yale Review* in 1956 (twenty years after the fact), though richly reminiscent of the little experiences with which it began — the blast of a shotgun, a scream in death agony, "a fat bullying whining man," a poor wife perjuring herself, a curvetting horse, a doleful tune — made it seem an even more absolute creation or invention than I had supposed on first reading.

That essay begins with almost a formula: "By the time a writer has reached the end of a story, he has lived it at least three times over — first, in the series of actual events that, directly or indirectly, have combined to set up the commotion in his mind and senses that causes him to write the story; second, in memory; and third, in the re-creation of the chaotic stuff." And toward the close of it she arrives at a more profound statement: "I do know why I remembered them" — that is to say, the shot, the scream, the horse, the tune (as it were, spark, pollen, seed, yeast) — "and why in my memory they slowly took on their separate lives in a story. It is because there radiated from each of those glimpses of strangers some element, some quality that arrested my attention at a vital moment of my own growth, and caused me, a child, to stop short and look outward,

away from myself; to look at another human being with that attention and wonder and speculation which ordinarily, and very naturally, I think, a child lavishes only on himself." To be noted for future
textbooks, components and instrumentalities of creative writing—
various accidental or incidental evidences of the senses, things the
writer sees and hears and feels, and their timing and sequence in
relation to the more general processes of his private and inner life;
a childish or childlike mind, maturing by fits and starts in one way
and another, peeping out of the hidey-hole of self, giving things a
second look, thinking things over, and lavishing its curiosity and
wonder.

Yeats said—did he not?—that certain of our nineteenth-century
classics, notably Emerson's essays and *Leaves of Grass,* were somewhat vitiated by their not incorporating or reflecting any large
and clear vision of evil. But certainly Hawthorne and Melville were
not limited to optimism and fond ecstasy. "Noon Wine" is of that
lineage, grandly and sorrowfully envisaging right and wrong, both
on the personal level, where something can be done about it, and in
the sense of the sublime, the insoluble. Let me call attention particularly to the power and the complexity of the characterization of
the villain in it, Hatch, a veritable Lucifer; brilliantly signifying
more, at every point, than the author actually tells us, faceted like a
diamond, flashing instructively in many directions. "Noon Wine"
would make a fine opera libretto for a composer able to write duets
and trios and quartets, without which (I think) music drama never
quite touches the heart.

It always pleases me to note how little continuousness, impinge-
ment, or repetition there is between one of Katherine Anne's stories
and another. In the case of most specialists in short fiction, as in that
of painters of easel pictures and composers of chamber music, one
finds some new order of artistry every few years; and between, only
variants of the same inspiration or the same method, efforts to perfect, or indeed a copying of themselves without much effort. Katherine Anne, when not hitting high spots, really has preferred not to
hit anything at all, at least not anything fictitious. She just keeps
turning the pages of her mind until she comes to one that is un-
touched, to which she then applies a new pen, silvery and needle-
sharp. Line the stories up: "Flowering Judas," "He," "The Jilting of
Granny Weatherall," "The Cracked Looking-Glass"; each advances
a separate proposition in morals or psychology, solves an unfamiliar
problem of form.

No theme except the given theme, one feels, could develop itself properly or transpire effectively in that particular setting and those circumstances. And yet she never forces the connection and congruity between the scene and the event. There is a minimum of anthropomorphism in her landscapes and changes of weather. Shapes and inanimate objects in her portrayal of the world are never geometrical or surrealistic or modernistic. Things are what they are; and what people do results directly from what *they* are. Everything is for the portraiture, inner portraiture mainly, and for the philosophy, which is almost entirely unspoken, and for the tale, the tale!

Her most recent collection of stories was published in 1944. Recently four admirable short narratives, not portions of *Ship of Fools,* have appeared in magazines; one of them, "St. Augustine and the Bullfight," is (I think) a masterpiece, in a strange new form, a hybrid of essay and tale, of which I expect her to make further use. Also occasionally she has produced valuable pieces of expository prose. In every type of short work she is a ready writer, given a green light, and a little removal from sociability, and certain facilities in the way of board and keep.

But never a ready novelist! All that time, a third of a lifetime, her struggle with *Ship of Fools* has been going on. With the everlasting problem of her delicate health, and the other difficulties and jeopardies that I have tried to describe without making a melodrama and a sentimentality of her life, certainly she has not worked at the novel uninterruptedly; but she has kept up her dedication of herself to it, only it, and staked her reputation and her self-respect on it. "Even when I was a little child," she once said to me, "I knew that youth was not for me"—a sentence wonderfully expressive of her particular lifelong uneasiness, responsiveness to her fate up ahead, and great patience from start to finish, knowing or sensing that she was going to grow old at the appointed, self-appointed task.

Troubles, jeopardies, hardships; note that I do not say misfortunes. The perils and disorders, even the wounds of a war scarcely seem deplorable to the home-coming soldier (or to his grateful countrymen), unless his battle has been lost; not even then, if he has shown heroism and if his story has been nobly reported. The fearsomeness of childbearing and the fatigues of parenthood are unhappy only if the children perish or turn out to be good for nothing. Likewise one cannot evaluate the experience of a literary genius unless and until one has perused all that has resulted from it. Obviously a great deal of heartbreak and travail has been Katherine Anne's lot. But, but, let us remind ourselves, no fortunate and facile youthful or even middle-aged person could have written *Ship of Fools*. It has required the better part of a lifetime of unshrinking participation in life and unshirking endeavor, or hardheadedness and heat of heart and almost fanaticism, and now we have the result; and surely it must seem to her, in her weariness and pride, cheap at the price.

So many writers of our generation brought forth novels in our twenties, immaturely. Often they were novels in name only, enlarged tales, family chronicles, disguised self-portraits. Some of us then hit upon a formula or worked out a method, so as to produce narrative reading matter wholesale; and some of us, on the other hand, simply got tired of the great form, or despaired of it. With lesser fish to fry, we let the white whale go. Not Katherine Anne! And when, twenty years ago, as a famed specialist in the short story, she let it be known that she had begun a novel, she meant precisely that: a large lifelike portrayal of a numerous and representative society, with contrasts of the classes and the masses and the generations and the ethnic groups, with causes and effects in the private psychology of one and all, and with their influences on one another —every man to some extent a part of every other man's fate—and all of this made manifest in behavior, action, plot! Despite destiny, unfavorable in some respects, despite passionate life and personal weakness and disadvantages in the day and age and in our present heterodox American culture, Katherine Anne would be a novelist, a novelist, or else! As the time passed, there arose in literary circles a murmur of skepticism or pessimism to which (I hope) she herself was deaf.

Let me confess that, at one point, when she had confided problems and despondencies to me, I began to write her a deplorable though well-meaning letter, advising her to give up the novel, as such; to salvage stories and sketches out of the incomplete manuscript; and to go on to whatever she had next on her agenda. Thank goodness, I was persuaded by my closest friend to consign this melancholy suggestion to the wastebasket, and presently I paid Katherine Anne a visit on her wooded hill in Connecticut, where, as she said, she lived "on guard and secretive and solitary as a woodchuck peeping out of its hidey-hole." And she read aloud several chapters that were new to me, and I suddenly caught sight of what was in her mind, the great novel structure; the whole so very much more than the sum of the parts. I came away repentant, exalted, and did not lose confidence in it or in her again.

*Ship of Fools* began with a sea voyage that she took in 1931, and specifically, she says, with an account of it in a letter to her friend and fellow writer, Caroline Gordon. Ten years later she began putting it in fiction form, and gradually, perhaps somewhat unintentionally, it ceased to be a reminiscence and a tale and became a true and full-length novel: The ship *Vera,* that is to say, Truth, but with no abstraction other than that, no symbolism, on its voyage from Veracruz in Mexico to Bremerhaven in Germany via four intermediate ports of call, a voyage only twenty-six days long in the narrated fact, but in the art of the telling, with reference to many of the passengers, lifelong, in that something of their past and something of their future is included in it all along, by means of great flashbacks and mirrorings of motive and fate, by means of a prophetic understanding of the patterns of their lives still to be lived; about three dozen of them clearly delineated and memorable, some unforgettable: a lot of Germans and a Swede and three Swiss and four Americans, and some Mexicans and Cubans and Spaniards (a vague pitiful collectivity of hundreds of the poorest Spaniards, deportees, in steerage); every age group; aristocrats and professional men and artists and various bourgeois and riffraff and merchant mariners (and that shadowy Spanish proletariat) diversely involved in love and lust and mortal illness and craziness and chauvinism and cruel intolerance and religiosity, actively involved, in brilliant incidents with hallucinating dialogue; all things motivating one another, all things illuminating one another.

What in the world made us so negative, Katherine Anne's friends and enemies, and all the literary gentry? With the long, solid, closely wrought, and polished work in hand, the grumpiness about it for so long seems strange. Occasionally, when publication had to be postponed again, and then again, did I not sometimes hear in certain voices, voices well-meaning enough as a rule, tones of what in psychoanalytical parlance used to be known as Schadenfreude, exhilaration-when-things-go-wrong? Have I ever been guilty of just that myself? I believe not. But who knows?

Though almost certainly she has had no notion of it, she has been enviable for years. Her fame has been out of proportion to the amount of her work, however highly one might think of it as to its excellence. At least in theory, a good many of us would willingly have experienced her sadnesses, shouldered her burdens, faced up

to her disappointments, in order to have produced just those few
volumes of her short fiction (even giving up hope of the legendary
novel) and to have felt her satisfaction in consequence. How proudly
she spoke of her vocation at times, almost as though she were a ruler
or as though she were a ruler or as though she were a saint! "I have
tossed a good many things considered generally desirable over the
windmill for that one intangible thing that money cannot buy, and
I find to my joy that I was right. There is no describing what my life
has been because of my one fixed desire to be a good artist, responsible to the last comma for what I write." Most of the time, at least
much of the time, even when things have been in no wise flourishing
for her, she has seemed somehow exultant, heroic, heroine-like.

Furthermore, she has a formidable wit, which may have troubled
some people. *Vide,* if you have not taken cognizance of this, her
satirical portrait of Gertrude Stein in *The Days Before,* or her more
recent minority opinion of *Lady Chatterley's Lover,* by which some
Lawrence admirers felt deflated as it were with beak and claw. I have
tried to think of some sample of her humor in its briefer and sometimes even fiercer form, a vive voix or by mail, that it might be
feasible to tell, naming no names. But hers is a type of humor that
cannot be appreciated if the target is veiled. Of course in a way one
is proud to be chastised with intellect and virtuosity like hers; at any
rate one prides oneself on taking it stoically; but it may leave sore-
nesses of scar tissue, reflexes of spite. No matter.

It occurs to me that there is a minimum of laughter of any kind
in *Ship of Fools.* George Moore maintained that humorousness
always has a bad effect in a novel, disruptive of the illusion in it,
drawing attention away from the characters in it to the humorous
disposition of the author. I have never heard Katherine Anne say
anything about this, but evidently her instinct has been in accord
with that of the influential, half-forgotten Irish writer. Humor is
one of the subjectivities, along with pathos and anger, powerful in
her letters, distilled out of her fiction, for fiction's sake. ...

Incidentally, I note this peculiarity of Katherine Anne's style:
she rarely indulges in figures of speech. One evening in my family
circle I read about thirty of these pages aloud, and only one simile
caught my eye: little greenish-pale Hans has freckles "like spots of
iodine." No one since Stendhal has written so plainly, so glass-
clearly; and my author carries about three times as much evidence
of the senses as the author of *Le Rouge et le Noir* ever did, and she

is much less inclined to infatuation and spite and eccentric argument than he was.

For a while after I have been reading her, my own way of writing —with impulsive images, with effects of cadence and pace, harmoniousness and dissonance, based on my way of reading things aloud, with ideas that I sometimes let language itself provide, and with a certain impressionism due to my having a memory at once excitable and faulty, resuccumbing to emotions of the past when I should be just mustering up the details—puts me to shame.

Now, to give a recapitulation and a close to this rambling study of my friend's lifework, let me quote another of her letters, somber once more, but blended with some of her malicious spirit; showing also her great virtue of steadfastness. It was written in Liege, Belgium, where she had been given a Fulbright Fellowship to teach at the university. In a letter to her I had vexed her with a weak reference of some sort to *my* age, and she chose to take it personally and struck back with an expression of some pathos and acerbity.

"When you and others younger than I, by I forget how many years, but a good number, complain of getting old, I think with dismay: What must they be thinking of me?"

Truly, I had not been (in that letter) thinking of her at all.

"I have had such a struggle to survive," she wrote," so many illnesses that nearly crippled me when I was young, so many intimations of mortality before my time; I felt more decrepit at twenty-four than I have since; and now I do not have a proper sense of time. It does not chop itself like stove wood into decades convenient for burning. It is a vast drift in which I float, eddying back and forth, spinning round now and then, moving always towards no fixed point; but one day it will dissolve and drop me into the abyss."

In any case, she went on to say, she could never trust other people's eyes or judgments in the matter. "When I was sixteen, a woman of middle age, when told *my* age, said 'Ha, she'll never see eighteen again!' And when I was twenty-eight, a man, not at all malicious, guessed my age to be forty. Oddly enough, when I was fifty, another man, who loved me, also thought me forty; and I told him about the other guess, and wondered if I was never to escape from that particular decade."

Why, she asked me, should she worry about her visible years when others were so happy to do that worrying for her? Though she did not blame *me* for my worrisomeness, this sentence struck home.

She then told me her favorite story about age. She was lunching in Hollywood with Charles Brackett, the distinguished screen writer (who is an old friend of hers and of mine) and two important film directors; a few tables away sat the then famous child actress, Margaret O'Brien, with her mother, her governess, her director, and someone else. "And the three men at my table looked her over as though she were a pony they were thinking of buying, and one of them said, 'How old is she now?' and another answered, 'Six years old,' and there was a pause, and then Charlie said, 'She looks older than that.' There was a kind of nod-around among them and the moment passed."

The concluding paragraph of this letter is a kind of prose poem:

"It is five o'clock, I am in a dowdy furnished apartment where the keys don't turn, the gas cocks stick, the bathroom gadgets work half way, the neighborhood is *tout-petit bourgeois,* the furnishings are from the Belgian branch of Sears Roebuck, the place is suburban, the wild yellow leaves are flying in a high bitter wind under a smoky sky, and I have come to world's end, and what was my errand here? There is nothing I wish to say to anyone here; does anybody want to listen? But it does look as if here again, with all the unlikeliness, the place and the time had met for me to sit at this table, three and one half feet square, and write something more of my own."

Amen to that, says her perennially grateful reader. She did not in fact write much in Liege. The autumn weather in that part of the world and the Fulbright schedule of lectures proved too much for her respiratory tract, and she had to come home. But it was not long afterward that she settled herself in Connecticut and began to see daylight as to her novel writing.

In that same letter of the dark night of her soul in Belgium, or, to be precise, teatime of her soul in Belgium, she declared that the only disturbing thing about the passage of time, for her, was the fact that she had four books all clearly conceived and partly begun and waiting to be finished. Now, three to go! And now perhaps not so many of us will care to bet against her.

# "Noon Wine": The Sources

*by Katherine Anne Porter*

This short novel, "Noon Wine" exists so fully and wholly in its own right in my mind, that when I attempt to trace its growth from the beginning, to follow all the clues to their sources in my memory, I am dismayed; because I am confronted with my own life, the whole society in which I was born and brought up, and the facts of it. My aim is to find the truth in it, and to this end my imagination works and re-works its recollections in a constant search for meanings. Yet in this endless remembering which surely must be the main occupation of the writer, events are changed, reshaped, interpreted again and again in different ways, and this is right and natural because it is the intention of the writer to write fiction, after all—real fiction, not a *roman a clef,* or a thinly disguised personal confession which better belongs to the psychoanalyst's seance. By the time I wrote "Noon Wine" it had become "real" to me almost in the sense that I felt not as if I had made that story out of my own memory of real events and imagined consequences, but as if I were quite simply reporting events I had heard or witnessed. This is not in the least true: the story is fiction; but it is made up of thousands of things that did happen to living human beings in a certain part of the country, at a certain time of my life, things that are still remembered by others as single incidents; not as I remembered them, floating and moving with their separate life and reality, meeting and parting and mingling in my thoughts, until they established their relationship. I could see and feel very clearly that all these events, episodes—hardly that, sometimes, but just mere glimpses and flashes here and there of lives strange or moving or astonishing to me—were forming a story, almost of themselves, it seemed; out of their apparent incoherence, unrelatedness, they grouped and clung in my mind in a form that

"'Noon Wine': The Sources." From Katherine Anne Porter, *Collected Essays* (New York: Delacorte Press/Seymour Lawrence, 1970). Reprinted by permission of the publishers.

gave a meaning to the whole that the individual parts had lacked. So I feel that this story is "true" in the way that a work of fiction should be true, created out of all the scattered particles of life I was able to absorb and combine and to shape into a living new being.

But why did this particular set of memories and early impressions combine in just this way to make this particular story? I do not in the least know. And though it is quite true that I intended to write fiction this story wove itself in my mind for years before I ever intended to write it, there were many other stories going on in my head at once, some of them evolved and were written, more were not. Why? This to me is the most interesting question, because I am sure there is an answer, but nobody knows it yet.

When the moment came to write this story, I knew it; and I had to make quite a number of practical arrangements to get the time free for it without fear of interruptions. I wrote it as it stands except for a few pen corrections in just seven days of trance-like absorption in a small room in an inn in rural Pennsylvania, from the early evening of November 7 to November 14, 1936. Yet I had written the central part, the scene between Mr. Hatch and Mr. Thompson, which leads up to the murder, in Basel, Switzerland, in the summer of 1932.

I had returned from Europe only fifteen days before I went to the inn in Pennsylvania: this was the end, as it turned out, of my living abroad, except for short visits back to Paris, Brittany, Rome, Belgium: but meantime I had, at a time of great awareness and active energy, spent nearly fourteen years of my life out of this country: in Mexico, Bermuda, various parts of Europe, but mostly by choice, Paris. Of my life in these places I felt then, and feel now, that it was all entirely right, timely, appropriate, exactly where I should have been and what doing at that very time. I did not feel exactly at home; I knew where home was; but the time had come for me to see the world for myself, and so I did, almost as naturally as a bird taking off on his new wingfeathers. In Europe, things were not so strange; sometimes I had a pleasant sense of having here and there touched home-base; if I was not at home, I was sometimes with friends. And all the time, I was making notes on stories—stories of my own place, my South—for my part of Texas was peopled almost entirely by Southerners from Virginia, Tennessee, the Carolinas, Kentucky—and I was almost instinctively living in a sustained state of mind and feeling, quietly and secretly, comparing one thing with another, always remembering and remembering; and all sorts of things were falling into their proper places, taking on their natural shapes and sizes, and going back and back clearly into right perspective—right for me as artist, I simply mean to say; and it was like breathing—I did not have consciously to urge myself to think about it. So my time in Europe served me in a way I had not dreamed of, even, besides its own charm and goodness; it gave me back my past and my own house and my own people—the native land of my heart.

This summer country of my childhood, this space and memory is filled with landscapes shimmering in light and color, moving with sounds and shapes I hardly ever describe or put in my stories in so many words; they form only the living background of what I am trying to tell, so familiar to my characters they would hardly notice them; the sound of mourning doves in the live-oaks, the childish voices of parrots chattering on every back porch in the little town, the hoverings of buzzards in the high blue air—all the life of that soft blackland farming country, full of fruits and flowers and birds, with good hunting and good fishing; with plenty of water, many little and big rivers. I shall name just a few of the rivers I remember—the San Antonio, the San Marcos, the Trinity, the Neuces, the Rio Grande, the Colorado, and the small clear branch of the Colorado—full of colored pebbles—Indian Creek, the place where I was born. The colors and tastes all had their smells, as the sounds have now their echoes: the bitter whiff of air over a sprawl of animal skeleton after the buzzards were gone; the smells and flavors of roses and melons, and peach bloom and ripe peaches, of cape jessamine in hedges blooming like popcorn, and the sickly sweetness of chinaberry florets; of honeysuckle in great swags on a trellised gallery; heavy tomatoes dead ripe and warm with the midday sun, eaten there, at the vine; the delicious milky green corn, and savory hot corn bread eaten with still-warm sweet milk; and the clinging brackish smell of the muddy little ponds where we caught, and boiled crawfish—in a discarded lard can—and ate them, then and there, we children, in the company of an old Negro who had once been my grandparents' slave, as I have told in another story. He was by our time only a servant, and a cantankerous old cuss very sure of his place in the household.

Uncle Jimbilly, for that was his name, was not the only one who knew exactly where he stood, and just about how far he could go in maintaining the right, privileges, exemptions of his status so long as he performed its duties. At this point, I want to give a rather generalized view of the society of that time and place as I remember it, and as talks with my elders since confirm it. (Not long ago I planned to visit a very wonderful old lady who was a girlhood friend of my mother. I wrote to my sister that I could not think of being a burden to Miss Cora, and would therefore stop at the little hotel in town and call on her. And my sister wrote back air-mail on the very day saying: "For God's sake, don't mention the word hotel to Miss Cora —she'll think you've lost your raising!") The elders all talked and behaved as if the final word had gone out long ago on manners, morality, religion, even politics: nothing was ever to change, they said, and even as they spoke, everything was changing, sliding, disappearing. This had been happening in fact ever since they were born; the greatest change, the fatal dividing change in this country, the war between the states, was taking place even as most of my father's generation were coming into the world. But it was the grandparents who still ruled in daily life; and they showed plainly in acts, words, and even looks—an enormously handsome generation they seemed to have been I remember—all those wonderful high noses with a diamond-shaped bony structure in the bridge!—the presence of good society, very well based on traditional Christian beliefs. These beliefs were mainly Protestant but not yet petty middle-class puritanism: there remained still an element fairly high stepping and wide gestured in its personal conduct. The petty middle class of fundamentalists who saw no difference between wine-drinking, dancing, card-playing, and adultery, had not yet got altogether the upper hand—in fact, never did except in certain limited areas; but it was making a brave try. It was not really a democratic society; if everybody had his place, sometimes very narrowly defined, at least he knew where it was, and so did everybody else. So too, the higher laws of morality and religion were defined; if a man offended against the one, or sinned against the other, he knew it, and so did his neighbors, and they called everything by its right name.

This firm view applied also to social standing. A man who had humble ancestors had a hard time getting away from them and rising in the world. If he prospered and took to leisurely ways of living, he was merely "getting above his raising." If he managed to marry into one of the good old families, he had simply "outmarried himself." If he went away and made a success somewhere else, when he returned for a visit he was still only "that Jimmerson boy who went No'th." There is—was, perhaps I should say—a whole level of society of the South where it was common knowledge that the mother's family outranked the father's by half, at least. This might be based on nothing more tangible than that the mother's family came from Richmond or Charleston, while the father's may have started out somewhere from Pennsylvania, or to have got bogged down one time or another in Arkansas. If they turned out well, the children of these matches were allowed their mother's status, for good family must never be denied, but father remained a member of the Plain People to the end. Yet there was nothing against any one hinting at better lineage, and a family past more dignified than the present, no matter how humble his present circumstances, nor how little proof he could offer for his claim. Aspiration to higher and better things was natural to all men, and a sign of proper respect for true blood and birth. Pride and hope may be denied to no one.

In this society of my childhood there were all sorts of tender ways of feeling and thinking, subtle understanding between people in matters of ritual and ceremony; I think in the main a civilized society, and yet, with the underlying, perpetual ominous presence of violence; violence potential that broke through the smooth surface almost without warning, or maybe just without warning to children, one learned later to know the signs. There were old cruel customs, the feud, for one, gradually dying out among the good families, never in fact prevalent among them—the men of that class fought duels, and abided—in theory at least—on the outcome; and country life, ranch life, was rough, in Texas, at least. I remember tall bearded booted men striding about with clanking spurs; and carrying loaded pistols inside their shirts next to their ribs, even to church. It was quite matter of course that you opened a closet door in a bedroom and stared down into the cold eyes of shotguns and rifles, stacked there because there was no more room in the gun closet. In the summer, in that sweet smelling flowery country, we children with our father or some grown-up in charge, spent long afternoons on a range, shooting at fixed targets or clay pigeons with the ordinary domestic firearms, pistols, rifles of several calibers, shotguns single and double. I never fired a shotgun, but I knew the sounds and could name any round of fire I heard, even at great distances.

Some one asked me once where I had ever heard that conversation in "Noon Wine" between two men about chewing tobacco—that apparently aimless talk between Mr. Hatch and Mr. Thompson which barely masks hatred and is leading towards a murder. It seems that I *must* have heard something of the sort somewhere, some time or another; I do not in the least remember it. But that whole countryside was full of tobacco-chewing men, whittling men, hard-working farming men perched on fences with their high heels caught on a rail, or squatting on their toes, gossiping idly and comfortably for hours at a time. I often wondered what they found to say to each other, day in day out year after year; but I should never have dared go near enough to listen profitably; yet I surely picked up something that came back whole and free as air that summer in Basel, Switzerland when I thought I was studying only the life of Erasmus and the Reformation. And I have seen them, many a time, take out their razor-sharp long-bladed knives and slice a "chew" as delicately and precisely as if they were cutting a cake. These knives were so keen, often I have watched my father, shelling pecans for me, cut off the ends of the hard shells in a slow circular single gesture; then split them down the sides in four strips and bring out the nut meat whole. This fascinated me, but it did not occur to me to come near the knife, or offer to touch it. In our country life, in summers, we were surrounded by sharpened blades—hatchets, axes, plough-shares, carving knives, bowie knives, straight razors. We were taught so early to avoid all these, I do not remember ever being tempted to take one in my hand. Living as we did among loaded guns and dangerous cutting edges, four wild, adventurous children always getting hurt in odd ways, we none of us were ever injured seriously. The worst thing that happened was, my elder sister got a broken collar bone from a fall, not as you might expect from a horse, for we almost lived on horseback, but from a three-foot fall off a fence where she had climbed to get a better view of a battle between two bulls. But these sharp blades slicing tobacco—did I remember it because it was an unusual sight? I think not, I must have seen it, as I remember it, dozens of times—but one day I really *saw* it; and it became part of Mr. Thompson's hallucinated vision when he killed Mr. Hatch, and afterward could not live without justifying himself.

There is an early memory, not the first, but certainly before my third year, always connected with this story, "Noon Wine"; it is the source, if there could be only one. I was a very small child. I know this by the remembered vastness of the world around me, the giant heights of grown-up people; a chair something to be scaled like a mountain; a table top to be peered over on tiptoe. It was late summer and near sunset, for the sky was a clear green-blue with long streaks of burning rose in it, and the air was full of the mournful sound of swooping bats. I was all alone in a wide grassy plain—it was the lawn on the east side of the house—and I was in that state of instinctive bliss which children only know, when there came like a blow of thunder echoing and rolling in that green sky, the explosion of a shotgun, not very far away; for it shook the air. There followed at once a high, thin, long-drawn scream, a sound I had never heard, but I knew what it was—it was the sound of death in the voice of a man. How did I know it was a shotgun? How should I not have known? How did I know it was death? We are born knowing death.

Let me examine this memory a little, which though it is of an actual event, is like a remembered dream; but then all my childhood is that; and if in parts of this story I am trying to tell you, I use poetic terms, it is because in such terms do I remember many things, and the feeling is valid, it cannot be left out, or denied.

In the first place, could I have been alone when this happened? It is most unlikely. I was one of four children, brought up in a houseful of adults of ripening age; a grandmother, a father, several Negro servants, among them two aged, former slaves; visiting relatives, uncles, aunts, cousins, grandmother's other grandchildren older than we, with always an ill-identified old soul or two, male or female, who seemed to be guests but helped out with stray chores. The house, which seemed so huge to me, was probably barely adequate to the population it accommodated; but of one thing I am certain — nobody was ever alone except for the most necessary privacies, and certainly no child at any time. Children had no necessary privacies. We were watched and herded and monitored and followed and spied upon and corrected and lectured and scolded (and kissed, let's be just, loved tenderly, and prayed over!) all day, every day, through the endless years of childhood—endless, but where did they go? So the evidence all points to the fact that I was not, could not have been, bodily speaking, alone in that few seconds when for the first time I heard the sound of murder. Who was with me? What did she say—for it was certainly one of the care-taking women around the house. Could I have known by instinct, of which I am so certain now, or did some one speak words I cannot remember which nonetheless told me what had happened? There is nothing more to tell, all speculations are useless; this memory is a spot of clear light and color and sound, of immense, mysterious illumination of feeling against a horizon of total darkness.

Yet, was it the next day? next summer? In that same place, that grassy shady yard, in board daylight I watched a poor little funeral procession creeping over the stony ridge of the near horizon, the dusty road out of town which led also to the cemetery. The hearse was just a spring wagon decently roofed and curtained with black oil cloth, poverty indeed, and some members of our household gathered on the front gallery to watch it pass, said, "Poor Pink Hodges—old man A _____got him just like he said he would." Had it been Pink Hodges, then, I had heard screaming death in the blissful sunset? And who was old man A, whose name I do not remember, and what became of him. I wonder? I'll never know. I remember only that the air of our house was full of pity for Pink Hodges, for his harmlessness, his helplessness, "so pitiful, poor thing," they said; and, "It's just not right," they said. But what did they do to bring old man A _____to justice, or at least a sense of his evil? Nothing, I am afraid. I began to ask all sorts of questions, and was silenced invariably by some elder who told me I was too young to understand such things.

Yet here I am coming to something quite clear, of which I am entirely certain. It happened in my ninth year, and again in that summer house in the little town near the farm, with the yard full of roses and irises and honeysuckle and hackberry trees, and the vegetable garden and the cow barn in back. It was already beginning to seem not so spacious to me; it went on dwindling year by year to the measure of my growing up.

One hot moist day after a great thunderstorm and heavy long rain, I saw a strange horse and buggy standing at the front gate. Neighbors and kin in the whole countryside knew each other's equipages as well as they did their own, and this outfit was not only strange, but not right; don't ask me why. It was not a good horse, and the buggy was not good either. There was something wrong with the whole thing, and I went full of curiosity to see why such strangers as would drive such a horse and buggy would be calling on my grandmother. (At this point say anything you please about the snobbism of children and dogs. It is real. As real as the snobbism of their parents and owners, and much more keen and direct.)

I stood just outside the living room door, unnoticed for a moment by my Grandmother, who was sitting rather stiffly, with an odd expression on her face: a doubtful smiling mouth, brows knitted in painful inquiry. She was a woman called upon for decisions, many decisions every day, wielding justice among her unruly family. Once she struck, justly or unjustly, she dared not retract—the whole pack would have torn her in pieces. They did not want justice in any case, but revenge, each in his own favor. But this situation had

nothing to do with her family, and there she sat, worried, unde-
cided. I had never seen her so, and it dismayed me.

Then I saw first a poor sad pale beaten-looking woman in a faded
cotton print dress and a wretched little straw hat with a wreath of
wilted forget-me-nots. She looked as if she had never eaten a good
dinner, or slept in a comfortable bed, the mark of life-starvation was
all over her. Her hands were twisted tight in her lap and she was
looking down at them in shame. Her eyes were covered with dark
glasses. While I stared at her, I heard the man sitting near her almost shouting in a course, roughened voice: "I swear, it was in self-
defense! His life or mine! If you don't believe me, ask my wife here.
She saw it. My wife won't lie!" Every time he repeated these words,
without lifting her head or moving, she would say in a low voice,
"Yes, that's right. I saw it."

In that moment, or in another moment later as this memory sank
in and worked in my feelings and understanding, it was quite clear
to me, and seems now to have been clear from the first, that he expected her to lie, was indeed forcing her to tell a lie; that she did it
unwillingly and unlovingly in bitter resignation to the double dis-
grace of her husband's crime and her own sin; and that he, stupid,
dishonest, soiled as he was, was imploring her as his only hope,
somehow to make his lie a truth.

I used this scene in "Noon Wine," but the man in real life was not
lean and gaunt and blindly, foolishly proud, like Mr. Thompson;
no, he was just a great loose-faced, blabbing man full of guilt and
fear, and he was bawling at my grandmother, his eyes bloodshot with
drink and tears, "Lady, if you don't believe me, ask my wife! She
won't lie!" At this point my grandmother noticed my presence and
sent me away with a look we children knew well and never dreamed
of disobeying. But I heard part of the story later, when my grandmother said to my father, with an unfamiliar coldness in her voice,
for she had made her decision about this affair, too: "I was never
asked to condone a murder before. Something new." My father said,
"Yes, and a cold-blooded murder too if ever there was one."

So, there was the dreary tale of violence again, this time with the
killer out on bail, going the rounds of the countryside with his
wretched wife, telling his side of it—whatever it was; I never knew
the end. In the meantime, in one summer or another, certainly before my eleventh year, for that year we left that country for good, I
had two other memorable glimpses. My father and I were driving
from the farm to town, when we met with a tall black-whiskered man

on horseback, sitting so straight his chin was level with his Adam's apple, dressed in clean mended blue denims, shirt open at the throat, a big devil-may-care black felt hat on the side of his head. He gave us a lordly gesture of greeting, caused his fine black horse to curvet and prance a little, and rode on, grandly. I asked my father who that could be, and he said, "That's Ralph Thomas, the proudest man in seven counties." I said, "What is he proud of?" And my father said, "I suppose the horse. It's a very fine horse," in a good-humored, joking tone, which made the poor man quite ridiculous, and yet not funny, but sad in some why I could not understand.

On another of these journeys I saw a bony, awkward, tired-look-ing man, tilted in a kitchen chair against the wall of his comfortless shack, set back from the road under the thin shade of hackberry trees, a thatch of bleached-looking hair between his eyebrows, blow-ing away at a doleful tune on his harmonica, in the hot dull cricket-whirring summer day: the very living image of loneliness. I was struck with pity for this stranger, his eyes closed against the alien scene, consoling himself with such poor music. I was told he was someone's Swedish hired man.

In time—when? how? Pink Hodges, whom I never knew except in the sound of his death-cry, merged with my glimpse of the Swedish hired man to become the eternal Victim; the fat bullying whining man in my grandmother's living room became the Killer. But noth-ing can remain so simple as that, this was only a beginning. Helton too, the Victim in my story, is also a murderer, with the dubious innocence of the madman; but no less in shedder of blood. Every-one in this story contributes, one way or another directly, or indirect-ly, to murder, or death by violence; even the two young sons of Mr. Thompson who turn on him in their fright and ignorance and side with their mother, who does not need them; they are guiltless, for they meant no harm, and they do not know what they have contributed to; indeed in their innocence they believe they are doing, not only right, but the only thing they could possibly do in the situation as they under-stand it: they must defend their mother....

And here I am brought to a pause, for almost without knowing it, I have begun to write about these characters in a story of mine as though they were real persons exactly as I have shown them. And these fragments of memory on which the story is based now seem to have a random look; they nowhere contain in themselves, together or separately, the story I finally wrote out of them; a story of the most painful moral and emotional confusions, in which every one concerned, yes, in his crooked way, even Mr. Hatch, is trying to do right.

It is only in the varying levels of quality in the individual nature that we are able finally more or less to measure the degree of virtue in each man. Mr. Thompson's motives are most certainly mixed, yet not ignoble; he helps some one who helps him in turn; while acting in defense of what he sees as the good in his own life, the thing worth trying to save at almost any cost, he is trying at the same time to defend another life—the life of Mr. Helton, who has proved himself the bringer of good, the present help, the true friend. Mr. Helton would have done as much for me, Mr. Thompson says, and he is right. Yet he hated Mr. Hatch on sight, wished to injure him before he had a reason: could it not be a sign of virtue in Mr. Thompson that he surmised and resisted at first glance the evil in Mr. Hatch? The whole countryside, let us remember, for this is most important, the relations of a man to his society, agrees with Mr. Burleigh the lawyer, and the jury and the judge that Mr. Thompson's deed was justifiable homicide: but this did not, as his neighbors confirmed, make it any less a murder. Mr. Thompson was not an evil man, he was only a poor sinner doing his best according to his lights, lights somewhat dimmed by his natural aptitude for Pride and Sloth. He still had his virtues, even if he did not quite know what they were, and so gave himself credit for some few that he had not.

But Hatch was the doomed man, evil by nature, a lover and do-er of evil, who did no good thing for any one, not even, in the long run, himself. He was evil in the most dangerous, irremediable way: one who works safely within the law, and has reasoned himself into believing that his motives, if not good, are at least no worse than any one else's: for he believes quite simply and naturally that the motives of others are no better than his own; and putting aside all nonsense about good, he will always be found on the side of custom and common sense and the letter of the law. When challenged he has his defense pat and ready, and there is nothing much wrong with it— it only lacks human decency, of which he has no conception beyond a faint hearsay. Mr. Helton is, by his madness, beyond good and evil, his own victim as well as the victim of others. Mrs. Thompson is a woman of the sort produced in numbers in that time, that place, that code: so trained to the practice of her prescribed womanly vocation of virtue as such—manifest, unrelenting, sacrificial, stupefying —she has almost lost her human qualities, and her spiritual courage

and insight, to boot. She commits the, to her, dreadful unforgivable
sin of lying; moreover, lying to shield a criminal, even if that criminal is her own husband. Having done this, to the infinite damage,
as she sees it, of her own soul (as well as her self-respect which is
founded on her feeling of irreproachability) she lacks the courage
and the love to see her sin through to its final good purpose; to commit it with her whole heart and with perfect acceptance of her guilt;
to say to her husband the words that might have saved them both,
soul and body—might have, I say only. I do not know and shall never
know. Mrs. Thompson was not that robust a character, and this story,
given all, must end as it does end...there is nothing in any of these
beings tough enough to work the miracle of redemption in them.

Suppose I imagine now that I really saw all of these persons in the
flesh at one time or another? I saw what I have told you, a few mere
flashes of a glimpse here and there, one time or another; but I do
know why I remembered them, and why in my memory they slowly
took on their separate lives in a story. It is because there radiated
from each one of those glimpses of strangers some element, some
quality that arrested my attention at a vital moment of my own
growth, and caused me, a child, to stop short and look outward, away
from myself; to look at another human being with that attention and
wonder and speculation which ordinarily, and very naturally, I
think, a child lavishes only on himself. It is not almost the sole end
of civilized education of all sorts to teach us to be more and more
highly, sensitively conscious of the reality of the existence, the essential being, of others, those around us so very like us and yet so
bafflingly, so mysteriously different? I do not know whether my
impressions were on the instant, as I now believe, or did they draw
to their magnet gradually with time and confirming experience?
That man on the fine horse, with his straight back, straight neck,
shabby and unshaven, riding like a cavalry officer, "the proudest
man in seven countries—" I saw him no doubt as my father saw him,
absurd, fatuous, but with some human claim on respect and not to
be laughed at, for all his simple vanity.

The woman I have called Mrs. Thompson—I never knew her
name—showed me for the first time I am certain the face of pure
shame; humiliation so nearly absolute it could not have been more
frightening if she had grovelled in the floor; and I knew that whatever the cause, it was mortal and beyond help. In that bawling sweating man with the loose mouth and staring eyes, I saw the fear that is

moral cowardice and I knew he was lying. In that yellow-haired, long-legged man playing his harmonica I felt almost the first glimmer of understanding and sympathy for any suffering not physical. Most certainly I had already done my share of weeping over lost or dying pets, or beside some one I loved who was very sick, or my own pains and accidents; but *this* was a spiritual enlightenment, some tenderness, some first wakening of charity in my self-centered heart. I am using here some very old fashioned noble words in their prime sense. They have perfect freshness and reality to me, they are the irreplaceable names of Realities. I know well what they mean, and I need them here to describe as well as I am able what happens to a child when the human feelings and the moral sense and the sense of charity are unfolding, and are touched once and for all in that first time when the soul is prepared for them; and I know that the all-important things in that way have all taken place long and long before we know the words for them.

# The Eye of the Story

*by Eudora Welty*

In "Old Mortality" how stirring the horse race is! At the finish
the crowd breaks into its long roar "like the falling walls of Jericho."
This we hear, and it is almost like seeing, and we know Miss Lucy
has won. But beyond a fleeting glimpse—the "mahogany streak" of
Miss Lucy on the track—we never get much sight of the race with
our eyes. What we see comes afterward. Then we have it up close:
Miss Lucy bleeding at the nose. For Miranda has got to say "That's
winning too." The race would never have got into the story except
that Miranda's heart is being prepared to reject victory, to reject
the glamor of the race and the cheering grandstand; to distrust from
now on all evidence except what she, out of her own experience, can
testify to. By the time we *see* Miss Lucy, she is a sight for Miranda's
eyes alone: as much symbol as horse.

Most good stories are about the interior of our lives, but Katherine
Anne Porter's stories take place there; they show surface only at her
choosing. Her use of the physical world is enough to meet her needs
and no more; she is not wasteful with anything. This artist, writing
her stories with a power that stamps them to their last detail on the
memory, does so to an extraordinary degree without sensory imagery.

I have the most common type of mind, the visual, and when first
I began to read her stories it stood in the way of my trust in my own
certainty of what was there that, for all my being bowled over by
them, I couldn't see them happening. This was a very good thing for
me. As her work has done in many other respects, it has shown me a
thing or two about the eye of fiction, about fiction's visibility and
invisibility, about its clarity, its radiance.

Heaven knows she can see. Katherine Anne Porter has seen all
her life, sees today, most intimately, most specifically, and down
to the bones, and she could date the bones. There is, above all, "Noon

Wine" to establish it forever that when she wants a story to be visible, it is. "Noon Wine" is visible all the way through, full of scenes charged with dramatic energy; everything is brought forth into movement, dialogue; the title itself is Mr. Helton's tune on the harmonica. "Noon Wine" is the most beautifully objective work she has done. And nothing has been sacrificed to its being so (or she wouldn't have done it); to the contrary. I find Mr. Hatch the scariest character she ever made, and he's just set down there in Texas, like a chair. There he stands, part of the everyday furniture of living. He's opaque, and he's the devil. Walking in at Mr. Thompson's gate —the same gate by which his tracked-down victim walked in first— he is that much more horrifying, almost too solid to the eyes to be countenanced. (So much for the visual mind.)

Katherine Anne Porter has not in general chosen to cast her stories in scenes. Her sense of human encounter is profound, is fundamental to her work, I believe, but she has not often allowed it the dramatic character it takes in "Noon Wine." We may not see the significant moment happen within the story's present; we may not watch it occur between the two characters it joins. Instead, a silent blow falls while one character is alone—the most alone in his life, perhaps. (And this is the case in "Noon Wine" too.) Often the revelation that pierces a character's mind and heart and shows him his life or his death comes in a dream, in retrospect, in illness or in utter defeat, the moment of vanishing hope, the moment of dying. What Miss Porter makes us see are those subjective worlds of hallucination, obsession, fever, guilt. The presence of death hovering about Granny Weatherall she makes as real and brings as near as Granny's own familiar room that stands about her bed—realer, nearer, for we recognize not only death's presence but the character death has come in for Granny Weatherall.

The flash of revelation is revelation but is unshared. But how unsuspecting we are to imagine so for a moment—it *is* shared, and by ourselves, her readers, who must share it feeling the doubled anguish of knowing this fact, doubled still again when it is borne in upon us how close to life this is, to *our* lives.

It is to be remembered that the world of fiction is not of itself visible. A story may or may not be born in sensory images in a given writer's mind. Experience itself is stored in no telling how many ways in a writer's memory. (It was "the sound of the sea, and Beryl fanning her hair at the window" that years later and thousands of miles away brought Katherine Mansfield to writing "At the Bay.")

But if the physical world *is* visible or audible in the story, it has to be made so. Its materialization is as much a created thing as are the story's characters and what they think or do or say.

Katherine Anne Porter shows us that we do not have to see a story happen to know what is taking place. For all we are to know, she is not looking at it happen herself when she writes it; for her eyes are always looking through the gauze of the passing scene, not distracted by the immediate and transitory; her vision is reflective.

Her imagery is as likely as not to belong to a time other than the story's present, and beyond that it always differs from it in nature; it is *memory* imagery, coming into the story from memory's remove. It is a distilled, a re-formed imagery, for it is part of a language made to speak directly of premonition, warning, surmise, anger, despair.

It was soon borne in upon me that Katherine Anne Porter's moral convictions have given her readers another way to see. Surely these convictions represent the fixed points about which her work has turned, and not only that but they govern her stories down to the smallest detail. Her work has formed a constellation, with its own North Star.

Is the writer who does not give us the pictures and bring us the sounds of a story as it unfolds shutting out part of life? In Katherine Anne Porter's stories the effect has surely been never to diminish life but always to intensify life in the part significant to her story. It is a darkening of the house as the curtain goes up on this stage of her own.

Her stories of Mexico, Germany, Texas all happen there: where love and hate, trust and betrayal happen. And so their author's gaze is turned not outward but inward, and has confronted the mysterious dark from her work's beginning.

Since her subject is what lies beneath the surface, her way—quite direct—is to penetrate, brush the stuff away. It is the writer like Chekov whose way of working is indirect. He moved indeed toward the same heart and core but by building up some corresponding illusion of life. Writers of Chekov's side of the family are themselves illusionists and have necessarily a certain fondness for, lenience toward, the whole shimmering fabric as such. Here we have the professional scientist, the good doctor, working with illusion and the born romantic artists—is she not?—working without it. Perhaps it is always the lyrical spirit that takes on instantaneous color, shape, pattern of motion in work, while the mediative spirit must fly as quickly as possible out of the shell.

All the stories she has written are moral stories about love and the hate that is love's twin, love's impostor and enemy and death. Rejection, betrayal, desertion, theft roam the pages of her stories as they roam the world. The madam kicking the girl in "Magic" and the rest of the brutality in the characters' treatment of one another; the thieving that in one form or another infects their relationships; the protests they make, from the weakness of false dreams or of lying down with a cold cloth over the eyes, on up to towering rages: all this is a way of showing to the inward eye: Look at what you are doing to human love.

We hear in how many more stories than the one the litany of the little boy at the end of "The Downward Path to Wisdom," his "comfortable, sleepy song": "I hate Papa, I hate Mama, I hate Grandma, I hate Uncle David, I hate Old Janet, I hate Marjory, I hate Papa, I hate Mama...." It is like the long list of remembered losses in the story "Theft" made vocal, and we remember how that loser's decision to go on and let herself be robbed coincides with the rising "in her blood" of "a deep almost murderous anger."

"If one is afraid of looking into a face one hits the face," remarked W. B. Yeats, and I think we must conclude that to Katherine Anne Porter's characters this face is the challenging face of love itself. And I think it is the faces—the inner, secret faces—of her characters, in their self-delusion, their venom and pain, that their author herself is contemplating. More than either looking at the face or hitting it, she has made a story out of her anger.

If outrage is the emotion she has most strongly expressed, she is using outgage as her cool instrument. She uses it with precision to show what monstrosities of feeling come about not from the lack of the existence of love but from love's repudiation, betrayal. From which there is no safety anywhere. Granny Weatherall, eighty, wise, affectionate and good, and now after a full life dying in her bed with the priest beside her, "knew hell when she saw it."

The anger that speaks everywhere in the stories would trouble the heart for their author whom we love except that her anger is pure, the reason for it evident and clear, and the effect exhilarating. She has made it the tool of her work; what we do is rejoice in it. We are aware of the compassion that guides it, as well. Only compassion could have looked where she looks, could have seen and probed what she sees. Real compassion is perhaps always in the end unsparing; it must make itself a part of knowing. Self-pity does not exist here; these stories come out trenchant, bold, defying; they are tough as sanity, unrelinquished sanity, is tough.

Despair is here, as well described as if it were Mexico. It is a despair, however, that is robust and sane, open to negotiation by the light of day. Life seen as a savage ordeal has been investigated by a straightforward courage, unshaken nerve, a rescuing wit, and above all with the searching intelligence that is quite plainly not to be daunted. In the end the stories move us not to despair ourselves but to an emotion quite opposite because they are so seriously and clear-sightedly pointing out what they have been formed to show: that which is true under the skin, that which will remain a fact of the spirit.

Miranda, by the end of "Old Mortality" rebelling against the ties of the blood, resenting their very existence, planning to run away now from these and as soon as she can from her own escape into marriage, Miranda saying "I hate loving and being loved," is hating what destroys loving and what prevents being loved. She is, in her own particular and her own right, fighting back at the cheat she has discovered in all that's been handed down to her as gospel truth.

Seeing what is not there, putting trust in a false picture of life, has been one of the worst nightmares that assail her characters. "My dreams never renege on me, Mr. Richards. They're all I have to go by," says Rosaleen. (The Irish are no better than the Southerners in this respect.) Not only in the comic and touching Rosaleen, the lovely and sentient and tragic Miranda, but in many other characters throughout the stories we watch the romantic and the anti-romantic pulling each other to pieces. Is the romantic ever scotched? I believe not. Even if there rises a new refrain, even if the most ecstatic words ever spoken turn out to be "I hate you," the battle is not over for good. That battle is in itself a romance.

Nothing is so naturally subject to false interpretation as the romantic, and in furnishing that interpretation the Old South can beat all the rest. Yet some romantic things happen also to be true. Miss Porter's stories are not so much a stand against the romantic as such, as a repudiation of the false. What alone can instruct the heart is the experience of living, experience which can be vile; but what can never do it any good, what harms it more than vileness, are those tales, those legends of more than any South, those universal false dreams, the hopes sentimental and ubiquitous, which are not on any account to be gone by.

For there comes a confrontation. It is then that Miss Porter's characters, behaving so entirely like ourselves, make the fatally wrong choice. Enter betrayal. Again and again, enter betrayal. We meet the betrayal that lies in rejection, in saying No to others or No to the self, or that lies with still more cunning in saying Yes when this time it should have been No.

And though we are all but sure what will happen, we are possessed by suspense.

It appears to me irrelevant whether or not the story is conceived and put down in sensory images, whether or not it is dramatic in construction, so long as its hold is a death-grip. In my own belief, the suspense—so acute and so real—in Katherine Anne Porter's work never did depend for its life on disclosure of the happenings of the narrative (nothing is going to turn out very well) but in the writing of the story, which becomes one single long sustained moment for the reader. Its suspense is one with its meaning. It must arise, then, from the mind, heart, spirit by which it moves and breathes.

It is a current like a strand of quicksilver through the serenity of her prose. In fiction of any substance, serenity can only be an achievement of the work itself, for any sentence that is alive with meaning is speaking out of passion. Serenity never belonged to the *now* of writing; it belongs to the later *now* offered its readers. In Katherine Anne Porter's work the forces of passion and self-possession seem equal, holding each other in balance from one moment to the next. The suspense born of the writing abides there in its own character, using the story for its realm, a quiet and well-commanded suspense, but a genie.

There was an instinct I had, trustworthy or not, that the matter of visibility in her stories had something to do with time. Time permeates them. It is a grave and formidable force.

Ask what time it is in her stories and you are certain to get the answer: the hour is fateful. It is not necessary to see the hands of the clock in her work. It is a time of racing urgency, and it is already too late. And then recall how many of her characters are surviving today only for the sake of tomorrow, are living on tomorrow's coming; think how we see them clearest in reference to tomorrow. Granny Weatherall, up to the last—when God gives her no sign acceptable to her and jilts her Himself—is thinking: "There was always so much to be done, let me see: tomorrow." Laura in "Flowering Judas" is "waiting for tomorrow with a bitter anxiety as if tomorrow may not come." Ordinary, self-respecting, and—up to a certain August day—fairly well blessed Mr. Thompson, because he has been the one to kill the abominable Mr. Hatch, is self-tried, self-pleaded for, and self-condemned to no tomorrow; neither does he leave his sons much of a tomorrow, and certainly he leaves still less of one to poor, red-eyed Mrs. Thompson, who had "so wanted to believe that tomorrow, or at least the day after, life, such a battle at best, was going to be better." In "Old Mortality" time takes Miranda by the hand and leads her into promising herself "in her hopefulness, her ignorance": "At least I can know the truth about what happens to me." In "Pale Horse, Pale Rider" the older Miranda asks Adam, out of her suffering, "Why can we not save each other?" and the straight answer is that there is no time. The story ends with the unforgettable words "Now there would be time for everything" because tomorrow has turned into oblivion, the ultimate betrayer is death itself.

But time, one of the main actors in her stories—teacher, fake healer, conspirator in betrayal, ally of death—is also, within the complete control of Miss Porter, with his inimical powers made use of, one of the movers of her writing, a friend to her work. It occurred to me that what is *seeing* the story is the dispassionate eye of time. Her passionate mind has asked itself, schooled itself, to use Time's eye. Perhaps Time is the genie's name.

Laura is stuck in time, we are told in "Flowering Judas"—and told in the timeless present tense of dreaming, a brilliant working upon our very nerves to let us know precisely Laura's dilemma. There is in all Katherine Anne Porter's work the strongest sense of unity in all the parts; and if it is in any degree a sound guess that an important dramatic element in the story has another role, a working role, in the writing of the story, might this not be one source of a unity so deeply felt? Such a thing in the practice of an art is unsurprising. Who can separate a story from the story's writing?

And there is too, in all the stories, a sense of long, learning life, the life that is the story's own, beginning from a long way back, extending somewhere into the future. As we read, the initial spark is not being struck before our eyes; the fire we see has already purified its nature and burns steadied by purpose, unwavering in meaning. It is no longer impulse, it is a signal, a beacon.

To me, it is the image of the eye of time that remains the longest in the mind at her story's end. There is a judgment to be passed. A moral judgment has to be, in all reason, what she has been getting at. But in a still further act of judiciousness, I feel, she lets Time pass that judgment.

Above all, I feel that what we are responding to in Katherine Anne Porter's work is the intensity of its life, which is more powerful and more profound than even its cry for justice.

They are excoriating stories. Does she have any hope for us at all? Well, do we not feel its implication everywhere—a desperate hope for the understanding that may come, if we use great effort, out of tomorrow, or if not then, maybe the day after? Clearly it has to become at some point an act of faith. It is toward this that her stories all point: here, it seems to me, is the North Star.

And how calm is the surface, the invisible surface of it all! In a style as invisible as the rhythm of a voice, and as much her own as her own voice, she tells her stories of horror and humiliation and in the doing fills her readers with a rising joy. The exemplary prose that is without waste or extravagance or self-indulgence or display, without any claim for its triumph, is full of pride. And her reader shares in that pride, as well he might: it is pride in the language, pride in using the language to search out human meanings, pride in the making of a good piece of work. A personal spell is about the stories, the something of her own that we refer to most often, perhaps, when we mention its beauty, and I think this comes from the *making* of the stories.

Readers have long been in the habit of praising (or could it be at times reproaching?) Katherine Anne Porter by calling her a perfectionist. I do not agree that this is the highest praise, and I would think the word misleading, suggesting as it does in the author a personal vanity in technique and a rigidity, even a deadness, in her prose. To me she is something more serious than a perfectionist. I celebrate her for being a blessed achiever. First she is an artist, of course, and as an artist she is an achiever.

That she hasn't wasted precious time repeating herself in her stories is sign enough, if it were needed, that she was never interested in doing the thing she knew already that she was able to bring off, that she hasn't been showing off for the sake of high marks (from whom?), but has patiently done what was to her her born necessity, quietly and in her own time, and each time the way she saw fit.

We are left with a sense of statement. Virginia Woolf set down in her diary, on the day when she felt she had seen that great brave difficult novel *The Waves* past a certain point in the writing: "But I think it possible that I have got my statues against the sky." It is the achieving of this crucial, this monumental moment in the work itself that we feel has mattered to Katherine Anne Porter. The reader who looks for the flawless result can find it, but looking for that alone he misses the true excitement, exhilaration, of reading, of re-reading. It is the achieving—in a constant present tense—of the work that shines in the mind when we think of her name; and in that achieving lies, it seems to me, the radiance of the work and our recognition of it as unmistakably her own.

And unmistakable is its source. Katherine Anne Porter's deep sense of fairness and justice, her ardent conviction that we need to give and to receive in loving kindness all the human warmth we can make—here is where her stories come from. If they are made by the mind and address the mind, they draw their eloquence from a passionate heart. And for all their pain, they draw their wit, do they not, from a reserve of natural gayety? I have wondered before now if it isn't those who were born gay who can devote themselves most wholeheartedly in their work to seriousness, who have seriousness to burn. The gay are the rich in feeling, and don't need to save any of it back.

Unmistakable, too, is what this artist has made. Order and form no more spring out of order and form than they come riding in to us upon seashells through the spray. In fiction they have to be made out of their very antithesis, life. The art of making is the thing that has meaning, and I think beauty is likely to be something that has for a time lain under good, patient hands. Whether the finished work of art was easy or hard to make, whether it demanded a few hours or many years, concerns nobody but the maker, but the making itself has shaped that work for good and all. In Katherine Anne Porter's stories we feel their making as a bestowal of grace.

It is out of the response to her particular order and form that I believe I may have learned the simplest and surest reason for why I cannot see her stories in their every passing minute, and why it was never necessary or intended that a reader should. Katherine Anne Porter is writing stories of the spirit, and the time that fills those moments is eternity.

# The Way of Dissent

## by Edward G. Schwartz

The way of dissent and the way of orthodoxy are apt to be one and the same. Although Katherine Anne Porter consistently attacks "the military police of orthodoxy" in her essays, she does so not out of lack of faith but by "compulsion of belief," because she, like Thomas Hardy, is committed to the faith of "the Inquirers."[1] The articles of this faith, which, I suppose, is what Miss Porter means when she speaks of the "continuous, central interest and preoccupation of [my] lifetime,"[2] include insistence that the artist be concerned with the fate of individual human beings, with the individual's need for recognizing, understanding, and accepting his human opportunities, responsibilities, and limitations as an animal in nature; emphasis upon the use of reason, tempered by a suspicion that mysterious, irrational forces working in man's unconscious mind may invalidate reason and cause him to rationalize, to delude himself; awareness of the seething internal realities which often are obscured by external appearances; rejection of dogmas that provide easy answers to problems that may, after all, have no solutions; tolerance of the inquisitive spirit in man which enables him to participate with joy in everyday life and which causes him to attempt to see through his illusions, to discover what is "true" for him. Concomitants of Miss Porter's creed are her devotion to truth-telling (i.e., the art of fiction), her skepticism of abstract theories, and her exalted view of the devout artist, who, though he is only human, endued with the responsibilities of other men, is as worthy as the saint. Because Miss Porter's preoccupation is essentially religious, it is appropriate that such expressions as "saints and artists," the "vocation" of the artist,

"The Way of Dissent" by Edward G. Schwartz. From *Western Humanities Review* (Spring 1954). Reprinted by permission of the Publisher.

[1]"Notes on a Criticism of Thomas Hardy," *Southern Review,* VI (1940), 150-161.
[2]*The Days Before* (New York: Harcourt, Brace and Co., 1952), p. vii.

and the poet's songs to the "greater glory of life" recur in her essays.[3]

Katherine Anne Porter's acceptance of her literary calling—"the basic and absorbing occupation, the line intact of my life, which directs my actions, determines my point of view, profoundly affects my character and personality, my social beliefs and economic status, and the kind of friendships I form"[4]—led to her early rejection of the orthodox religious and social beliefs accepted for generations by her family. Born in Indian Creek, Texas, on May 15, 1890, Miss Porter belongs to "the last generation" that reached maturity in the twenties, the jazz age. The world she knew as a child was governed by a fixed code administered by her Kentucky grandmother, her father, her uncles and aunts. This old order, nurtured during the Victorian age, knew what to expect from a young girl of good family and proper upbringing. But Miss Porter, a proud great-great-great granddaughter of Daniel Boone,* confounded the family's expectations: when she was sixteen, she ran away from a Catholic convent school and was married.[5] The following year she left Texas, as she later commented, to escape "the South because I didn't want to be regarded as a freak. That was how they regarded a woman who tried to write. I had to make a rebellion.... When I left, they were all certain I was going to live an immoral life. It was a confining society in those days."[6]

But Miss Porter's rebellion was not complete; she did not intend it to be. Wherever she lived, whether in New Orleans, Chicago, Denver, New York, Hollywood, Bermuda, Mexico City, France, Spain, Germany, or Switzerland, she discovered within herself a past which somehow seemed to shape her present life, to determine her character and her fate. She desired to understand that past, to rediscover that childhood world and the familiar, though, enigmatic, human beings who peopled it. In a far-off country where she could be fascinated by a new landscape with its mysterious inhabitants, Miss

---

[3] *The Days Before, passim.*

[4] Autobiographical Sketch," *Authors Yesterday and Today*, ed. S. J. Kunitz (New York: H. W. Wilson Co., 1933), p. 538.

*[See page 0 in this volume.—Ed.]

[5] Three years later, she was divorced. She was subsequently married (in 1933) to Eugene Pressly, an American career diplomat, and (in 1938) to Albert R. Erskine, Jr., an English teacher at Louisiana State University. These marriages also ended in divorces.

[6] Archer Winsten, "The Portrait of an Artist," *New York Post,* May 6, 1937, p. 17. (An early interview.)

Porter found the "constant exercise of memory...to be the chief occupation of my mind, and all my experience seems to be simply memory with continuity, marginal notes, constant revision and comparison of one thing with another."[7] Neither abstract speculation nor rationalization about the meaning of life, but exact memory of past events concerned her. She set about to resist "one of the most disturbing habits of the human mind...its willful and destructive forgetting of whatever in its past does not confirm or flatter its present point of view."[8] Like Henry James, Miss Porter was determined to obtain "knowledge at the price of finally, utterly 'seeing through' everything"[9] —everything, even a sheltered childhood, which by most standards was fortunate and happy.

Critical as Miss Porter is of the inadequacies of the old order, she does not completely reject it or despise it. She understands what it can mean to live in a world in which people do not share ideas, intuitions, habits, and customs; so she values the stable society in which "there is no groping for motives, no divided faith: [the Mexican peons] love their past with that uncritical, unquestioning devotion which is beyond logic and above reason. Order and precision they know by heart. Instinctive obedience to the changeless laws of nature, strait fidelity to their inner sense mark all they do."[10] And she admires Henry James partly because

> nothing came to supplant or dislocate in any way [his] early affections and attachments and admirations. This is not to say he never grew beyond them, nor that he did not live to question them, for he did both; but surely no one ever projected more lovingly and exactly the climate of youth, of budding imagination, the growth of the tender, perceptive mind, the particular freshness and keenness of feeling, the unconscious generosity and warmth of heart of the young brought up in the dangerous illusion of safety; and though no writer ever "grew up" with more sobriety and pure intelligence, still there lay at the back of his mind the memory of a lost paradise; it was in the long run the standard by which he measured the world he learned so thoroughly....[11]

For Miss Porter, too, the old stable order provides the standard by

[7]"Notes on Writing," *New Directions,* 1940, ed. James Laughlin (Norfolk, Conn.: New Directions, 1940), p. 203.

[8]*Ibid.,* p. 203.

[9]"The Days Before," *Kenyon Review,* V (Autumn, 1943), 492.

[10]*Outline of Mexican Popular Arts and Crafts* (Los Angeles: Young & M'Callister, Inc., 1922), p. 39.

[11]"The Days Before," p. 494.

which the failures (and the occasional successes) of modern man in a chaotic, mechanized world are measured. But for her the old order shares the responsibility for some of the failures of the new. And Miss Porter's memories of the matriarchal world of her childhood did not permit her to describe it as a lost paradise, because the old order had its serious failures, too, its abnegation of important human needs and desires.

Victorian morality, the bulwark of the old, settled Southern society of Miss Porter's childhood, was based on such orthodox dogmas as original sin, the existence of a personal God, the purposiveness of all human life, the need for regarding man's life on earth as preparation for a refined spiritual life after death. When Miss Porter left the care of her family and moved out of the South, she revolted against not only the customs of the old order but also its fundamental convictions. The traditional dogmas of orthodox Christianity, Miss Porter came to believe, could only hinder the artist, who must find his own answers, his own truths. In a violent attack upon T. S. Eliot for his criticism of Thomas Hardy, Miss Porter renounces the tradition of orthodoxy and moves, with Hardy, "into another tradition of equal antiquity, equal importance, equal seriousness, a body of opinion running parallel throughout history to the body of law in church and state: the tradition of dissent."[12]

Recognizing "the unbridgable abyss" between the questions posed by Hardy and the answers offered by the orthodox Mr. Eliot, Miss Porter asserts that "the yawning abyss between question and answer remains the same, and until this abyss is closed the dissent will remain, persistent, obdurate, a kind of church in itself, with its leaders, teachers, saints, martyrs, heroes; a thorn in the flesh of Orthodoxy, but I think not necessarily of the devil on that account."[13] Intent upon probing her own world for the meaning of what she sees, hears, feels, thinks, Miss Porter is unwilling to relinquish her calling, the art of fiction, by accepting the catechism she was taught at the convent school; but she concedes that "there is at the heart of the universe a riddle no man can solve, and in the end God may be the answer."[14]

Perhaps what Miss Porter most deplores about organized religion is its misdirection of men, its cynicism and false otherworldly orien-

---

[12]"Notes on a Criticism of Thomas Hardy," p. 153.
[13]*Ibid.*, pp. 153-154.
[14]*Ibid.*, p. 155.

tation. Man's mysticism, Miss Porter complains, "has been harnessed rudely to machinery of the most mundane sort, and has been made to serve the ends of an organization which ruling under divine guidance, has rules very little better, and in some respects, worse, than certain frankly man-made systems of government."[15] Organized religion, she continues, has justified "the most cynical expedients of worldly government by a high morality" and committed "the most savage crimes against human life for the love of God."[16] Furthermore, the leaders of the church, often "God-intoxicated mystics and untidy saints with only a white blaze of divine love where their minds should have been," are "perpetually creating as much disorder within the law as outside it."[17] Miss Porter, aware of man's self-deception, distrusts mystics because "the most dangerous people in the world are the illuminated ones through whom forces act when they themselves are unconscious of their own motives."[18]

The proper concern of man, according to Miss Porter, is the visible world. She rejects the theological notion that "the world [is] a testing ground for the soul of man in preparation for eternity, and that his sufferings [are] part of a 'divine' plan, or indeed, so far as the personal fate of mankind [is] concerned, of any plan at all."[19] Instead, she insists upon a humanistic, this-worldly orientation, for "both malevolence and benevolence originated in the mind of man, and the warring forces [are] within him alone; such plan as [exists] in regard to him he [has] created for himself, his Good and his Evil [are] alike the mysterious inventions of his own mind."[20] The tangible world was the one Miss Porter would have, so she, like Henry James, "strained and struggled outward to meet it, to absorb it, to understand it, to be part of it."[21]

Since Miss Porter believes that men bring evil upon themselves by attributing human ills to divine providence and by preparing for a

[15]*Ibid.*, p. 155.
[16]*Ibid.*, p. 155.
[17]*Ibid.*, p. 154.
[18]"James' *The Turn of the Screw*," *New Invitation to Learning*, ed. Mark Van Doren (New York: Random House, 1942), p. 230. Cf. "A Bright Particular Faith," *Hound and Horn*, VII (January, 1934), 246-257; and "A Goat for Azazel," *Partisan Review*, VII (May, 1940), 188-199. In these chapters from an unfinished biography of Cotton Mather, Miss Porter seems most impressed with the egotism, pride, and self-deception of the early American "saint."
[19]"Notes on a Criticism of Thomas Hardy," p. 157.
[20]*Ibid.*, p. 157.
[21]"The Days Before," p. 492.

spiritual after-life instead of concerning themselves with the every-day world, she insists upon the efficacy of social reform: "man could make the earth a more endurable place for himself if he would."[22] She believes, with Hardy, in the use of "reasonableness: the use of intelligence directed towards the best human solution of human ills."[23] But, while Miss Porter expects men to use reason to amelio-rate human suffering, she qualifies whatever optimism might be implicit in her faith in reasonableness by her conviction that "the refusal to acknowledge the evils in ourselves which therefore are implicit in any human situation is as unworkable a proposition as the doctrine of total depravity."[24] These evils are inherent in man's unconscious life; they belong to that part of human nature which is "not grounded in commonsense, [that] deep place...where the mind does not go, where the blind monsters sleep and wake, war among themselves and feed upon death."[25] This irrational element in human nature is "not subject to mathematical equation or the water-tight theories of dogma, and this intransigent, measureless force [is] divided against itself, in conflict with its own system of laws and the unknown laws of the universe."[26]

Respect for the dignity of the individual, whose complicated life, both conscious and unconscious, cannot be explained away by in-genious theories or impressive abstract words, enables Miss Porter to reject the dogmatic line of political parties as well as religious sects. The artist, Miss Porter believes, cannot restrict his view by adhering to a party line because "all working practical political systems...are based upon and operate in contempt of human life and the individual fate; in accepting any one of them and shaping his mind and work to that mold, the artist dehumanizes himself, un-fits himself for the practice of an art."[27] Commending Eudora Welty for escaping "a militant social consciousness," Miss Porter observes that Miss Welty is supported by "an ancient system of ethics, an un-answerable, indispensable moral law," which has "never been the particular property of any party or creed or nation," but which re-lates to "that true and human world of which the artist is a living

[22]"Notes on a Criticism of Thomas Hardy," p. 156.
[23]*Ibid.*, p. 156.
[24]"Love and Hate," *Mademoiselle*, October, 1948, p. 204.
[25]"Notes on a Criticism of Thomas Hardy," p. 157.
[26]*Ibid.*, p. 157.

[27]Introduction, *A Curtain of Green*, by Eudora Welty (New York: Doubleday, Doran and Co., 1941), pp. xii-xiv.

part; and when he dissociates himself from it in favor of political, which is to say, inhuman, rules, he cuts himself away from his proper society—living men."[28]

The artist's job of work is to deal with the "true and human world" he himself knows. He does this not as that "parochial visitor," Mr. Eliot, legislates, for the edification of his audience; "in the regions of art, as religion, edification is not the highest form of intellectual or spiritual existence."[29] The artist's creations, Miss Porter believes, "are considerably richer, invoked out of deeper sources in the human consciousness, more substantially nourishing than this lukewarm word can express."[30] Thus, her own work has been an attempt "to discover and understand human motives, human feelings, to make a distillation of what human relations and experiences my mind has been able to absorb."[31] And her admiration is for the writer who, like Katherine Mansfield, with "fine objectivity" bares "a moment of experience, real experience, in the life of some human being; [Miss Mansfield] states no belief, gives no motives, airs no theories, but simply presents to the reader a situation, a place, and a character, and there it is; and the emotional content is present implicitly as the germ is in the wheat."[32] This comes very close to being a description of Miss Porter's own method of composition, which is to record objectively her exact memory of life as she knows it, to avoid rationalizations, to trust her reader to find within the story or short novel the unifying and informing theme or symbol. Miss Porter begins with an image, an incident, a character: "a section here and a section there has been written—little general scenes explored and developed. Or scenes or sketches of characters which were never intended to be incorporated in the finished work have been developed in the process of trying to understand the full potentiality of the material."[33] At the critical moment, "thousands of memories converge, harmonize, arrange themselves around a central idea in a coherent form, and I write a story."[34]

Since Miss Porter's "aesthetic bias, [her] one aim is to tell a straight

[28]*Ibid.*, p. xiii. Cf. "Corridos," *Survey,* LII (May, 1924), 158. "Such things [as revolution] are ephemerae to the maker of ballads. He is concerned with the eternal verities."

[29]"Notes on a Criticism of Thomas Hardy," p. 154.

[30]*Ibid.*, p. 154.

[31]"The Situation in American Writing," *Partisan Review,* VI (Summer, 1939), 38.

[32]"The Art of Katherine Mansfield," *Nation,* CXLV (October 23, 1937), 436.

[33]"Notes on Writing," p. 203.

[34]*Ibid.*, p. 203.

story and to give true testimony,"[35] she is convinced that the artist must retain a close, vital connection with society. She agrees with Diego Rivera's objection to early Mexican artists who "were still thrall to the idea that the artist is an entity distinct from the human world about him, mysteriously set apart from the community;... they still regarded painting as a priestly function. This is an old superstition, and though the artist did not invent it, he became ultimately its victim."[36] While Miss Porter looks upon her work as a "vocation," a "calling,"[37] and sometimes feels that "only the work of saints and artists gives us any reason to believe the human race is worth belonging to,"[38] she distrusts the romantic, illuminated artist: "I think the influence of Whitman on certain American writers has been disastrous, for he encourages them in the vices of self-love (often disguised as love of humanity, or the working classes, or God), the assumption of prophetic powers, of romantic superiority to the limitations of craftsmanship, inflated feeling, and slovenly expression."[39] Like Rivera, she feels that "when art becomes a cult of individual eccentricity, a meager precious and neurasthenic body struggling for breath; when it becomes modish and exclusive, the aristocratic pleasure of the few, it is a dead thing,"[40] Miss Porter considers the artist's obligations to society to be "the plain and simple responsibility of any other human being, for I refuse to separate the artist from the human race."[41] The artist should expect no special privileges from society, no "guarantee of economic security"; for he "cannot be a hostile critic of society and expect society to feed [him] regularly. The artist of the present is demanding (I think childishly) that he be given, free, a great many irreconcilable rights and privileges."[42]

Preferring the kind of art that aims at "a perfect realism, a complete statement of the thing [the artist] sees," Miss Porter expects the artist to write about his own familiar country, the world and peo-

[35]"Autobiographical Sketch," p. 539.

[36]"The Guild Spirit in Mexican Art" (as told to Katherine Anne Porter by Diego Rivera), *Survey,* LII (May, 1924), 175.

[37]Cf. "Homage to Ford Madox Ford," *New Directions, Number 7,* ed. James Laughlin (Norfold, Conn.: New Directions, 1942), p. 175.

[38]"Transplanted Writers," *Books Abroad,* XVI (July, 1942), 274.

[39]"The Situation in American Writing," p. 36.

[40]"The Guild Spirit in Mexican Art," p. 175. Cf. 'Gertrude Stein: A Self-Portrait," *Harper's,* CXCV (December, 1947), 519-528.

[41]"The Situation in American Writing," p. 39. Cf. "Transplanted Writers," p. 274.

[42]*Ibid.,* p. 38.

ple he knows best.[43] She early took issue with critics who complained that the guild art of Mexico was provincial and lacked sophistication: "a peasant art," she wrote, "is what it is, what it should be."[44] Miss Porter also disagreed with the editors of *Partisan Review* who (when it was fashionable) were critical of the renewed emphasis in American literature on the specifically native elements in contemporary culture; she thought "the 'specifically American' things might not be the worst things for us to cultivate, since this is America and we are Americans, and our history is not altogether disgraceful."[45] Thus her enthusiasm could be aroused by such a writer as Willa Cather, who was

> a provincial, and I hope not the last. She was a good artist, and all true art is provincial in the most realistic sense: of the very time and place of its making, out of human beings who are so particularly limited by their situation, whose faces and names are real and whose lives begin each one at an individual unique center. Indeed, Willa Cather was as provincial as Hawthorne, or Flaubert, or Turgenev, or Jane Austen.[46]

Besides reflecting Miss Porter's special interest in her own particular region, her strong defense of provincialism is an extension of her skepticism of modern industrial progress, which, she fears, destroys individuality and results in an empty uniformitarianism. Miss Porter further suspects that should the artist be removed from his "fructifying contact with his mother earth, condemned daily to touch instead the mechanics and artifices of modern progress, he might succumb as do the aristocratic arts,... to the overwhelming forces of a world turned dizzyingly by a machine."[47] While Miss Porter directs her irony at the "myth creativeness which has always marked the ideas of man pitiably eager to explain himself to himself, to open the door to eternity with the key of his human imagination," she values the "symbols of the racial mind" that the artist

[43]*Outline of Mexican Popular Arts and Crafts*, p. 42. Cf. "Defoe's *Moll Flanders*," *New Invitation to Learning*, p. 143. "I like the introspective novel very much,... but I do think that the weakness of it is that when a novelist gets inside a character, he finds only himself, and the great art really is to be able to look at the world and individuals and present characters that readers will recognize and will know or feel they know." Cf. "The Days Before," p. 491.

[44]*Ibid.*, p. 33.

[45]"The Situation in American Writing," p. 38.

[46]The Calm, Pure Art of Willa Cather," *New York Times Book Review*, Sept. 25, 1949, p. 1.

[47]*Outline of Mexican Popular Arts and Crafts*, p. 38.

can discover by concerning himself with individuals of a particular time and place.[48]

Related to Miss Porter's taste for provincial literature is her conviction that really good art, like the early twentieth-century peasant art of Mexico, must be natural, organic—"a living thing that grows as a tree grows, thrusting up from its roots and saps, knots and fruits and tormented branches, without an uneasy feeling that it should be refined for art's sake."[49] The writer, too, must come by his art organically; artistic technique "is an internal matter."[50] A writer is "dyed in his own color; it is useless to ask him to change his faults or his virtues; he must...work out his own salvation."[51] The art of fiction "cannot be taught, but only learned by the individual in his own way, at his own pace and his own time."[52] Or, as Miss Porter once advised young writers, "if you have any personality of your own, you will have a style of your own; it grows, as your ideas grow, and as your knowledge of your craft increases."[53]

Although Miss Porter seems to accept an organic theory of art, she prefers Henry James to such an "organic" writer as Whitman, because she holds with "the conscious disciplined artist, the serious expert against the expansive, indiscriminately 'cosmic' sort."[54] Her skepticism moves in two directions—against the academic teacher and the literary cult that obstructs the artist from following his calling in his own individual way, and against the egotistical artist who wants to express himself, to become (as Emerson wanted to) the mystical eyeball of the universe. Miss Porter considers the artist's job to be the creation of order, of form, but she does not value technical virtuosity for its own sake: "unless my material, my feelings, my problems on each new...work are not well ahead of my technical skill at the moment, I should distrust the whole thing. When virtuosity gets the upper hand of your theme, or is better than your idea, it is time to quit."[55] Miss Porter's concern with problems of style, then, stems from her desire to curb the artist's emotional tendencies and to make his ideas more precise.

[48] *Ibid.,* pp. 5, 9.
  *Ibid.,* p. 33.
[50] "Notes on Writing," p. 195.
[51] "The Situation in American Writing," p. 35.
[52] Introduction, *A Curtain of Green,* p. xii.
[53] "No Plot, My Dear, No Story," *Writer,* LV (1942), 168.
[54] "The Situation in American Writing," p. 34.
[55] "Notes on Writing," p. 196.

Miss Porter's interest in the technical problems of her craft also results from her affinity for "the new way of writing."[56] But the new movement in literature involved much more than a change of style; it included a view of reality that (its adherents thought) was radically different from that of Arnold Bennett or H. G. Wells or other Edwardian writers. The Edwardians described the fabric of things, the externals, but the new writers were to be concerned with the internal reality, the truth of the human heart. Miss Porter found in Virginia Woolf's first novel, *The Voyage Out,* "the same sense of truth I had got in early youth from Laurence Sterne..., from Jane Austen, from Emily Bronte, from Henry James."[57] These and W. B. Yeats, James Joyce, T. S. Eliot, and Ezra Pound seemed "in the most personal way...to be my contemporaries; their various visions of reality merged for me into one vision, one world view."[58]

To express this vision of reality adequately a writer needed new techniques, new forms; he needed to develop an exact, nondiscursive fiction which could simultaneously contain detailed, objective description and intricate patterns of symbols. In his own way, each writer Miss Porter admires had developed the necessary tools. Miss Porter values James' "extreme sense of the appearance of things, manners, dress, social customs, [through which] he could convey mysterious but deep impressions of individual character."[59] She also could admire in Katherine Mansfield's stories "the sense of human beings living on many planes at once with all the elements justly ordered and in right proportion."[60] Miss Porter's acceptance of the new world view and her desire to find a proper vehicle to contain it result in her "deeply personal interest" in the kind of story "where external act and the internal voiceless life of the imagination almost meet and mingle on the mysterious threshold between dream and waking, one reality refusing to admit or confirm the existence of the other, yet both conspiring toward the same end."[61]

Like Willa Cather, Katherine Anne Porter never has been primarily concerned with literary theory. And so Miss Porter's critical position may sometimes seem ambiguous, at times even contradictory. Her preference for the conscious artist who is alert to the technical

---

[56]"Example to the Young," *New Republic,* LXVI (April 22, 1931), 279.
[57]"Virginia Woolf's Essays," *New York Times Book Review,* May 7, 1950, p. 3.
[58]*Ibid.,* p. 3.
[59]"The Days Before," p. 491.
[60]"The Art of Katherine Mansfield," p. 436.
[61]Introduction, *A Curtain of Green,* p. xviii.

problems of his craft, for instance, may seem to contradict her advocacy of an organic theory apparently akin to that of Whitman, whose "expansive, indiscriminate 'cosmic'" impulse the skeptical, rational Miss Porter distrusts. And her concept of the poet as a "seer" set apart and to be trusted more than other men may not be entirely compatible with her notion of the poet as being like other men, with the usual social responsibilities and privileges.[62]

But the most striking paradox in Miss Porter's position emerges from her consistent definition of the nature of her devotion to her "basic and absorbing occupation," for Miss Porter's language suggests religious devotion and faith: she speaks of art as a "calling," of "saints and artists." of giving "true testimony," of the "indispensable moral law," of the necessity for "order and precision," of the "only two possibilities for any real order: art and religion." The paradox of Miss Porter's negation of the orthodoxy of her Catholic[63] family, of her denial of social and political authoritarianism, is that its end is affirmation: extremes meet; "the way up and the way down is one and the same," as Heraclitus was wont to say and as the orthodox T. S. Eliot seems to agree (in "Burnt Norton"). For Miss Porter —ironically, in view of her skepticism—declares her faith in the continuity of human life through art. The arts, Miss Porter declares,

> do live continuously, and they live literally by faith; their names and their shapes and their uses and their basic meanings survive unchanged in all that matters through times of interruption, diminishment, neglect; they outlive governments and creeds and the societies, even the very civilizations that produced them. They cannot be destroyed altogether because they represent the substance of faith and the only reality. They are what we find again when the ruins are cleared away. And even the smallest and most incomplete offering at this time can be a proud act of faith in defense of that faith.[64]

Like Henry James, Miss Porter's quest for moral definition led not to philosophy or religion but to art. She thus became the inheritor of a great tradition—the tradition of dissent and inquiry, of selfless devotion of the search for meaning and order to the world of fiction.

---

[62]Cf. "Quetzalcoatl," *New York Herald Tribune Books*, March 7, 1926, p. 1; and The Situation in American Writing," p. 39.

[63]The Porter family was, apparently, Methodist.—Ed.]

[64]Introduction, *Flowering Judas and Other Stories* (New York: Modern Library, 1940), p. ii.

# Irony with a Center

## by Robert Penn Warren

The fiction of Katherine Anne Porter, despite widespread critical adulation, has never found the public which its distinction merits.
Many of her stories are unsurpassed in modern fiction, and some are
not often equaled. She belongs to the relatively small group of writers—extraordinarily small, when one considers the vast number of
stories published every year in English and American magazines—
who have done serious, consistent, original, and vital work in the
form of short fiction—the group which would include James Joyce,
Katherine Mansfield, Sherwood Anderson, and Ernest Hemingway.
This list does not include a considerable number of other writers
who, though often finding other forms more congenial—the novel
or poetry—have scored occasional triumphs in the field of short
fiction. Then, of course, there is a very large group of writers who
have a great facility, a great mechanical competence, and sometimes
moments of real perception, but who work from no fundamental and
central conviction.

It was once fashionable to argue complacently that the popular
magazine had created the short story—had provided the market and
had cultivated an appetite for the product. It is true that the magazine did provide the market, but at the same time, and progressively,
the magazine has corrupted the short story. What the magazine encourages is not so much the short story as a conscious or unconscious
division of the artistic self of the writer. One can still discover (as
in an address delivered by Mr. Frederick Lewis Allen to the American Philosophical Society) a genial self-congratulation in the face of
"mass appreciation." But, writes Mr. R. P. Blackmur in reply:

> In fact, mass appreciation of the kind which Mr. Allen approves rep-
> resents the constant danger to the artist of any serious sort: *the danger*

*of popularization before creation.* ... The difference between great art and popular art is relatively small; but the difference between either and popularized art is radical, and absolute. Popular art is topical and natural, great art is deliberate and thematic. What can be popularized in either is only what can be sold...a scheme which requires the constant replacement of the shoddy goods. He (Mr. Allen) does not mean to avow this; he no doubt means the contrary; but there it is. Until American or any other society is educated either up to the level or back to the level of art with standards, whether popular or great, it can be sold nothing but art without standards....

The fact that Miss Porter has not attempted a compromise may account for the relatively small body of her published fiction. There was the collection of stories published in 1931 under the title *Flowering Judas;* an enlarged collection, under the same title in 1935, which includes two novelettes, "The Cracked Looking-Glass" and "Hacienda," the latter of which had been previously published by Harrison, in Paris; a collection of three novelettes under the title *Pale Horse, Pale Rider,* in 1939; the Modern Library edition of *Flowering Judas;* and a few pieces, not yet in book form, which have appeared in various magazines—for instance, sections of the uncompleted biography of Cotton Mather and the brilliant story "A Day's Work."[1]

Her method of composition does not, in itself, bend readily to the compromise. In many instances, a story or novelette has not been composed straight off. Instead, a section here and a section there have been written—little germinal scenes explored and developed. Or scenes or sketches of character which were never intended to be incorporated in the finished work have been developed in the process of trying to understand the full potentiality of the material. One might guess at an approach something like this: a special, local excitement provoked by the material—character or incident; an attempt to define the nature of that local excitement, as local—to squeeze it and not lose a drop; an attempt to understand the relationships of the local excitements and to define the implications—to arrive at theme; the struggle to reduce theme to pattern. That would seem to be the natural history of the characteristic story. Certainly, it is a method which requires time, scrupulosity, and contemplation.

The method itself is an index to the characteristics of Miss Porter's fiction—the rich surface detail scattered with apparently casual profuseness and the close structure which makes such detail meaning-

[1]Since included in the volume *The Leaning Tower.*

ful; the great compression and economy which one discovers upon analysis; the precision of psychology and observation, the texture of the style.

Most reviewers, commenting upon Miss Porter's distinction, refer to her "style"—struck, no doubt, by an exceptional felicity of phrase, a precision in the use of metaphor, and a subtlety of rhythm. It is not only the appreciation of the obviously poetical strain in Miss Porter's work that has tended to give her reputation some flavor of the special and exquisite, but also the appreciation of the exceptional precision of her language. When one eminent critic praises her for an "English of a purity and precision almost unique in contemporary American fiction," he is giving praise richly merited and praise for a most important quality, but this praise, sad to relate as a commentary on our times, is a kind that does encourage the special reputation. This same eminent critic also praises Miss Porter as an artist, which goes to say that he himself knows very well that her language is but one aspect of her creations; but even so, the word *artist* carries its own overtones of exquisiteness.

The heart of the potential reader may have been chilled—and I believe quite rightly—by the praise of "beautiful style." He is put off by a reviewer's easy abstracting of style for comment and praise; his innocence repudiates the fallacy of agreeable style. The famous common reader is not much concerned with English as such, pure or impure, precise or imprecise, and he is no more concerned with the artist as artist. He is concerned with what the English will say to him, and with what the artist will do for him, or to him.

It is, of course, just and proper for us to praise Miss Porter for her English and her artistry, but we should remind ourselves that we prize those things because she uses them to create vivid and significant images of life. All this is not to say that we are taking the easy moralistic, or easy Philistine, view of English or artistry. We know that the vividness and the significance of any literary work exist only in the proper medium, and that only because of a feeling for the medium and an understanding of artistry did the writer succeed, in the first place, in discovering vividness and significance. We hope that we shall never have to remind ourselves of that fact, and now we remind ourselves of the vividness and significance in which Miss Porter's English and artistry eventuate, only because we would balance praise for the special with praise for the general, praise for subtlety with praise for strength, praise for sensibility with praise for intellect.

But let us linger upon the matter of Miss Porter's style in the hope that it can be used as a point of departure. Take, for example, a paragraph from the title story of *Flowering Judas,* the description of Braggioni, the half-Italian, half-Indian revolutionist in Mexico, "a leader of men, skilled revolutionist, and his skin has been punctured in honorable warfare." His followers "warm themselves in his reflected glory and say to each other, 'He has a real nobility, a love of humanity raised above mere personal affections.' The excess of this self-love has flowed out, inconveniently for her, over Laura"—the puzzled American girl who has been lured to Mexico by revolutionary enthusiasm and before whom he sits with his guitar and sings sentimental songs, while his wife weeps at home. But here is the passage.

> Braggioni...leans forward, balancing his paunch between his spread knees, and sings with tremendous emphasis, weighing his words. He has, the song relates, no father and no mother, nor even a friend to console him; lonely as a wave of the sea he comes and goes, lonely as a wave. His mouth opens round and yearns sideways, his balloon cheeks grow oily with the labor of song. He bulges marvelously in his expensive garments. Over his lavender collar, crushed upon a purple necktie, held by a diamond hoop: over his ammunition belt of tooled leather worked in silver, buckled cruelly around his gasping middle: over the tops of his glossy yellow shoes Braggioni swells with ominous ripeness, his mauve silk hose stretched taut, his ankles bound with the stout leather thongs of his shoes.
>
> When he stretches his eyelids at Laura she notes again that his eyes are the true tawny yellow cat's eyes. He is rich, not in money, he tells her, but in power, and this power brings with it the blameless ownership of things, and the right to indulge his love of small luxuries. "I have a taste for the elegant refinements," he said once, flourishing a yellow silk handkerchief before her nose. "Smell that? It is Jockey Club, imported from New York." Nonetheless he is wounded by life. He will say so presently. "It is true everything turns to dust in the hand, to gall on the tongue." He sighs and his leather belt creaks like a saddle girth.

The passage is sharp and evocative. Its phrasing embodies a mixture, a fusion, of the shock of surprise and the satisfaction of precision —a resolved tension, which may do much to account for the resonance and vibration of the passage. We have in it the statement, "His mouth opens round and yearns sideways"—and we note the two words *yearns* and *sideways;* in the phrase, "labor of song"; in, "he bulges marvelously"; in, "Braggioni swells with ominous ripeness." But upon inspection it may be discovered that the effect of these details is not merely a local effect. The subtle local evocations really involve us in the center of the scene; we are taken to the core of the meaning of the scene, and thence to the central impulse of the story; and thence, possibly to the germinal idea of all of this author's fiction. All of these filaments cannot be pursued back through the web—the occasion does not permit; but perhaps a few can be traced to the meaning of the scene itself in the story.

What we have here is the revolutionist who loves luxury, who feels that power gives blameless justification to the love of elegant refinements, but whose skin has been punctured in "honorable warfare"; who is a competent leader of men, but who is vain and indolent; who is sentimental and self-pitying, but, at the same time, ruthless; who betrays his wife and yet, upon his return home, will weep with his wife as she washes his feet and weeps; who labors for the good of man, but is filled with self-love.

We have here a tissue of contradictions, and the very phraseology takes us to these contradictions. For instance, the word *yearns* involves the sentimental, blurred emotion, but immediately afterward the words *sideways* and *oily* remind us of the grossness, the brutality, the physical appetite. So when the implied paradox in the "labor of song." The ammunition belt, we recall, is buckled *cruelly* about his "gasping middle." The ammunition belt reminds us that this indolent, fat, apparently soft, vain man is capable of violent action, is a man of violent profession, and sets the stage for the word *cruelly*, which involves the paradox of the man who loves mankind and is capable of individual cruelties, and which, further, reminds us that he punishes himself out of physical vanity and punishes himself by defining himself in his calling—the only thing that belts in his sprawling, meaningless animality. He swells with "ominous ripeness"—and we sense the violent threat in the man as contrasted with his softness, a kind of great overripe plum as dangerous as a grenade, a feeling of corruption mixed with sentimental sweetness; and specifically we are reminded of the threat to Laura in the situation. We come to the phrase "wounded by life," and we pick up again the motif hinted at in the song and in the lingering rhythms: "He has, the song relates, no father and no mother, nor even a friend to console him; lonely as a wave of the sea he comes and goes, lonely as a wave." In nothing is there to be found a balm—not in revolution, in vanity, in love—for the "vast cureless wound of his self-esteem."

Then, after the bit about the wound, we find the sentence: "He sighs and his leather belt creaks like a saddle girth." The defeated, sentimental sigh, the cureless wound, and the bestial creaking of the leather.

If this reading of the passage is acceptable, the passage itself is a rendering of the problem which the character of Braggioni poses to Laura. It is stated, in bare, synoptic form, elsewhere:

> The gluttonous bulk of Braggioni has become a symbol of her many disillusions, for a revolutionist should be lean, animated by heroic faith, a vessel of abstract virtues. This is nonsense, she knows it now and is ashamed of it. Revolution must have leaders, and leadership is a career for energetic men. She is, her comrades tell her, full of romantic error, for what she defines as a cynicism is to them merely a developed sense of reality.

What is the moral reality here? This question is, I should say, the theme of the story, which exists in an intricate tissue of paradox, and is posed only in the dream Laura has at the end, a dream which embodies but does not resolve the question.

With all the enchanting glitter of style and all the purity of language and all the flow and flicker of feeling, Miss Porter's imagination, as a matter of fact, is best appreciated if we appreciate its essential austerity, its devotion to the fact drenched in God's direct daylight, its concern with the inwardness of character, and its delight in the rigorous and discriminating deployment of a theme. Let us take another passage from her work, a passage from the novelette "Noon Wine," the description of Mr. Thompson, a poor dirt-farmer in Texas, busy at his churning, a task that he, in his masculine pride and bitter incompetence, finds contemptible and demeaning:

> Mr. Thompson was a tough weather-beaten man with stiff black hair and a week's growth of black whiskers. He was a noisy proud man who held his neck so straight his whole face stood level with his Adam's apple, and the whiskers continued down his neck and disappeared into a black thatch under his open collar. The churn rumbled and swished like the belly of a trotting horse, and Mr. Thompson seemed somehow to be driving a horse with one hand, reining it in and urging it forward; and every now and then he turned halfway around and squirted a tremendous spit of tobacco juice out over the steps. The door stones were brown and gleaming with fresh tobacco juice.

This passage is simple and unpretending, a casual introductory description near the beginning of a story, but it succeeds in having its own kind of glitter and purity and flow. Here those things come, as in so much of Miss Porter's fiction, from the writer's rigorous repudiation of obvious literary resources, resources which, on other occasions, she can use so brilliantly. The things that stir our admiration in the passage from "Flowering Judas" are notably absent here, are notably eschewed. Here the style is of the utmost transparency, and our eye and ear are captivated by the very ordinariness of the ordinary items presented to us, the trotting motion of the churn, the swish of the milk, the tobacco juice glittering on the door stones. Miss Porter has the power of isolating common things, the power that Chekhov or Frost or Ibsen or, sometimes, Pound has, the power to make the common thing glow with an Eden-innocence by the mere fact of the isolation. It is a kind of indicative poetry.

Miss Porter's eye and ear, however, do not seize with merely random and innocent delight on the objects of the world, even though we may take that kind of delight in the objects she so lovingly places before us, transmuted in their ordinariness. If the fact drenched in daylight commands her unfaltering devotion, it is because such facts are in themselves a deep language, or can be made to utter a language of the deepest burden. What are the simple facts saying in the paragraph just quoted?

They are saying something about Mr. Thompson, poor Mr. Thompson who will die of a self-inflicted gunshot wound before many pages have passed, and will die of it because he is all the things we might have surmised of him if we had been able to understand beforehand the language of the simple facts of the scene at the churn. The pridefully stiff neck and the black whiskers, they tell us something. He is the sort of man who ought, or thinks he ought, to be holding the reins of a spanking horse and not the cord of a churn, and his very gesture has a kind of childish play acting. Somewhere in his deepest being, he is reminded of the spanking horse with the belly swishing in the trot, the horse such a fine manly man ought to have under his hand, if luck just weren't so ornery and unreasonable, and so he plays the game with himself. But he can't quite convince himself. It is only a poor old churn, after all, woman's work on a rundown and debt-bit shirt-tail farm, with kids and an ailing wife, and so he spits his tremendous spits of masculine protest against fate, and the brown juice gleams with its silly, innocent assertiveness on the stones the woman's broom has, so many times, swept clean of this and that. In the end, looking back, we can see that the story is the story of a noisy, proud, stiff-necked man whose pride has constantly suffered under failure, who salves his hurt pride by harmless bluster with his wife and children, and who, in the end, stumbles into a situation which takes the last prop of certainty from his life.

Our first glimpse of Mrs. Thompson is in the "front room," where she lies with the green shade down and a wet cloth over her poor weak eyes. But in spite of the weeping eyes, the longing for the cool dark, and all her sad incompetence, on the one hand, and Mr. Thompson's bluster and hurt pride on the other, there is a warm secret life between them:

> "Tell *you* the truth, Ellie," said Mr. Thompson, picking his teeth with a fork and leaning back in the best of humors, "I always thought your granma was a ter'ble ole fool. She'd just say the first thing that popped into her head and call it God's wisdom."
>
> "My granma wasn't anybody's fool. Nine times out of ten she knew what she was talking about. I always say, the first thing you think is the best thing you can say."
>
> "Well," said Mr. Thompson, going into another shout, "you're so ree*fined* about that goat story, you just try speaking out in mixed comp'ny sometime! You just try it. S'pose you happened to be thinking about a hen and a rooster, hey? I reckon you'd shock the Babtist preacher!" He gave her a good pinch on her thin little rump. "No more meat on you than a rabbit," he said, fondly. "Now I like 'em cornfed."
>
> Mrs. Thompson looked at him open-eyed and blushed. She could see better by lamplight. "Why, Mr. Thompson, sometimes I think you're the evilest-minded man that ever lived." She took a handful of hair on the crown of his head and gave it a good, slow pull. "That's to show you how it feels, pinching so hard when you're supposed to be playing," she said, gently.

This little glimpse of their secret life, Mr. Thompson's masculine, affectionate bragging and bullying and teasing, and Mrs. Thompson's shy and embarrassed playfulness, comes as a surprise in the middle of their drab world, a sudden brightness and warmth. Without this episode we should never get the full force of Mr. Thompson's bafflement and anger when Mr. Hatch, the baleful stranger, misinterprets Mr. Thompson's prideful talk of his wife's ill health and says that he himself would get rid of a puny wife mighty quick. And without this episode we should never sense how that bafflement and anger flow, as one more component, into the moment when Mr. Thompson sees, or thinks he sees, the blade of Mr. Hatch's bowie knife go into the poor Swede's stomach, and he brings his axe down on Hatch's head, as though stunning a beef.

We are, however, getting ahead of ourselves. Let us summarize

the apparently simple story. On Mr. Thompson's poverty-bit farm a
stranger appears, a Swede, Mr. Helton, who takes work at a low wage,
plays the harmonica in his off hours, and seems to inhabit some
vague and lonely inner world. But Mr. Helton is a worker, and for
the first time the farm begins to pay. Mr. Thompson can give up
"woman's work," can do the big important things that become a man,
and can bask in the new prosperity. Nine years later, to interrupt
the new prosperity, another stranger appears, a Mr. Hatch, who
reveals that the Swede is a murderer and a lunatic whom he will
arrest and take back north to the asylum. When the Swede appears,
Mr. Thompson sees, or thinks he sees, Mr. Hatch's knife going into
his stomach. With his axe he kills Mr. Hatch, defending the Swede,
defending what, he does not know.

After the deed, there isn't, strangely enough, a scratch on the
Swede's stomach. This doesn't bother the jury, and Mr. Thompson
is acquitted in no time at all. But it does bother Mr. Thompson. He
simply can't understand things, how he could see the knife go in and
then find it not true, and all the other things he can't understand. He
had never intended to do it, he was just protecting the poor Swede.
But we are aware that there had been the slow building up of the
mysterious anger against Mr. Hatch, of the fear that Mr. Hatch
threatened the new prosperity of the farm. And in the trial Mr.
Thompson has been caught in a web of little lies, small distortions
of fact, nothing serious, nothing needed to prove he wasn't guilty,
just little twists to make everything clearer and simpler.

Is Mr. Thompson innocent or guilty? He doesn't really know.
Caught in the mysteriousness of himself, caught in all the impulses
which he had never been able to face, caught in all the little lies
which had really meant no harm, he can't know the truth about anything. He can't stand the moral uncertainty of this situation, but he
does not know what it is that most deeply he can't stand. He can't
stand not knowing what he himself really is. His pride can't stand
that kind of nothingness. Not knowing what it is he can't stand, he is
under the compulsion to go, day after day, around the countryside,
explaining himself, explaining how he had not meant to do it, how it
was defense of the Swede, how it was self-defense, all the while
plunging deeper and deeper into the morass of his fate. Then he
finds that his own family have, all along, thought him guilty. So the
proud man has to kill himself to prove, in his last pride, that he is
really innocent.

That, however, is the one thing that can never be proved, for the story is about the difficult definition of guilt and innocence. Mr. Thompson, not able to trust his own innocence, or understand the nature of whatever guilt is his, has taken refuge in the lie, and the lie, in the end, kills him. The issue here, as in "Flowering Judas," is not be be decided simply. It is, in a sense, left suspended, the terms defined, but the argument left only at a provisional resolution. Poor Mr. Thompson—innocent and yet guilty, and in his pride unable to live by the provisional.

"The Cracked Looking-Glass," too, is about guilt and innocence. It is the story of a high-spirited, pleasure-loving Irish girl, married to a much older man, faithful to him, yet needing the society of young fun-provoking men, to whom she takes a motherly or sisterly attitude. She lives a kind of lie—in fact, she can't tell anything without giving it a romantic embroidery. Then she is horrified to discover that her Connecticut neighbors think her a bad woman, suspect her of infidelities. At the end, sitting in her tight kitchen with Old Dennis, "while beyond were far off places full of life and gaiety ...and beyond everything like a green field with morning sun on it lay youth and Ireland," she leans over and puts her hand on her husband's knee, and asks him, in an ordinary voice: 'Whyever did ye marry a woman like Me?'"

Dennis says mind, she doesn't tip the chair over, and adds that he knew he could never do better. Then:

> She sat up and felt his sleeves carefully. "I want you to wrap up warm this bitter weather, Dennis," she told him. "With two pairs of socks and the chest protector, for if anything happened to you, whatever would become of me in this world?"
>
> "Let's not think of it," said Dennis, shuffling his feet.
>
> "Let's not, then," said Rosaleen. "For I could cry if you crooked a finger at me."

Again the provisional resolution of the forces of the story: not a solution which Rosaleen can live by with surety, but one which she must re-learn and re-earn every day.

With the theme of "The Cracked Looking-Glass" in mind, let us take another of the novelettes, "Old Mortality."

To begin, "Old Mortality" is relatively short, some twenty thousand words, but it gives an impression of the mass of a novel. One factor contributing to this effect is the length of the time span; the novelette falls into three sections, dated 1885-1902, 1904, and 1912. Another factor is the considerable number of the characters, who, despite the brevity of the story, are sketched in with great precision; we know little about them, but that little means much. Another, and not quite so obvious but perhaps more important, factor is the rich circumstantiality and easy discursiveness, especially in Part I, which sets the tone of the piece. The author lingers on anecdote, apparently just to relish the anecdote, to extract the humor or pathos—but in the end we discover that there has been no casual self-indulgence, or indulgence of the reader; the details of the easy anecdote, which seemed to exist at the moment for itself alone, have been working busily in the cellarage of our minds.

Part I, 1885-1902, introduces us to two little girls, Maria and Miranda, aged twelve and eight, through whose eyes we see the family. There is the grandmother, who takes no part in the action of the story, but whose brief characterization, we discover, is important— the old lady who, "twice a year compelled in her blood by the change of seasons, would sit nearly all day beside old trunks and boxes in the lumber room, unfolding layers of garments and small keepsakes ...unwrapping locks of hair and dried flowers, crying gently and easily as if tears were the only pleasure she had left." (Her piety— stirred by the equinoxes, as unreflecting as tropism—provides the basic contrast for the end of the story; her piety does not achieve the form of legend—merely a compulsion of the blood, the focus of old affections.) There is the father, "a pleasant everyday sort of man"— who once shot to protect the family "honor" and had to run to Mexico. There is Cousin Eva, chinless and unbeautiful amidst the belles, who, when we first meet her, teaches Latin in a female seminary and tries to interest Maria and Miranda in that study by telling them the story of John Wilkes Booth, "who, handsomely garbed in a long black cloak"—so the story is recast by the little girls—"had leaped to the stage after assassinating President Lincoln. Sic semper tyrannis,' he had shouted superbly, in spite of his broken leg." There is Amy, dead, already a legend, a beautiful sad family story, the girl who almost had a duel fought over her in New Orleans, who drove her suitor, Cousin Gabriel, almost to distraction before she married him, and who died under mysterious circumstances a few weeks after her marriage. There is Gabriel himself, fond of the races, cut off by his grandfather without a penny, a victim of the bottle in his bereavement; he marries Miss Honey, who can never compete with the legend of the dead Amy. In this section, the little girls attempt to make the people they know and the stories they have heard fit together, make sense; and always at the center is the story of Amy.

Part II, in contrast with Part I with its discursiveness, its blurring of time, its anecdotal richness, gives a single fully developed scene, dated 1904. The father takes the little girls, on holiday from their convent school, to the races. There, out of family piety, they bet their dollar on Uncle Gabriel's horse—a poor hundred-to-one shot. (Piety and common sense—they know even at their tender years that a hundred-to-one bet is no bet at all—are in conflict, and piety wins only because of the father's pressure.) But Gabriel's horse comes in, and they see for the first time their romantic Uncle Gabriel—"a shabby fat man with bloodshot blue eyes...and a big melancholy laugh like a groan"—now drunk, and after his victory, weeping. But he takes them to meet Miss Honey, Amy's successor, in his shabby apartment, and the little girls know that Miss Honey hates them all.

Part III, 1912, shows us Miranda on a train going to the funeral of Uncle Gabriel, who has died in Lexington, Kentucky, but has been brought home to lie beside Amy—to whom he belongs. On the train Miranda, now a young lady recently married, meets Cousin Eva, whom she has not seen for many years, who has, since the days at the seminary, crusaded for woman suffrage and gone to jail for her convictions. The talk goes back to the family story, to Amy. "Everybody loved Amy," Miranda remarks, but Cousin Eva replies: "Not everybody by a long shot.... She had enemies. If she knew she pretended she didn't.... She was sweet as honeycomb to everybody. ...That was the trouble. She went through life like a spoiled darling, doing as she pleased and letting other people suffer for it." Then: "'I never believed for one moment,' says Cousin Eva, putting her mouth close to Miranda's ear and breathing peppermint hotly into it, 'that Amy was an impure woman. Never! But let me tell you there were plenty who did believe it.'" So Cousin Eva begins to reinterpret the past, all the romantic past, the legend of Amy, who, according to Cousin Eva, was not beautiful, just good-looking, whose illness hadn't been romantic, and who had, she says, committed suicide.

Cousin Eva defines the bitter rivalry under the gaiety of the legend, the vicious competition among the belles. And more:

> Cousin Eva wrung her hands. "It was just sex," she said in despair;
> [The word *despair,* caught in the frustrated and yet victorious old
> woman's casual gesture, is important—a resonance from her personal
> story which gives an echo to the theme of the story itself.] "their minds
> dwelt on nothing else. They didn't call it that, it was all smothered
> under pretty names, but that's all it was, sex."

So Cousin Eva, who has given her life to learning and a progressive cause, defines all the legend in terms of economics and biology. "They simply festered inside," she says of all the Amys, "they festered."

But Miranda, catching a Baudelairean vision of "corruption concealed under lace and flowers," thinks quite coldly: "Of course, it was not like that. This is no more true than what I was told before, it's every bit as romantic." And in revulsion from Cousin Eva, she wants to get home, though she is grown and married now, and see her father and sister, who are solid and alive, are not merely "definitions."

But when she arrives her father cannot take her in, in the old way. He turns to Cousin Eva. And the two old people, who represent the competing views of the past—love and poetry opposed to biology and economics—sit down together in a world, their world of the past, which excludes Miranda, Miranda thinks: "Where are my own people and my own time?" She thinks, and the thought concludes the story: "Let them go on explaining how things happened. I don't care. At least I can know the truth about what happens to me, she assured herself silently, making a promise to herself, in her hopefulness, her ignorance."

So much for the action of the story. We see immediately that it is a story about legend, and it is an easy extension to the symbol for tradition, the meaning of the past for the present. We gradually become acquainted with the particular legend through the little girls, but the little girls themselves, in their innocence, criticize the legend. Their father, speaking of Amy's slimness, for instance, says: 'There were never any fat women in the family, thank God." But the little girls remember Aunt Keziah, in Kentucky, who was famous for her heft. (Such an anecdote is developed richly and humorously, with no obvious pointing to the theme, beyond the logic of the context.) Such details, in Part I, develop the first criticism of the legend, the criticism by innocent common sense. In Part II, the contrast between Gabriel as legend and Gabriel as real extends the same type of criticism, but more dramatically; but here another, a moral criticism, enters in, for we have the effect of Amy on other people's lives, on Gabriel and Miss Honey. This, however, is not specified; it merely charges the scene of the meeting between Miranda and Cousin Eva on the way to Gabriel's funeral. Part III at first gives us, in Cousin Eva's words, the modern critical method applied to the legend—as if invoking Marx and Freud.

Up to this point, the line of the story has been developed fairly directly, though under a complicated surface. The story could end here, a story of repudiation, and some readers have interpreted it as such. But—and here comes the first reversal of the field—Miranda repudiates Cousin Eva's version, as romantic, too, in favor of the "reality" of her father, whom she is soon to see. But there is another shift. Miranda discovers that she is cut off from her father, who turns to Cousin Eva, whose "myth" contradicts his "myth," but whose world he can share. Miranda, cut off, determines to leave them to their own sterile pursuit of trying to understand the past. She will understand herself, the truth of what happens to her. This would provide another point of rest for the story—a story about the brave younger generation, their hope, courage, and honesty, and some readers have taken it thus. But—withheld cunningly until the end, until the last few words—there is a last reversal of the field. Miranda, makes her promise to herself in "her hopefulness, her ignorance." And those two words, *hopefulness, ignorance,* suddenly echo throughout the story.

Miranda will find *a* truth, as it were, but it, too, will be a myth, for it will not be translatable, or, finally, communicable. But it will be the only truth she can win, and for better or worse she will have to live by it. She must live by her own myth. But she must earn her myth in the process of living. Her myth will be a new myth, different from the mutually competing myths of her father and Cousin Eva, but stemming from that antinomy. Those competing myths will simply provide the terms of her own dialectic of living.

We remember that the heroine's name is Miranda, and we may remember Miranda of Shakespeare's *Tempest,* who exclaims, "O brave new world, that has such people in it!" Perhaps the identity of the name is not an accident. Miranda of "Old Mortality" has passed a step beyond that moment of that exclamation, but she, too, has seen the pageant raised by Prospero's wand—the pageant evoked by her father, the pleasant everyday sort of father, who, however, is a Prospero, though lacking the other Prospero's irony. For "Old Mortality, like *The Tempest,* is about illusion and reality, and comes to rest upon a perilous irony.

In "Old Mortality" Miss Porter has used very conventional materials; the conventional materials, however, are revitalized by the intellectual scope of the interpretation and the precision and subtlety of structure. But Miss Porter has not committed herself to one type of material. The world of balls and horsemanship and romance is exchanged in "Noon Wine," as we have seen, for a poverty-ridden Texas farm; in "Pale Horse, Pale Rider," for a newspaper office and a rooming house at the time of World War I; in "Hacienda," "Flowering Judas" and "María Concepción," for Mexico. We may ask, What is the common denominator of these stories, aside from the obvious similarities of style (though the style itself is very flexible)? What is the central "view," the central intuition?

In these stories, and, as I believe, in many others, there is the same paradoxical problem of definition, the same delicate balancing of rival considerations, the same scrupulous development of competing claims to attention and action, the same interplay of the humorous and the serious, the same refusal to take the straight line, the formula, through the material at hand. This has implied for some readers that the underlying attitude is one of skepticism, negation, refusal to confront the need for immediate, watertight, foolproof solutions. The skeptical and ironical bias is, I think, important in Miss Porter's work, and it is true that her work wears an air of detachment and contemplation. But, I should say, her irony is an irony with a center, never an irony for irony's sake. It simply implies, I think, a refusal to accept the formula, the ready-made solution, the hand-me-down morality, the word for the spirit. It affirms, rather, the constant need for exercising discrimination, the arduous obligation of the intellect in the face of conflicting dogmas, the need for a dialectical approach to matters of definition, the need for exercising as much of the human faculty as possible.

This basic attitude finds its correlation in her work, in the delicacy of phrase, the close structure, the counterpoint of incident and implication. That is, a story must test its thematic line at every point against its total circumstantiality; the thematic considerations must, as it were, be validated in terms of circumstance and experience, and never be resolved in the poverty of statement.

In one sense, it is the intellectual rigor and discrimination that gives Miss Porter's work its classic distinction and control—that is, if any one quality can be said to be uniquely responsible. No, no single quality can take that credit, but where many writers have achieved stories of perception, feeling, sensibility, strength, or charm, few have been able to achieve stories of a deep philosophic urgency in the narrow space, and fewer still have been able to achieve the kind of thematic integration of a body of stories, the mark of the masters, the thing that makes us think first of the central significance of a writer rather than of some incidental and individual triumph. For Miss Porter's bright indicative poetry is, at long last, a literally metaphysical poetry, too. The luminosity is from inward.

# The Collected Stories of
# Katherine Anne Porter

*by V. S. Pritchett*

The novelist is concerned with many things: the short-story writer with one thing that implies many. Singularity and intensity are the essence of his art. This is obvious in the finest practitioners. They depend on a marked personal attitude. Where the novelist is immolated eventually in his subject, the story writer seems to depend on being perpetually visible...

Katherine Anne Porter's stories have rightly had the highest reputation in America since they first appeared in the early Thirties. Her scene changes often, a good sign. Her subjects bear out O'Connor's theory: Mexico, but in revolution; life in the decaying American South, in rootless New York, in hysterical post-1914 Berlin. Where she settles she writes from the inside. Her singularity is truthfulness: it comes out in the portrait of Laura, the virginal but reckless American school-teacher in "Flowering Judas" who has ventured her political and personal chastity among the vanities and squalors of the Mexican revolution, perhaps as a religious exercise. She is a good old Calvinist-Catholic:

> But she cannot help feeling that she has been betrayed irresponsibly by the disunion between her way of living and her feeling of what life should be, and at times she is almost contented to rest in this sense of grievance as a private consolation. Sometimes she wishes to run away but she stays.

Laura wishes to live near enough to violent passion to be singed by it and is willing to pay for the experience in terrifying dreams. The Mexicans appeal to her because of their boundless vanity, their violence, their ability to forget and their indifference: Miss Porter austerely tests her characters against things that are elemental or in-

"The Collected Stories of Katherine Anne Porter" by V. S. Pritchett. From *New Statesman* (January 10, 1964), pp. 41-43. Reprinted by permission of the publisher.

eluctable—a classical writer. There is a point at which life or circumstance does not give: when human beings come to this point she
is ready for them, Braggoni, the Stalin-like Mexican revolutionary
leader, is at this point: he is identified in a frightening, yet slightly
fatuous and amicable way with the shady needs of revolution.

In the tale "María Concepción" it is the respectable churchwoman,
with her classical Christian sense of the rights of jealousy and ven-
geance, who murders and who is backed up by the villagers. Her husband will punish her: she accepts that. In "Noon Wine" we have an
incompetent poor white farmer whose fortunes are saved by a Swedish hired hand down from Dakota. The hand speaks to no one, slaves
night and day and consoles himself only by playing the harmonica.
Years pass and then a blackmailer comes down from Dakota to reveal that the Swede is a murderous escaped lunatic. The farmer,
faced with losing his saviour, kills the blackmailer. The Swede runs
away, consoled by his harmonica. The poor farmer has nothing but a
sense of social injustice. He kills himself out of self-pity.

Katherine Anne Porter does not find her tests only in these Verga-
like subjects. The girl reporter and the soldier-boy in [Denver] "dig
in" in spiritual self-defence against the hysteria of the 1914 war. The
choice is between reality and illusion and the reality is harder to
bear. It is no reward. It is the same  in the comic tale of the Depression: the domestic war between the out-of-work Irishman turned
windbag and drunk and his avaricious and scornful wife who keeps
him and ends by beating him up with a knotted towel. Violent:
these classical heroes and heroines are always that. Again, in the
comical sad history of the old Southern aunts and cousins one sees
that Aunt Amy was wild, amusing, cruel and destructive because she
knew she would soon die: she had inner knowledge of Fate Killed,
she could be a killer. Old Granny Weatherall fights to the last drop
of consciousness on her death-bed because her pride will not really
accept, even now, that she was once jilted as a girl. And that is not
funny, it is terrifying. To every human being there eventually comes
—Miss Porter seems to say—the shock of perception of something
violent or rock-like in themselves, in others, or in circumstance.
We awaken to primitive knowledge and become impersonal in our
tragedies. There will arise a terrible moment of crisis, a kind of illness, when, for Laura, there will be *no* disunion between her way of
living and her feeling for what life should be. She will discover what
life is. It is something out of one's control, scarcely belonging to one,
and that has to be borne as if one were a stone.

Miss Porter's singularity as a writer is in her truthful explorations of a complete consciousness of life. Her prose is severe and exact; her ironies are subtle but hard. If she is arbitrary it is because she identifies a conservative with a classical view of human nature. Laura listens to Braggoni with "pitiless courtesy" because she dare not smile at his bad performance on the guitar:

> He is so vain of his talents and so sensitive to slights that it would require a cruelty and vanity greater than his own to lay a finger on the vast cureless wound of his self-esteem.

Miss Porter has a fine power of nervous observation. Her picture of Berlin in the Isherwood period is eerie and searching. She sees everything that disturbs. She notices peculiar local things that one realises afterwards are true: how often, for example, the Berliners' eyes filled with tears when they were suddenly faced with small dilemmas. Hysteria is near to the surface. Yet the tears were a kind of mannerism. Her power to make a landscape, a room, a group of people, thinkingly alive is not the vague, brutal talent of the post-Hemingway reporter but belongs to the explicit Jamesian period and suggests the whole rather than the surface of a life. Her stories are thoroughly planted. It is true that she is chastely on the edge of her subjects, that one catches the wild look of the runaway in her eye; but if her manner is astringent it is not precious. She is an important writer in the genre because she solves the essential problem: how to satisfy exhaustively in writing briefly.

# On "The Grave"

## by Cleanth Brooks

If I had to choose a particular short story of Katherine Anne Porter's to illustrate her genius as a writer—the choice is not an easy one—I think that I should choose "The Grave." I did choose it some months ago for a lecture in Athens, where the special nature of the audience, whose English ranged from excellent to moderately competent, provided a severe test. The ability of such an audience to understand and appreciate this story underlines some of Miss Porter's special virtues as a writer. Hers is an art of apparent simplicity, with nothing forced or mannered, and yet the simplicity is rich, not thin, full of subtleties and sensitive insights. Her work is compact and almost unbelievably economical.

The story has to do with a young brother and sister on a Texas farm in the year 1903. Their grandmother, who in some sense had dominated the family, had survived her husband for many years. He had died in the neighboring state of Louisiana, but she had removed his body to Texas. Later, when her Texas farm was sold and with it the small family cemetery, she had once more moved her husband's body, and those of the other members of the family, to a plot in the big new public cemetery. One day the two grandchildren, out rabbit hunting with their small rifles, find themselves in the old abandoned family cemetery.

> Miranda leaped into the pit that had held her grandfather's bones. Scratching round aimlessly and pleasurably as any young animal, she scooped up a lump of earth and weighed it in her palm. It had a pleasantly sweet, corrupt smell, being mixed with cedar needles and small leaves, and as the crumbs fell apart, she saw a silver dove no larger than a hazel nut, with spread wings and a neat fan-shaped tail.

Miranda's brother recognizes what the curious little ornament is—the screw-head for a coffin. Paul has found something too—a small

"On 'The Grave'" by Cleanth Brooks. From *Yale Review* (Winter 1966). Reprinted by permission of the author.

gold ring—and the children soon make an exchange of their treasures, Miranda fitting the gold ring onto her thumb.

Paul soon becomes interested in hunting again, and looks about
for rabbits, but the ring,

> shining with the serene purity of fine gold on [the little girl's] rather
> grubby thumb, turned her feelings against her overalls and sockless
> feet. ... She wanted to go back to the farm house, take a good cold
> bath, dust herself with plenty of Maria's violet talcum powder...put
> on the thinnest, most becoming dress she ever owned, with a big sash,
> and sit in the wicker chair under the trees.

The little girl is thoroughly feminine, and though she has enjoyed
knocking about with her brother, wearing her summer roughing
outfit, the world of boys and sports and hunting and all that goes
with it is beginning to pall.

Then something happens. Paul starts up a rabbit, kills it with one
shot, and skins it expertly as Miranda watches admiringly. "Brother
lifted the oddly bloated belly. 'Look,' he said, in a low amazed voice.
'It was going to have young ones.'" Seeing the baby rabbits in all
their perfection, "their sleek wet down lying in minute even ripples
like a baby's head just washed, their unbelievably small delicate ears
folded close," Miranda is "excited but not frightened." Then she
touches one of them, and exclaims, "Ah, there's blood running over
them!" and begins to tremble. "She had wanted most deeply to see
and to know. Having seen, she felt at once as if she had known all
along."

The meaning of life and fertility and of her own body begins to
take shape in the little girl's mind as she sees the tiny creatures just
taken from their mother's womb. The little boy says to her "cautious-
ly, as if he were talking about something forbidden: 'They were just
about ready to be born.' 'I know,' said Miranda, 'like kittens. I know,
like babies.' She was quietly and terribly agitated, standing again
with her rifle under her arm, looking down at the bloody heap."
Paul buries the rabbits and cautions his sister "with an eager friendliness, a confidential tone quite unusual in him, as if he were taking
her into an important secret on equal terms: Listen now.... Don't
tell a soul."

The story ends with one more paragraph, and because the ending
is told with such beautiful economy and such care for the disposition
of incidents and even the choice of words, one dares not paraphrase
it.

Miranda never told, she did not even wish to tell anybody. She thought about the whole worrisome affair with confused unhappiness for a few days. Then it sank quietly into her mind and was heaped over by accumulated thousands of impressions, for nearly twenty years. One day she was picking her path among the puddles and crushed refuse of a market street in a strange city of a strange country, when without warning, plain and clear in its true colors as if she looked through a frame upon a scene that had not stirred nor changed since the moment it happened, the episode of that far-off day leaped from its burial place before her mind's eye. She was so reasonlessly horrified she halted suddenly staring, the scene before her eyes dimmed by the vision back of them. An Indian vendor had held up before her a tray of dyed sugar sweets, in the shapes of all kinds of small creatures: birds, baby chicks, baby rabbits, lambs, baby pigs. They were in gay colors and smelled of vanilla, maybe. . . . It was a very hot day and the smell in the market, with its piles of raw flesh and wilting flowers, was like the mingled sweetness and corruption she had smelled that other day in the empty cemetery at home: the day she had remembered always until now vaguely as the time she and her brother had found treasure in the opened graves. Instantly upon this thought the dreadful vision faded, and she saw clearly her brother, whose childhood face she had forgotten, standing again in the blazing sunshine, again twelve years old, a pleased sober smile in his eyes, turning the silver dove over and over in his hands.

The story is so rich, it has so many meanings that bear close and subtle relations to each other, that a brief summary of what the story means will oversimplify it and fail to do justice to its depth, but I shall venture a few comments.

Obviously the story is about growing up and going through a kind of initiation into the mysteries of adult life. It is thus the story of the discovery of truth. Miranda learns about birth and her own destiny as a woman; she learns these things suddenly, unexpectedly, in circumstances that connect birth with death. Extending this comment a little further, one might say that the story is about the paradoxical nature of truth: truth wears a double face—it is not simple but complex. The secret of birth is revealed in the place of death and through a kind of bloody sacrifice. If there is beauty in the discovery, there is also awe and even terror.

These meanings are dramatized by their presentation through a particular action, which takes place in a particular setting. Something more than illustration of a statement is involved—something more than mere vividness or the presentation of a generalization in a form to catch the reader's eye. One notices, for example, how important is the fact of the grandmother's anxiety to keep the family together, even the bodies of the family dead. And the grandmother's solicitude is not mentioned merely to account for the physical fact of the abandoned cemetery in which Miranda makes her discovery about life and death. Throughout this story, birth and death are seen through a family perspective.

Miranda is, for example, thoroughly conscious of how her family is regarded in the community. We are told that her father had been criticized for letting his girls dress like boys and career "around astride barebacked horses." Miranda herself had encountered such criticism from old women whom she met on the road—women who smoked corncob pipes. They had always "treated her grandmother with most sincere respect," but they ask her "What yo Pappy thinkin about?" This matter of clothes, and the social sense, and the role of women in the society are brought into the story unobtrusively, but they powerfully influence its meaning. For if the story is about a rite of initiation, an initiation into the meaning of sex, the subject is not treated in a doctrinaire polemical way. In this story sex is considered in a much larger context, in a social and even a philosophical context.

How important the special context is will become apparent if we ask ourselves why the story ends as it does. Years later, in the hot tropical sunlight of a Mexican city, Miranda sees a tray of dyed sugar sweets, moulded in the form of baby pigs and baby rabbits. They smell of vanilla, but this smell mingles with the other odors of the marketplace, including that of raw flesh, and Miranda is suddenly reminded of the "sweetness and corruption" that she had smelled long before as she stood in the empty grave in the family burial plot. What is it that makes the experience not finally horrifying or nauseating? What steadies Miranda and redeems the experience for her? I quote again the concluding sentence:

> Instantly upon this thought the dreadful vision faded, and she saw clearly her brother, whose childhood face she had forgotten, standing again in the blazing sunshine, again twelve years old, a pleased sober smile in his eyes, turning the silver dove over and over in his hands.

I mentioned earlier the richness and subtlety of his beautiful story. It needs no further illustration; yet one can hardly forbear reminding oneself how skilfully, and apparently almost effortlessly, the author has rendered the physical and social context that gives point to Miranda's discovery of truth and has effected the modulation of her shifting attitudes—toward the grave, the buried ring, her hunting clothes, the dead rabbit—reconciling these various and conflicting attitudes and, in the closing sentences, bringing into precise focus the underlying theme.

# "Holiday": A Version of Pastoral

## by George Core

For Henry James the ideal form of fiction on the "dimensional ground" is the "beautiful and blest *nouvelle*," that indeterminate measure which falls between the short story and the novel, a genre which is his favorite and of which he is master. The same can be said of Katherine Anne Porter who would agree with James that the "forms of wrought things" are "all exquisitely and effectively, the things; so that, for the delight of mankind, form might compete with form and might correspond to fitness; might...have an inevitability, a marked felicity." James in his magisterial way does not often bother with matters of precise definition, and in this instance he makes no distinction between the longer short story and the short novel. Miss Porter, herself a great admirer of James and the most deliberate and severe perfectionist writing American short fiction since his death, has noted that difference in the preface to her *Collected Stories*. For her there are four forms of fiction: short stories, long stories, short novels, and novels. Miss Porter's best work is in the short novel: "Pale Horse, Pale Rider," "Old Mortality," and "Noon Wine"; of these (all fine works) the last is the best—and a masterpiece. Her long stories—"The Cracked Looking-Glass," "Hacienda," "The Leaning Tower," and "Holiday"—are not so good on the whole as the short novels—or the short stories. Of the long stories "Holiday" is easily the finest: it is a story which will endure because form and idea are one—technique provides a window to a fable of universal proportions—and because the action in its totality—in its confluence of language, metaphor, theme, movement: in short, in its life— carries with it an absolute inevitability.

It is easy enough to stake out the preliminary ground on which

"'Holiday': A Version of Pastoral." From Lodwick Hartley and George Core, eds., *Katherine Anne Porter: A Critical Symposium* (Athens, Ga.: the University of Georgia Press, 1969), pp. 149-58. Copyright 1969 by the University of Georgia Press. Reprinted by permission of the author and the publisher.

this story should be examined: it is a narrative which dramatizes what William Empson calls a version of pastoral, that subject which finds its archetypal lineage in man's impulse to return to the Garden, to a prelapsarian world forever green and innocent. "Holiday" is characteristic of Miss Porter's art in that it is faultlessly written, closely wrought, and economically presented through a sharp, clear perspective and a gradually and firmly evolving focus which narrows to a view that is at once tentative and final, innocent and ironic, luminous and dark. The center of composition is here, but beyond this the mystery of the art remains almost inviolate.

The total configuration of "Holiday" possesses a self-sufficient order and achieves a symmetrical unity even though the life it desscribes, and embodies is far from neat and orderly, being rife with the terrible stresses and disrelations which are typical of the human lot even at its best. In many respects this story is a celebration of the soil which is tilled by those who know and understand it deeply and intuitively. Yet at the same time "Holiday" contains a tragic dimension which moves the reader to awe, regret, and finally acceptance, as the narrator herself is moved in the course of the action. It is a double story of sorts in which the two lines of action meet. On the one hand it is the narrator's story of a chapter in her life, involving a real but unexplained crisis—a psychic turning point; on the other it is almost a typical episode in the Mullers' lives from which they do not attempt to wrest a philosophic and religious meaning: a spring which brings birth, marriage, and death. The element of death brings a uniqueness to an action which is otherwise typical of the Mullers' lives, and it gives the plot a necessary and moving dramatic context.

At the beginning the narrator is haunted by troubles of her own, and she runs to the home of the Mullers to lose and to find herself. Through the persona Miss Porter states in the opening paragraph what might appear to be the "moral" of the story:

> ...this story I am about to tell you happened before this great truth impressed itself upon me—that we do not run from the troubles and dangers which are truly ours, and it is better to learn what they are earlier than later, and if we don't run from the others, we are fools.

The obvious theme of individual responsibility versus common obligation is soon joined to the governing theme—the fools-of-life motif which appears in St. Paul. So this *apparently* artless tale begins—as a simple story, not a polished literary artifice, told much in the manner of the lyric or ballad; and the tone of a certain naivete and undeniable humility is in perfect accord.

It is at this point—the outset of "Holiday"—that the story stands a chance of foundering, for the narrator's unexplained troubles and her removal to the country are a bit disingenuous and forced, and the reader may feel that he is getting bogged down in merely referential narrative. All, however, comes right in short order, and the drama unfolds steadily and surely as the plot moves toward complication. The action must be viewed and reported by a stranger—an articulate compassionate reflector who in this case represents the vantage point of the larger cosmopolitan world. Her general attitude and particular frame of mind are important, and they must be established early in the story as indeed they are. Therefore the reader is all the more impressed with the narrator's sympathetic portrayal of the Muller family. The stranger's narrative voice contributes in no small part to the unfolding design of "Holiday." The unnamed persona certainly reminds us of Miranda, a Miranda living some time between the period of "Old Mortality" and "Pale Horse, Pale Rider"; but there is no reason to suppose once and for all that she is, for unlike Miranda in "Pale Horse, Pale Rider" and many stories in *The Old Order,* she is on the periphery of the action, and she interprets as well as reports the events, as does the nameless narrator of "Hacienda."

On any level "Holiday" is about the Muller family. The larger frame of the story, the enveloping action, deals with the family as a whole and the archetypal experiences that affect all families; whereas the particular instance of this larger pattern that provides the main action involves one member of the family. All the Mullers work unceasingly to increase the already abundant store of the Muller dynasty. They are German peasants who oil with great reward in East Texas: the crops abound and the livestock multiply while the Mullers marry and increase. In the course of the story the youngest daughter, Hatsy, is married; and another daughter, Gretchen, bears one of many third-generation Mullers. All live under the same roof. All are curiously alike, save one:

> I got a powerful impression that they were all, even the sons-in-law, one human being divided into several separate appearances. The crippled servant girl brought in more food and gathered up plates and went away in her limping run, and she seemed to me the only individual in the house. ... She was whole, and belonged nowhere.

The narrator gradually realizes that the servant, Ottilie, is an older sister of Hatsy, Gretchen, and a third sister, Annetje. Ottilie has been terribly and hopelessly transfigured by a nameless childhood accident, and what remains is a grotesque distortion of humanity. She is pictured as a frenzied automaton, "a mere machine of torture," working in "aimless, driven haste," preparing and serving "that endless food that represented all her life's labors." Yet paradoxically Ottilie is the most human and sympathetic character in the story (and it is her story): she ironically achieves humanity in inhumanity, whereas the remainder of her family do not. The mystery of this paradox is at the heart of the story, and here Miss Porter's irony finds its true center in "Holiday."

Despite the success of the Mullers there are deficiencies which the narrator does not articulate so much as sense, and we, through her deepening consciousness, perceive the terrible shortcomings of the Mullers—and of humanity. We see the typical contradiction of the German character: Father Muller reads *Das Kapital* religiously every evening and knows whole passages by heart:

> And here was this respectable old farmer who accepted its dogma as a religion—that is to say, its legendary inapplicable precepts were just, right, proper, one must believe in them, of course, but life, everyday living, was another and unrelated thing.

The dimension of satire is coming into play. The "natural man" is bemused by the sophisticated life of the outside world to the extent that he reads Marx; but sensing that Marx's abstractions have nothing whatever to do with his essential life, he ignores them. The obvious satiric motif directed toward a national type—the phlegmatic German—and the concomitant irony quickly deepen as the conflict of the story develops and the lines of action gather.

These same respectable Mullers have forgotten that Ottilie is a member of their family. We want to be indignant, but the matter is not so simple as that, because the narrator sympathizes in large part with the Mullers:

> It is not a society or a class that pampered its invalids and the unfit. So long as one lived, one did one's share. This was her place, in this family she had been born and must die; did she suffer? No one asked, no one looked to see. Suffering went with life, suffering and labor. While one lived one worked, and that was all, and without complaints, for no one had time to listen, and everybody had his own troubles. So, what else could they have done with Ottilie? As for me, I could do

nothing but promise myself that I would forget her, too; and to remember her for the rest of my life.

The last sentence reminds one of Robert Penn Warren's lines in
*Brother to Dragons:* "Forgetting is just another kind of remembering." In this patriarchial world Ottilie has lost her original place as
child, wife, and mother—functions which are fulfilled by all her
sisters, but she is assigned another place, and in and through it she
works out her own salvation, while at once remembering her past.

In the simplest sense the story is about suffering and labor, about
the labor of the farm, the labor of childbirth, the labor of life, and the
labor of death. For there is not only marriage and childbirth, but
death. Mother Muller dies as the result of her struggles in a storm
which ravages the countryside and blights the land. The order of
nature is thrown into discord, and so is the order of the family when
Mother Muller is stricken: "The family crowded into the room,
unnerved in panic, lost unless the sick woman should come to herself and tell them what to do for her." Father Muller cries, "'Ach,
Gott, Gott. A hundert tousand tollars in the bank...and tell me, tell,
what goot does it do?'" With the understatement and directness of
her creator the narrator tells us: "This frightened them, and all at
once, together, they screamed and called and implored her in a
tumolt utterly beyond control. The noise of their grief and terror
filled the place. In the midst of this, Mother Muller died."

The death is the turning point of "Holiday" and the author deftly
works out the complications in the remaining few pages of the story.
We are concerned with the reactions of the Mullers to the death, of
Ottilie on the one hand and the remainder of the family on the other.
There is finally no one right attitude, any more than there is a clearly wrong one. The resolution comes in the bringing of the conflicting attitudes and tensions to a sharp and dramatic but deliberately
ambiguous focus.

Only moments before Hatsy, accompanied by her shy new husband, has shouted at Ottilie, who is apparently frightened by the
storm, "in a high, penetrating voice as if to a deaf person or one at a
great distance, 'Ottilie! Suppertime. We are hungry!'" Hatsy and her
husband then go on to care for a sick lamb. Ottilie, the human lamb,
is sacrificed to the needs of the family. This implicit comparison of
animal life to human life is one of the most striking aspects of the
story. Shortly after she arrives at the farm the narrator watches Hatsy and Mother Muller separate nursing calves from their mothers

so the dams can be milked. When Gretchen's child is born, she nurses like "a young calf." (One is reminded of "The Grave" when Miranda and her brother discover the tiny unborn litter in the dead mother rabbit, and Miranda begins to understand the mystery of life and death.) Later in "Holiday," immediately after Ottilie has appeared to clear the table, Annetje expresses fear that her brother will trap Kuno, a German shepherd. The narrator observes that "Annetje was full of silent, tender solicitudes. . . . Still, she seemed to have forgotten that Ottilie was her sister. So had all the others. . . . She moved among them as invisible to their imaginations as a ghost." For the family Ottilie is a ghost from the past, preserved only in the photograph she keeps. Theirs is a cruel, practical, and necessary accommodation. On the day of Mother Muller's funeral the narrator dreams that she hears the howls of Kuno who is caught in a 'possum trap. But it is not Kuno the narrator hears: it is Ottilie, caught in a far more vicious trap, and nightmare becomes waking life. Ottilie, like Benjy Compson, bellows against disorder in her world. She howls "with a great wrench of her body, an upward reach of the neck, without tears."

The [narrator] thinks that Ottilie wants to join the funeral procession, and they start out together in the ludicrous spring wagon that has brought the narrator to the farm. The story here is coming full circle, as spring, which had just begun when the narrator arrived at the farm, is coming into full bloom against the "peacock green of the heavens," with its "sun westering gently." Time and life go on in the same ways despite death. Suddenly Ottilie laughs, "a kind of yelp, but unmistakably laughter." The speaker then sees her "ironical mistake":

> There was nothing I could do for Ottilie, selfishly as I wished to ease my heart of her; she was beyond my reach as well as any other human reach, and yet, had I not come nearer to her than I had to anyone else in my attempt to deny and bridge the distance between us, or rather, her distance from me? Well, we were both equally fools of life, equally fellow fugitives from death. We had escaped for one day more at least. We would celebrate our good luck, we would have a little stolen holiday, a breath of spring air and freedom on this lovely, festive afternoon.

We do not know why Ottilie laughs. It may be a triumphant laugh since she is still among the living. She is perhaps once again trying to affirm her humanity as she has done poignantly earlier when she has shown to the speaker her picture as a normal healthy child. Here is one of the most compassionate and compelling scenes in all literature: its tenderness and pathos are unforgettable. Ottilie's entire predicament is brilliantly rendered and starkly portrayed in this vignette. Her joy seems blasphemous on the funeral day, the family holy day with which the holiday is ended. Yet is not the family's treatment of her equally blasphemous, and why is the afternoon "festive"? Ottilie's laughter is best regarded as an affirmation amidst almost unbearable suffering and sorrow; and Ottilie celebrates the triumphant return of spring and the continuance of life amidst grief and death, even as the other Mullers turn their thoughts toward the future while they are fashioning the coffin for Mother Muller and preparing her body for burial. "For a while they would visit the grave and remember, and then life would arrange itself in another order, yet it would be the same."

So Ottilie assumes life in our minds which the other Mullers do not assume in their "mystical inertia" of mind and their "muscular life." Ottilie, the caricature who is once described as unreal, is more human and real than the remainder of the family. As Father Muller has realized for them, they are the fools of life. Ottilie, physically and mentally and psychically wrenched by fate, is still less a fool and more a person, and she celebrates her "good luck," her "stolen holiday," even while returning to the kitchen to continue her suffering. It is a final irony that Ottilie is able to steal a holiday only when her mother has died.

One should note that Miss Porter is unafraid of coming dangerously close to telling the reader what the themes of "Holiday" are as the story comes to an end. She does this elsewhere with equal boldness, especially in "Old Mortality." There are the old themes revolving around the life-cycle and its fundamental rhythms, but the answer is not so easy as it looks on the surface, for there is also the question of appearance, illusion, and reality. The fools-of-life theme is both Christian and existential, and Miss Porter uses it in a darker sense in "Pale Horse, Pale Rider" and *Ship of Fools.* Miranda returns from her sojourn with the Pale Rider to feel that she has been tricked, and it is ironical to her that she has been placed "once more safely in the road that would lead her again to death." Throughout her fiction Miss Porter shows us the truth of St. Paul's statement: "Let no man deceive himself. If any man among you seemeth to be wise in this world, let him become a fool, that he may be wise." Miranda, the narrator of "Holiday," and Ottilie achieve wisdom thus, although they come to it in radically different ways, and Ottilie's perception, like her howl and her laugh, is of a very special and finally unknowable order.

The life of "Holiday" demands our attention a moment longer. This microcosm of the human community is a bountiful world with a shared simple life, but it is also "a house of perpetual exile," as the narrator says. Its people are "solid, practical, hard-bitten, land-holding German peasants, who struck their mattocks into the earth deep and held fast wherever they were, because of them life and the land were one indivisible thing; but never in any wise did they confuse nationality with habitation." So the Mullers are typical plain (if wealthy) folk of an agrarian world and characteristic Germans; they are of the land and yet are alienated from its principal inhabitants. Here is revealed another deep irony in the story, and through touches such as these (which are deliberate and which count significantly in the ultimate meaning of the fable) the author is able to suggest a spreading field of meaning and value. Miss Porter triumphantly explores what Empson calls one assumption of pastoral: "You can say everything about complex people by a complete consideration of simple people." To put it another way, simple people fully considered are no longer simple. So it is with the Mullers, whose lives are something more than tranquil, orderly, and perfectly consistent.

The apparent simplicity and neatness of the Mullers' lives leads the narrator to flee there and make a haven of their home, but she soon finds out life in both its manifest forms and unpredictable nature continues any and everywhere, despite man's best efforts to avoid it. The mystery of the human experience remains, whether he be in tenement or field, townhouse or cottage. One thinks at the outset that the life of the Mullers inheres in the good since it is straightforward, free of duplicity and cunning, and since it is, for all intents and purposes, wholly successful. But it turns out that not a little of the old German atavism is present: we catch hints of dynastic rule and heavy-handed politics. If Mr. Muller is not Marx's *Kapital* (as he says), he still smacks of the German tribal chieftain and rules his house and lands with the close grip of the beneficent dictator.

Because Miss Porter quite characteristically qualifies her sympathy, the Mullers are believable and interesting: they have human failings as well as human virtues. That is one reason why the reader assents to the donnees of the story and is caught up in its action. There is primitivism in "Holiday," but not of the romantic sort: the view of man in the natural world is hard—not soft—and is tough-minded and realistic. As J. F. Powers has said, "Nobody else could have written the story 'Holiday,'" a story which is an example of what he calls "the nearest thing yet to reality in American fiction." The reality emerges because Katherine Anne Porter "has approached life reverently in her stories, and it lives on in them." And, in the words of Robert Penn Warren, the story is "paradoxically, both a question asked of life and a celebration of life; and the author of it knows in her bones that the more corrosive the question asked, the more powerful may be the celebration."

The version of pastoral in "Holiday" is neither propaganda nor idyll: it is realistic in its depiction of a world which is both elemental and communal, and the sharpness of detail and accuracy of picture contribute in no small way to our understanding of this microcosm of the human community. If to the unwary reader this world seems narrow and artificial, then he should examine it more closely. As Empson has shrewdly remarked, "The feeling that life is essentially inadequate to the human spirit, and yet that a good life must avoid saying so, is naturally at home with most versions of pastoral; in pastoral you take a limited life and pretend it is the full and normal one, and a suggestion that one must do this with all life, because the normal is itself limited, is easily put into the trick." Within these boundaries (which are in some respects those of all art) the action of "Holiday" embodies a full and convincing world, invested with all the appurtenances of life and charged with visceral (and cerebral) forces: indeed the still center of the story involves the senses and emotions in an almost painfully real and palpable way: it is the intense yet sure feeling one encounters often in the best Russian fiction—in *A Sportsman's Sketches* and in parts of *Anna Karenina*. All in all "Holiday" is an utterly believable confluence of elements which are caught and held—radiantly—in the living tapestry of the art—a pastoral in which form, the shape of the art, and substance, the fable within the art, are one: the form of the wrought thing is the thing itself—and the configuration of the whole is both beautiful and blest.

# Katherine Anne Porter

## by Edmund Wilson

Miss Katherine Anne Porter has published a new book of stories, her third: *The Leaning Tower and Other Stories.* To the reviewer, Miss Porter is baffling because one cannot take hold of her work in any of the obvious ways. She makes none of the melodramatic or ironic points that are the stock in trade of ordinary short story writers; she falls into none of the usual patterns and she does not show anyone's influence. She does not exploit her personality either inside or outside her work, and her writing itself makes a surface so smooth that the critic has little opportunity to point out peculiarities of color or weave. If he is tempted to say that the effect is pale, he is prevented by the realization that Miss Porter writes English of a purity and precision almost unique in contemporary American fiction. If he tries to demur that some given piece fails to mount with the accelerating pace or arrive at the final intensity that he is in the habit of expecting in short stories, he is deterred by a nibbling suspicion that he may not have grasped its meaning and have it hit him with a sudden impact some minutes after he has closed the book.

Not that this meaning is simple to formulate even after one has felt its emotional force. The limpidity of the sentence, the exactitude of the phrase, are deceptive in that the thing they convey continues to seem elusive even after it has been communicated. These stories are not illustrations of anything that is reducible to a moral law or a political or social analysis or even a principle of human behavior. What they show us are human relations in their constantly shifting phases and in the moments of which their existence is made. There is no place for general reflections; you are to live through the experience as the characters do. And yet the writer has managed to say something about the values involved in the experience. But what is

"Katherine Anne Porter." From Edmund Wilson, *Classics and Commercials* (New York: Farrar, Straus & Giroux, Inc., 1950), pp. 219-23. Copyright 1950 by Edmund Wilson. Reprinted with the permission of Farrar, Straus & Giroux, Inc.

it? I shall try to suggest, though I am afraid I shall land in ineptitude.

Miss Porter's short stories lend themselves to being sorted into three fairly distinct groups. There are the studies of family life in working-class or middle-class households (there are two of these in *The Leaning Tower*), which, in spite of the fact that the author is technically sympathetic with her people, tend to be rather bitter and bleak, and, remarkable though they are, seem to me less satisfactory than the best of her other stories. The impression we get from these pieces is that the qualities that are most amiable in human life are being gradually done to death in the milieux she is presenting, but Miss Porter does not really much like these people or feel comfortable in their dismal homes, and so we, in turn, don't really much care. Another section of her work, however, contains what may be called pictures of foreign parts, and here Miss Porter is much more successful. The story which gives its name to her new collection and which takes up two-fifths of the volume belongs to this category. It is a study of Germany between the two wars in terms of a travelling American and his landlady and fellow-lodgers in a Berlin rooming house. By its material and its point of view, it rather recalls Christopher Isherwood's *Goodbye to Berlin*, but it is more poetic in treatment and more general in implication. The little plaster leaning tower of Pisa which has been cherished by the Viennese landlady but gets broken by her American tenant stands for something in the destruction of which not merely the Germans but also the Americans have somehow taken a criminal part (though the American is himself an artist, he finds that he can mean nothing to the Germans but the power of American money). So, in a fine earlier story, "Hacienda" a Mexican peon is somehow destroyed — with no direct responsibility on the part of any of the elements concerned — by a combination of Soviet Russians intent on making a Communist movie, their American business manager and a family of Mexican landowners.

In both cases, we are left with the feeling that, caught in the meshes of interwoven forces, some important human value has been crushed. These stories especially, one gathers, are examples of what Miss Porter means when she says, in her foreword to *Flowering Judas* in the Modern Library edition, that most of her "energies of mind and spirit have been spent in the effort to grasp the meaning" of the threats of world catastrophe in her time, "to trace them to their sources and to understand the logic of this majestic and terrible failure of the life of man in the Western world."

But perhaps the most interesting section of Katherine Anne Porter's work is composed of her stories about women — particularly her heroine Miranda, who figured in two of the three novelettes that made up her previous volume, *Pale Horse, Pale Rider*. The first six pieces of *The Leaning Tower* deal with Miranda's childhood and her family background of Louisianians living in southern Texas. This is the setting in which Miss Porter is most at home, and one finds in it the origins of that spirit of which the starvation and violation elsewhere make the subjects of her other stories. One recognizes it in the firm little sketches that show the relations between Miranda's grandmother and her lifelong colored companion, the relations between the members of the family and the relations between the family and the Negro servants in general. Somewhere behind Miss Porter's stories there is a conception of a natural human spirit in terms of their bearing on which all the other forces of society are appraised. This spirit is never really idealized, it is not even sentimentalized; it can be generous and loving and charming, but it can also be indifferent and careless, inconsequent, irresponsible and silly. If the meaning of these stories is elusive, it is because this essential spirit is so hard to isolate or pin down. It is peculiar to Louisianians in Texas, yet one misses it in a boarding house in Berlin. It is the special personality of a woman, yet is is involved with international issues. It evades all the most admirable moralities, it escapes through the social net, and it resists the tremendous oppressions of national bankruptcies and national wars. It is outlawed, driven underground, exiled; it becomes rather unsure of itself and may be able, as in "Pale Horse, Pale Rider," to assert itself only in the delirium that lights up at the edge of death to save Miranda from extinction by war flu. It suffers often from a guilty conscience, knowing too well its moral weakness; but it can also rally bravely if vaguely in vindication of some instinct of its being which seems to point toward justice and truth.

But I said that this review would be clumsy. I am spoiling Miss Porter's stories by attempting to find a formula for them when I ought simply to be telling you to read them (and not merely the last volume but also its two predecessors). She is absolutely a first-rate artist, and what she wants other people to know she imparts to them by creating an object, the self-developing organism of a work of prose. The only general opinion on anything which, in her books, she has put on record has been a statement about her craft of prose fiction, and I may quote it — from the foreword to which I have re-

ferred—as more to the purpose than anything that the present critic
could say. Here is the manifesto of the builder of this solid little
sanctuary, so beautifully proportioned and finished, for the queer
uncontrollable spirit that it seems to her important to save:

> In the face of such shape and weight of present misfortune, the voice
> of the individual artist may seem perhaps of no more consequence
> than the whirring of a cricket in the grass, but the arts do live con-
> tinuously, and they live literally by faith; their names and their shapes
> and their uses and their basic meanings survive unchanged in all that
> matters through times of interruption, diminishment, neglect; they
> outlive governments and creeds and the societies, even the very
> civilizations that produced them. They cannot be destroyed altogether
> because they represent the substance of faith and the only reality.
> They are what we find again when the ruins are cleared away. And
> even the smallest and most incomplete offering at this time can be a
> proud act in defense of that faith.

# We're All on the Passenger List

## by Mark Schorer

This novel has been famous for years. It has been awaited through an entire literary generation. Publishers and foundations, like many once hopeful readers, long ago gave it up. Now it is suddenly, superbly here. It would have been worth waiting for for another thirty years if one had had any hope of having them. It is our good fortune that it comes at last still in our time. It will endure, one hardly risks anything in saying, far beyond it, for many literary generations.

The novel is set in 1931. It opens on Aug. 22 in Veracruz, Mexico, when the *Vera,* "a mixed freight and passenger ship," is about to sail, and it ends on Sept. 17, when its passengers disembark in Bremerhaven. There are about fifty important characters, at least half of whom are major. Seventeen of the twenty-five major characters are Germans, returning to the homeland after a stay of one kind or another in Mexico. There are three Swiss, four Americans, a Swede, and a miscellany of Spaniards, Cubans and Mexicans.

Having for some years used *No Safe Harbor* as her working title, Katherine Anne Porter's final title acknowledges the organizing source of her conception in *Das Narrenschiff,* Sebastian Brant's late fifteenth-century satire. Brant stayed only sporadically with his narrative conception of a shipload of fools sailing for the Land of Fools, digressing in all manner of didactic apostrophe, polemic, allusions and parallels, allegorical swellings. Miss Porter's voyage is a very real one, based, indeed, on her first passage to Europe.

If, like Brant's book, hers moves constantly from character to character, the dramatic point of view continually shifting, yet the controlling point of view, her perfectly poised ironical intelligence, is constant and in complete authority. If, now and then, her precise

"We're All on the Passenger List." From Mark Schorer's review of *Ship of Fools, New York Times* (April 1, 1962). © 1962 by The New York Times Company. Reprinted by permission.

prose opens audibly into the overtones of allegory, these cannot be abstracted from the concrete details of the voyage. Yet all the time, as with any great work of art, something larger is in the air, and we know that we are on another ship as well, another voyage, sailing to another harbor.

Sebastian Brant did not exempt himself from the charge of folly but went so far as to make himself the captain of his ship of fools. Miss Porter says simply at the end of her little foreword, "I am a passenger on that ship." It will be a reader myopic to the point of blindness who does not find his name on her passenger list.

Probably many an eager graduate student is about to brush up on his German (Brant's dialect was Swabian) in order to read old Brant, and presently in certain periodicals we will be coming upon earnest analogical studies of the sort that followed upon the publication of Joyce's *Ulysses.* Who knows what ingenious discoveries will be made? The Seven Deadly Sins will be marched out (and they are all unquestionably if most delicately here, but chiefly, and in every guise, "Accidia"—spiritual torpor, the paralysis of love), and someone may find in Miss Porter's two perfunctory priests not two perfunctory priests but modern instances of the corruption of the clergy in the late Middle Ages. Any such effort to get at the center of this novel would, of course, be nonsensical. *Ship of Fools,* universal as its reverberating implications are, is a unique imaginative achievement.

If, as a conceptual convenience, Miss Porter has associated her novel with a medieval tradition of peculiarly harsh and not very witty satire, there is nothing (or almost nothing) harsh in her book. There is much that is comic, much even that is hilarious, and everything throughout is always flashing into brilliance through the illuminations of this great ironic style. At the same time, almost everything that is comic is simultaneously pathetic; what is funny is also sad, moving to the point of pain, nearly of heartbreak.

No, all that is conceivably harsh in this novel is its magnificent lack of illusion about human nature and especially the human sexual relationship. Even that is not really harsh because all the sharp perception and unsparing wit of this total candor is exercised by an imaginative sympathy that is not withheld from even the greatest fool, not even from the Texan oaf, Denny, whom the gracious Mrs. Treadwell, suddenly outraged beyond endurance, beats into insensibility with the sharp heel of her lovely golden slipper.

There is no plot, not even, really, a story. Most of the major characters are presented in groups, chiefly family groups, each group with its own problem or project, and then there are a few solitary figures wandering the decks in isolation. And while the various groups become acquainted with one another and each reacts critically to the others and all interact, they are in fact all isolated. When they are not indifferent to one another, they are impelled by active hostility or chill malice. When they appear, within the groups, to be loving one another, they are usually destroying one another and themselves, if they have not already done so.

There are the Swiss Lutzes, with their stolid, unmarriageable daughter; the childless Huttens with their repulsive white bulldog, Bebe, who is nearly drowned, unfortunately not; the Baumgartners, he a hopeless alcoholic, and their frightened, defeated little boy; Jenny angel and David darling, Americans who are lovers but occupy separate cabins and who are hopelessly bound together in a symbiotic relationship based on hate and self-hate. There are an aged, miserly religious enthusiast, dying in a wheelchair, and his trapped young nephew; eight Spaniards who make up a zarzuela company, the women tarts, the men pimps, and their two demonic children, called Ric and Rac. It is the Spaniards who organize the ship's party, which turns into a marvelous and absolutely disastrous Walpurgisnacht, in which every appearance of order is at last shattered and the real state of moral dishevelment is exposed in character after character, group after group of which I have named only a few.

Among the solitaries are the charming Mrs. Treadwell, a divorcee incapable of love; the attractive, gaudy Condesa, a political exile from Cuba put off on Tenerife, loved too late by the ship's doctor; the handsome Herr Freytag, returning to Germany to bring out before it is too late his beautiful Jewish wife, whom he is already beginning to resent. There are also Herr Lowenthal, the ship's pariah, a Jewish salesman of Catholic Church furnishings, a self-pitying hunchback, the Texas lout who pursues women like a sniffing dog and gets his highly satisfactory and entirely unexpected comeuppance.

Such catalogues as these cannot begin to suggest the brilliance and variety of characterization, nor the thematic unity (the fated and clumsy human quest for love and affection explicitly observed by Mrs. Treadwell) that binds all these together in the work of art even as separation is their condition in life. The Germans are particularly wonderful and horrifying creations, but even the best of the others do not escape the lash of irony or the relentless sharp prick of perception.

Set as the novel is in the years just before Hitler, and involved as it is with so many Germans and the impending German-Jewish crisis, one almost irresistibly compares it with another recent novel, Richard Hughes' *The Fox in the Attic*. (The comparison is a little unfair since the Hughes work is only the novel's first volume.) When Mr. Hughes moves from British manners to German politics, all becomes over-simplified, diagrammatic. Miss Porter, approaching the same historical situation, involves one more and more deeply in the sheer mess of human materials—these dreadful domestic relations, at once so funny and so unbearably sad.

If one is to make useful comparisons of *Ship of Fools* with other work they should be with neither Sebastian Brant nor Richard Hughes, but with the greatest novels of the past hundred years. Call it, for convenience, the *Middlemarch* of a later day. And be grateful.

# *Ship of Fools* and the Critics

## *by Theodore Solotaroff*

Whatever the problems were that kept Katherine Anne Porter's *Ship of Fools* from appearing during the past twenty years, it has been leading a charmed life ever since it was published late last March. In virtually a single voice, a little cracked and breathless with excitement, the reviewers announced that Miss Porter's long-awaited first novel was a "triumph," a "masterpiece," a "work of genius...a momentous work of fiction," "a phenomenal, rich, and delectable book," a "literary event of the highest magnitude." Whether it was Mark Schorer in the *New York Times Book Review* delivering a lecture, both learned and lyrical, on the source, sensibility, and stature of the novel ("Call it...the *Middlemarch* of a later day"), or a daily reviewer for the San Francisco *Call Bulletin* confessing that "not once [had] he started a review with so much admiration for its author, with such critical impotence"—in the end it came to the same thing.

Riding the crest of this wave of acclaim, *Ship of Fools* made its way to the top of the best-seller lists in record time and it is still there as I write in mid-September. During these four months, it has encountered virtually as little opposition in taking its place among the classics of literature as it did in taking and holding its place on the best-seller lists. A few critics like Robert Drake in the *National Review,* Stanley Kauffmann in the *New Republic,* Granville Hicks in the *Saturday Review,* and Howard Moss in the *New Yorker,* wound up by saying that *Ship of Fools* fell somewhat short of greatness, but only after taking the book's claim to greatness with respectful seriousness. Some of the solid citizens among the reviewers, like

John K. Hutchens, found the novel to be dull and said so. Here and there, mainly in the hinterlands, a handful of independent spirits ... suspected that the book was a failure. But who was listening?

Prominent among the circumstances which have helped to make a run-away best seller and a *succes d'estime* out of this massive, un-exciting, and saturnine novel was the aura of interest, partly senti-mental and partly deserved, that Miss Porter's long struggle with it had produced. Most of the reviews begin in the same way: a dis-tinguished American short-story writer at the age of seventy-one has finally finished her first novel after twenty years of working on it. As this point was developed, it tended to establish the dominant tone of many reviews—that of an elated witness to a unique personal triumph, almost as though this indomitable septuagenarian had not written a book, but had done something even more remarkable— like swimming the English Channel.

The more sophisticated magazine critics approached the novel mainly in terms of the expectancy that Miss Porter's previous work had created. In Mark Schorer's words, *Ship of Fools* had been "eagerly awaited by an entire literary generation," which may overstate the matter but does point to the fact that over the years Miss Porter has become one of the representative figures of the heroic days in modern American letters—"the stylist of the 1920's to the last," to quote John Chamberlain's review. For the survivors of her literary generation, as well as for many members of a later one, this has given her something of the same appeal that Mrs. Roosevelt enjoys among Democrats. Miss Porter's reputation is particularly strong in the academy where she has taught off and on over the years and where her stories have been studied with special zeal and affection.

In short, the objective interest that Miss Porter's previous work had inspired usually contained an element of reverence, and in reading the reviews, one had the feeling that almost everyone in the academy and in New York literary circles (where, as *Time* put it, this "gracious...Southern gentlewoman" has long been a "charming chatterer") was either awed by or pulling for her—particularly those "in the know" who were aware of the troubles that she had had in writing her novel.

If the first paragraph of the reviews was likely to dote in one way or another on Miss Porter, the second was likely to dote upon the universal dimensions of her new book. More often than not, this universality was demonstrated by quoting the Preface: particularly Miss Porter's statement that at the center of her design is nothing less than the "image of the ship of this world on its voyage to eternity." However grandiose the claim might seem, the reviewers accepted it without question and lauded *Ship of Fools* as a novel whose theme "is the human race," as a "parable of a corrupt faithless world," as "a great moral allegory of man's fate," and so forth. That the only real sign of allegory in *Ship of Fools* is provided by the Preface (there are a few other details—the German ship's name is *Vera*, etc.) and that the novel, if it is anything at all, is a straightforward and grimly realistic account of a voyage from Veracruz to Bremerhaven in 1931, that the characters are drawn as literally as one could imagine, that the surface of the writing is completely univalent— none of this stopped any of the more enthusiastic reviewers from finding themselves in the presence of a great symbolic vision of human life and destiny. As Dayton Kohler, an English professor writing in the Richmond (Va.), *News Leader,* put it, *"Ship of Fools* is an attempt to confront the mystery of being. ... Here in microcosm is the world man has made."

Another feeling repeatedly expressed by the reviews was that the return of Miss Porter had ended a winter of general discontent with recent fiction. At one level, this feeling took the form of an impatience with the genial popular novel that neatly solves the problems of its characters. However, a number of other reviewers were less inclined to express their gratitude for *Ship of Fools* by repudiating *kitsch* than by repudiating their image of what passes for serious fiction today. In their desire to behold again the "solid" novel that they had been deprived of by the idiosyncracy, morbidity, and super-subtlety of serious contemporary fiction, such reviewers were inclined to see in *Ship of Fools* a somewhat different book from the one Miss Porter had actually written. If *Ship of Fools* does not have a "flimsy plot" (Winston-Salem *Journal and Sentinel),* this is only because it does not have any plot at all. If it has no "case histories" (Winston-Salem again) its cast of characters nevertheless includes a dipsomaniac (Herr Baumgartner), a nymphomaniac and drug addict (La Condesa), a religious maniac (Herr Graf), two paranoids (Herr Rieber and Herr Lowenthal), two child psychopaths (Ric and Rac), and—transfixed by their frustrations, compulsions, and illusions—a dozen or more thoroughgoing neurotics. Similarly, one needs to read only the first ten pages to see that Miss

Porter re-creates "persons and events on their own terms" (Chicago *Sun-Times*) about as much as her title would indicate. For these reasons, among others, the novel has very little power, "rugged" *(Newsweek)* or otherwise, and its "myriad insights" *(Newsweek* again) all lie along the same fixed line of vision and impart much the same judgment of human experience.

Yet it is not hard to see what these reviewers had in mind. *Ship of Fools* suggests many of the qualities of the traditional "solid" novel that has virtually dropped out of sight in recent years. Like the 19th-century classics, it comes at life in a straightforward and comprehensive way, while at the same time it shows itself to be a very modern novel in its form and sensibility. There are many characters and they all have the uncomplicated distinctiveness, bordering on caricature, that allows the reader to keep them straight, and to know where he is with each of them. Miss Porter's steady, clear notation of the strongly marked and typical manners and attitudes of her German burghers, pedagogues, and naval men, of her American natives and expatriates, of her Hispanic priests and revolutionaries, aristocrats and peasants, thus provides the sort of large-scale social inventory that used to be one of the leading features of the major novel. Though she has dispensed with the old-fashioned elaborate plot, she does contrive an almost continual movement of the narrative among the characters which serves much the same purpose as complicated plotting once did: it brings different classes (in this case nationalities) and types into relation and into the kind of revealing patterns of specific connection and conflict that can take on a large public significance. And tied as the novel is to crucial historical events such as the worldwide depression of the 1930's and the coming of fascism, the over-all effect is that of a novelist, as confident in her sense of moral order as Dickens or Balzac, creating the private history of an age.

Seen, then, from a respectful distance, *Ship of Fools* can easily look like the real thing come back again—a spacious, resonant, self-assured novel that the reader can settle down with instead of the highly mannered, oblique, claustral novel of recent years, confined to the academy or the suburb or a vaguely specified limbo, equivocal if not hostile toward normative values. At the same time, the unconventional anecdotal structure eliminates the Victorian furniture of an elaborate and artificial "story" and gives *Ship of Fools* a lean, functional, modern look that accords with its distinctly contemporary *Weltanschauung.* In other words, it is a book not only for the coffee table but for the room whose main point of taste is the well-upholstered Danish armchair and the print from Picasso's Blue Period.

All of which provides a few of the more obvious reasons why Miss Porter was able to win over about 80 per cent of the reviewers and presumably the hundreds of thousands of readers whose currents of taste the reviewers both direct and mirror. The other reasons are more subtle. Virginia Pasley, book editor of *Newsday,* a Long Island daily, remarked that the novel's lack of an immediate story interest and its "incisive indictment of humanity" would put off many readers. "It was not written to please. It won't," she concluded. Yet Miss Pasley was completely wrong—for many of the reviewers chose to recommend *Ship of Fools* precisely for the two reasons that she had dismissed it as a possible best seller. Indeed, the reception of the novel seemed a good deal less like another gathering of the philistines than a massive act of aspiration—even of conversion. It was seized upon both as an opportunity to move the level of popular literary appreciation up a full notch, and to declare, once and for all, that life has come to be as unsatisfying and immoral as Miss Porter so "objectively" pictures it to be.

The efforts at literary enlightenment turned mainly upon the discussions of the novel's action—the absence of a developing narrative, of any appreciable dividend of suspense, cumulative interest, or reversal of expectations that results from the highly episodic structure and the panoramic treatment of the characters. There was a good deal of talk about "the interplay of character" taking precedence over "the strategy of plotting," of "vibrant tension" rather then mere "suspense," of the writer's "vision of chaos" and use of "thematic structure." All of which indicated that a half century after the innovations of Proust, Joyce, Kafka, Mann, *et al.,* the idea that the happenings in a novel are far less significant or even moving than the underlying design, usually symbolic, to which they point, appears to have filtered down into the popular literary mind. But the result of this theorizing was to shift the ground of discussion almost immediately from the novel's narrative qualities to its themes, which led most of the reviewers to overlook its crucial weaknesses *as* a novel.

The main such weakness is that no effective principle of change operates on the action or on the main characters or on the ideas, and hence the book has virtually no power to sustain, complicate, and intensify either our intellectual interests or emotional attachments. Several reviewers have compared *Ship of Fools* to Mann's *The Magic Mountain* but the comparison immediately discloses the differences between a plot of ideas that changes with the development of the central figure and a collection of incidents that are strung along a few themes. In *The Magic Mountain,* there is an order of development whose nature is uncertain and problematic as the central figure, young Hans Castorp, passes through a series of intellectual and spiritual influences that resumes much of the cultural history of pre-World War I Europe. The slow, subtle transformation of Castorp's consciousness holds the various episodes together and also provides for a kind of intellectual suspense that merges with the drama of character. In *Ship of Fools* there is little such drama or suspense, for no character or idea is kept open long enough to provide for them. As Marie Louise Aswell noted in her review, Miss Porter's narrative technique betrays at almost every point the hand of the unreconstructed short-story writer. Over and over again she isolates a single point of significance in an incident (peoples' failure to communicate, their self-deception, their emotional barrenness, moral bestiality, intellectual folly, etc.) and one or two salient traits in a character (Denny's bigotry and prurience, Mrs. Treadwell's boredom and indifference, Captain Thiele's childish authoritarianism, Fraulein Spockenkieker's stridency, etc.). As a result, the personages on the ship soon become predictable, and when their behavior is not merely repetitious, it is usually abortive and inconsequential, leading to no significant change or complication and merely further illustrating one or another of the themes of human hunger, animality, or evil. The sense of sameness spreads like a yawn and, as one of the characters remarks herself, "this voyage... must undoubtedly be described as somewhat on the dull side."

The second type of missionary work that was done by the reviewers centered around Miss Porter's characters. In general, two claims were made in behalf of this extraordinary collection of inveterate boors, malcontents, and moral cripples, who are mixed in with the grosser pathological cases. The first was that they were all superb creations ("any one or two of which," as Louis D. Rubin remarked, "would be the making of a lesser writer's reputation"); the second was that they are, individually and collectively, ourselves.

The favorite characters of the reviewers appeared to be La Condesa and Dr. Schumann. The former, with her young men and her

drugs and her wise heart is little more than a stock theatrical voice
crooning or shrieking in the wilderness inhabited by the fallen
ladies of literature. Dr. Schumann—for all that he is supposed to be
the main figure who experiences the truth of the substantial reality
of evil by virtue of his sober, humane intelligence and his corrupt-
ing passion for La Condesa—is too enfeebled by a weak heart and
a prudish malaise to have much force either as the victim or raison-
neur of man's sinfulness. Also this good gray physician becomes not
a little absurd during the course of the banal romance—a kind of
higher literary soap opera—that he and La Condesa are given to
act out:

> "...oh do you know what it is, coming so late, so strangely, no wonder
> I couldn't understand it. It is that innocent romantic love I should
> have had in my girlhood!...Well, here we are. Innocent love is the
> most painful kind of all, isn't it?"
>
> "I have not loved you innocently," said Dr. Schulmann, "but guiltily
> and I have done you great wrong, and I have ruined my life..."
>
> "My life was ruined so long ago I have forgotten what it was like
> before," said La Condesa. "So you are not to have me on your mind.
> ...I shall find a way out of everything. And now, now my love, let's
> kiss again really this time in broad daylight and wish each other well,
> for it is time for us to say good-bye."
>
> "Death, death," said Dr. Schumann, as if to some presence standing
> to one side of them casting a long shadow. "Death," he said, and
> feared his heart would burst.

The other two characters that tended to be singled out for special
praise by the reviewers were the two American woman, Jenny Brown
and Mrs. Treadwell. What the reviewers sensed, though tended to
sentimentalize, is that both women possess an intermittent auton-
omy, denied to the other characters, by virtue of a special fund of
feeling that Miss Porter has for them. Jenny, an embittered and
hollow version of the earlier autobiographical heroine (Miranda in
"Old Mortality" and "Pale Horse, Pale Rider," Laura in "Flowering
Judas"), is shown in the grip of a personal despair whose force is
sufficient to shake her alive from time to time, so that she becomes
something more than the stereotype of the liberated American and
reveals something deeper and less predictable than her foolishness.
To a lesser extent, this is also true of Mrs. Treadwell, an emotional-
ly fragile divorcee with the rest of her life to kill. Otherwise, the
characters lead lives on the ship that are tightly circumscribed by
the baleful vision of human folly in which they are suspended, by

the particular disfigurements, both personal and cultural, that they are fashioned to reveal. Unlike Dante's Brunetto Latino, or Chaucer's Pardoner, or Shakespeare's Angelo, or Stendahl's Sansfin (Miss Porter was compared to these and other masters by the reviewers in hailing her understanding of human nature), her figures are caricatures of moral infirmity and as such have only so much to reveal. After fifty pages they are predictable; after a hundred they are less revealing of human nature than they are of Miss Porter's design and sensibility.

In fact, once the characters begin to be brought into relation or to have their innards exposed at all, the attentive reader can smell the formaldehyde of an overdetermined simulation of real experience. Thus Frau Rittersdorf comes aboard the *Vera*. Her first act is to take over the lower berth, though she has been assigned an upper; her second act is to place in vases "two enormous floral offerings she had sent herself" with cards from two male admirers. After dressing and ogling herself, she opens her diary and writes:

> "So in a way, let me admit, this adventure—for is not all life an adventure?—has not ended as I hoped, yet nothing is changed for indeed I may yet see the all-guiding Will of my race in it. A German woman should not marry into a dark race. ...There are the fatal centuries in Spain when all too insidiously Jewish and Moorish blood must certainly have crept in—who knows what else?..."

Elsewhere on the ship, Herr Rieber is already defending German honor and frolicking with the shrieking Lizzi Spockenkieker ("How he admired and followed the tall thin girls with long scissor-legs like storks striding under their fluttering skirts, with long narrow feet on the ends of them"); William Denny is leering at two "Chili Queens"; and David Scott, Jenny's cold-hearted lover, is instancing his hatred of her and his horror of life ("There was no place, no place at all to go"). In one stateroom, Frau Baumgartner is taking out her hostility to her husband (a helpless alcoholic and hypochondriac) on their sickly little boy, whom, despite the intense Mexican heat, she has kept dressed in a heavy leather cowboy costume. ("Mayn't I just take off my jacket?' he persisted hopelessly.") And nearby, the supernaturally pedantic Professor Hutten is lecturing to his wife about their bottlefed bulldog Bebe ("We need not look for any radical change in his organic constitution"), while "in round maternal tones" she croons to the dog: "Don't think your little Vati and Mutti are deserting you, my precious one."

And so it goes for the next 460 pages, with only a few time-outs for an act of relative candor, dignity, or decency. All of which is supposed to constitute a true picture of human nature, and so it was generally taken to be.

This is the most remarkable feature of the reviews. One wonders which of those hapless or vicious grotesques Mark Schorer (who said that "It will be a reader myopic to the point of blindness who does not find his name on her passenger list") found to represent himself, or what qualities Louis Auchincloss ("how easy it would be for anyone to turn into even the most repellent of these incipient Nazis") would own up to that brings him so close to Herr Rieber with his clownish lust and serious wish to throw the steerage passengers into gas ovens. Moreover, one wonders why so many of the popular reviewers ("Katherine Anne Porter has seen all of us plain") took as gospel the most sour and morbid indictment of humanity to appear in years.

There is reason to suspect that something more than reviewers' can't was involved here, for the willingness of the reviewers to see themselves in Miss Porter's characters bears a remarkable resemblance to the reaction of the American press to the disclosures of the Eichmann trial last year. Bypassing the specific circumstances that had produced and empowered an Eichmann, most of the editorial writers hastened to phrases like "man's inhumanity to man," which collapsed all political and moral distinctions, not to say the purpose of the trial itself. And in the mood of moral malaise that the trial seems mainly to have inspired, it apparently became increasingly easy to assert that we are all Adolf Eichmann, which immediately transformed Eichmann from a very special kind of 20th-century political figure into merely one more example of the imperfectibility of man.*

By and large, *Ship of Fools* was read as another brief in the same abstract trial of mankind, vaguely centering upon the Nazi treatment of Jews. "In 1931 the foulness [of the world] was the rise of pride-injured German nationalism..." *(Time)*. "To the author, anti-Semitism of any description is only one form of humanity's general failure to perceive the commonness of all humanity." *(Newsweek)*. In some cases the reviewers were proceeding on the basis of a statement Miss Porter made in 1940 that the stories collected in *Flowering Judas* were part of a "much larger plan," whose ultimate purpose

---

*I am indebted for this point to a study by Midge Decter of American press reaction to the Eichmann trial.

was "to understand the logic of this majestic and terrible failure of the life of man in the Western world." But they were also reading the novel. That Miss Porter has no use for her Germans is perfectly clear, and in almost every case they are seen to be well along the road to Nazism (the book is set in 1931). But since she has no more use for most of her Mexicans, Swiss, Americans, and Spaniards, the road to Nazism soon becomes indistinguishable from the general highway to hell that runs down the middle of her novel, along which the various characters clown, scheme, or stagger. The only power of active evil is given to the troupe of Spanish dancers; in the main, the Germans merely sit nervously at the Captain's table and speak their different varieties of Aryan cant while they bolt their food and look for chances to devour each other. There is no sense at all of the *force* of that monstrous romanticism, of the potential for *active* evil in the character of German nationalism, with its commitments not only to the purity of order but to the purity of chaos and self-immolation. In his recent novel, *The Fox in the Attic,* Richard Hughes understands these matters far more deeply than does Miss Porter. Hughes, too, sees the ludicrous pretensions of the early Hitler and his cohorts, but he also grasps not only the mythos but the energy of that "insane idealism" of hatred and love that created *Lebensraum* and death camps. It is the argument of *Ship of Fools,* indeed the main theme of the book as Dr. Schumann states it, that most people's "collusion with evil is only negative, consent by default," and that it is the "mere mass and weight of negative evil [which] threatened to rule the world." This last may be merely Schumann's own proto-fascist proclivities but it is difficult to distinguish his attitude from that of the writer who has been speaking through him. In any event, Miss Porter's theme of man's paltry sinfulness once translated, say, into the figures of Captain Thiele and Herr Rieber produces merely a bilious stuffed shirt whose fantasies of violence come from American gangster movies and an impotent buffoon who eventually cavorts around the ship in a baby bonnet. The threat of "the terrible failure of the life of man" that lurks at the Captain's table is far less that of genocide than of sloth and gastritis.

This insistence upon a "general failure" of humanity creates not only a feeble portent of Hitler's Germany but in time a brutally indiscriminate one. Among the Germans on board the *Vera,* there is none more wretched and repulsive than the Jew Julius Lowenthal, with his whining, puny hatred of the *goyim;* with his lack of curiosity, much less passion, for anything in life save kosher cooking and the opportunities to make a killing off the Catholics; with his tendency to spit disgustedly into the wind. A caricature of Jewish vulgarity, Lowenthal is otherwise coldly reduced to an abstract tribal paranoia. Thinking himself snubbed by Captain Thiele, he broods for hours:

> He wished for death, or thought he did. He retired into the dark and airless ghetto of his soul and lamented with all the grieving wailing company he found there; for he was never alone in that place. He... mourned in one voice with his fated people, wordlessly he bewailed their nameless eternal wrongs and sorrows; then feeling somewhat soothed, the inspired core of his being began to search for its ancient justification and its means of revenge. But it should be slow and secret.

In brief, this successful peddler to the Catholics is the stage Jew of the modern literary tradition whom other Christian writers of sensibility (among them T. S. Eliot) have dragged out of the ghetto to represent the vulgar and menacing dislocations of traditional order:

> My house is a decayed house,
> And the jew squats on the window sill,
>         the owner,
> Spawned in some estaminet of Antwerp,
> Blistered in Brussels, patched and peeled
>         in London.

Far from exerting any understanding of or sympathy for Lowenthal —which he might have claimed if only because of the far from "nameless wrongs and sorrows" that he and his people will soon have to face in Germany—Miss Porter uses him in a situation whose implications are both historically misleading and morally vicious. At the dramatic center of the novel—both in terms of placement and by being the only conflict in the book that affects any appreciable group of characters—is an incident in which Herr Freytag, Miss Porter's other well-intentioned but ineffectual German, is removed from the Captain's table because it has been discovered that his wife is Jewish. He is then seated with the isolated Lowenthal, who immediately begins to persecute him and his absent wife:

> She's the kind of Jewish girl that makes disgrace for all the rest of us... I never laid a finger on a Gentile woman in my life, and the thought of touching one makes me sick; why can't you Goyim leave our girls alone, isn't your own kind good enough for you?...Be ashamed, Herr Freytag—when you wrong Jewish girls, you wrong the whole race. ...

While Lowenthal baits him, Freytag thinks, "Here it comes again, from the other side. ...I can't sit here either." And indeed the hostility toward him that he has also found in his wife's circle, along with the contempt he receives from his fellow Germans, has the force of making him repent of his marriage and renew his identification with the mentality and destiny of the Fatherland.

Thus, the historical significance that *Ship of Fools* is designed to possess—and all of its detail of national and cultural traits as well as its supposed symbolic resonance are nothing if not pretensions to such significance—becomes a matter of implying that the fate of Germany and its Jews reduces to the encounter of two particularly obnoxious breeds of inhumanity, with the decent but weak German liberals caught in the middle, where they become the victims of their own milder impulses toward evil.

Such an implication (and there is little to complicate, much less correct it, in the course of the novel) bespeaks not simply a failure of historical understanding, but what is more inexcusable for a novelist, it indicates a failure of consciousness, a glib refusal to acknowledge any of the imponderables of Lowenthal's fate:

> All he wanted in the world was the right to be himself, to go where he pleased and do what he wanted without any interference from them [the goyim]. That no race or nation in the world, nor in all human history had enjoyed such rights made no difference to Herr Lowenthal: he should worry about things none of his business.

And the trifling attitude that lies behind the treatment of Lowenthal is only one example of Miss Porter's compulsive tendency to simplify and close her characters and issues, to look down upon life from the perspective of a towering arrogance, contempt, and disgust.

It is just here that the reviewers went most astray in reading and puffing the novel. As some of the cleverer ones saw, *Ship of Fools* is not a novel of action or character or ideas, but one that is held together and given significance by its point of view, that is to say by the presence and pressure of Miss Porter's sensibility. However, the personal aura of Miss Porter, that we began by noting, was particularly protective in this respect, for it guarded her against direct criticism of the main weakness of the book—the spirit in which it was written. To judge this spirit was inevitably to judge the "gracious ...gentle-woman," "the distinguished humanist" of acquaintance and reputation. The better critics—such as Stanley Edgar Hyman and Stanley Kauffmann—stopped just short of doing so. The others spoke of Miss Porter's "compassion" and "concern," "candor" and "objectivity," "wit" and "humor." The critic who went to greatest lengths to define and exult over Miss Porter's sensibility was Mark Schorer:

> There is nothing (or almost nothing) harsh in her book. There is much that is comic, much even that is hilarious, and everything throughout is always flashing into brilliance through the illumination of this great ironic style. At the same time, almost everything that is comic is simultaneously pathetic...moving to the point of pain, nearly of heartbreak. No, all that is conceivably harsh in this book is its magnificent lack of illusion about human nature and especially the human sexual relationship. Even that is not really harsh because all the sharp perception and unsparing wit is exercised by an imaginative sympathy that is not withheld from even the greatest fool, not even from the Texan oaf, Denny, whom the gracious Mrs. Treadwell, suddenly outraged beyond endurance, beats into insensibility with the sharp heel of her lovely golden slipper.

The remarkable thing about this passage, from what must have been the most influential review of the book, is that it does not contain a single word of critical truth. There is simply nothing funny about *Ship of Fools* and its pathos is represented by the type of artful corn that was quoted some pages back in connection with La Condesa and Dr. Schumann's relationship. Seldom does anything "flash into brilliance," for the "great ironic style" of the author who wrote "Noon Wine" no longer belongs to Miss Porter. Under the cold, smooth plaster of her prose is not a "magnificent lack of illusion about human nature," but an alternately smug or exasperated or queasy hostility toward most of the behavior she is describing. This takes incessant little forms of showing up and putting down her characters, and almost any passage of description or dialogue brings out some of them. As I said earlier, Jenny Brown is one of the few characters that her author has any feeling for; yet not even she is allowed to escape from Miss Porter's subtle, habitual snideness:

> She hesitated and then spoke the word "soul" very tentatively, for it was one of David's tabus, along with God, spirit, spiritual, virtue— especially that one!—and love. None of these words *flowered particularly* in Jenny's daily speech, though now and then in some *stray* warmth of feeling she *seemed* to need one or the other; but David

could not endure the sound of any of them. ...He could translate them
into obscene terms and pronounce them with a sexual fervor of en-
joyment; and Jenny, who blasphemed as *harmlessly as a well-taught
parrot*, was in turn offended by what she *prudishly* described as
"David's dirty mind." ...

My italics underscore the small jabs, the kind of compulsive catti-
ness with which Miss Porter's "sensibility" operates. The most
persistent and revealing example of her "sharp perception and
unsparing wit" is in her relentless comparisons of almost all her
characters to a whole menagerie of animals and birds — the idea
being that their behavior is at bottom no different from the chain of
greedy, malicious animosity that has been illustrated in the opening
pages by the relations between a cat, a monkey, a parrot, and a dog.
As for Miss Porter's "imaginative sympathy," one can read the frigid
description of the incident Schorer notes in which the "gracious"
Mrs. Treadwell, having alternately teased and pushed away a young
officer on the ship through a whole evening, and having drunk
herself into a stupor in her stateroom, squats over the unconscious
Denny. With "her lips drawn back and her teeth set, she beat him
with such furious pleasure [that] a sharp pain started up in her
right wrist..."

Mrs. Treadwell's violence is not directed at Denny so much as
at "the human sexual relationship" she fears and hates and which
he, like most of the other characters, embodies in a particularly
hideous manner. Miss Porter's attitude in this respect is most apparent in the treatment of the Spanish dancing troupe — particularly
the two six-year-old twins — who are the evil characters in the novel,
the focus of most of the speculations about original sin. From the
moment they appear on the scene, the girls' "sleazy black skirts too
tight around their slender hips...their eyes flashing and their hips
waving in all directions," a sense of fascinated revulsion settles into
the tone of the narrative and continues throughout the novel as the
dominant strain of Miss Porter's misanthropy. In its most overt
form, it fixates upon the incestuous relations of the two six-year-old
psychopaths, Ric and Rac; upon the malign sexual power and corruption of the adult dancers as they glide about the decks; upon the
wildly lascivious Concha teasing one of the young passengers nearly
to the point of murdering his grandfather in order to get some
money to sleep with her; upon the sexual relations of the dancers
themselves:

Their supple dancers' legs writhed together for a moment like a nest of snakes. They sniffed, nibbled, bit, licked and sucked each other's flesh with small moans of pleasure. ...She saved herself like a miser in the dull plungings and poundings of those men who were her business, and spent herself upon Pepe, who was tricky as a monkey and as coldly long-lasting as a frog.

However, the atmosphere of cold, queasy sexuality, and the accompanying imagery of revulsion, radiates outward from the dancers to condition each of the other sexual relationships. La Condesa croons seductively to Dr. Schumann and he has "a savage impulse to strike her from him, this diabolical possession, this incubus fastened upon him like a bat." Even when the incredibly stuffy Huttens make love, the reader finds himself back with Pepe and Amparo: the same stressed male violence, the same abased female satisfaction, the same description of their bodies "grappled together like frogs." Sex on Miss Porter's "ship of this world" is Denny's constant goatish leer; it is the chasing of the "pig-snout" Rieber after the "peahen" Spockenkieker; it is the "monkey-faced" snickering of the Cuban students and the impassioned face of La Condesa, "her eyes...wild and inhuman as a monkey's"; sex is Jenny's gesture, "unselfconscious as a cat," of slapping her inner thigh; it is the Baumgartners' terrifying their child who lies awake in the next berth; in sum, it is David Scott's moment of introspection when "slowly there poured through all his veins again that deep qualm of loathing and intolerable sexual fury, a poisonous mingling of sickness and death-like pleasure."

This is what Miss Porter's "magnificent lack of illusion" comes to. Her contemptuous and morbid attitude toward human sexuality plays a large part in deflecting her sensibility to its incessant quarrel with human nature and in leading it by inevitable stages to a vision of life that is less vice and folly than a hideously choking slow death. For Miss Porter's versions of political action, artistic creation, religious belief, teaching, and so forth are no less skewed and embittered than her versions of copulation. Further, this clammy connection between sex and evil appears to rule out any feeling toward her characters other than a nagging exasperated irony, and to remove the possibility of any struggle toward deeper insight. As a result, the consciousness that is operating in the book, for all its range of view, is standing, so to speak, on a dime, and has little contact with the sources of imaginative vitality and moral power that renew a long work of fiction.

One can begin to understand, then, why *Ship of Fools*—apart from problems of technique and theme—remains so stagnant and repetitive; why there is neither the humor nor the pathos that Schorer raves about; and why there is nothing either "majestic" or "terrible" about Miss Porter's image of human failure. Far from being a profound account of the "ship of this world on its voyage to eternity," *Ship of Fools* is simply what it is: an account of a tedious voyage to Europe three decades ago that has been labored over for twenty years by a writer who, late in life, is venturing, hence revealing, little more than misanthropy and clever technique. *"Ship of Fools* is a work of mechanical art," as Elizabeth N. Hoyt of the Cedar-Rapids *Gazette* put it—cutting through the sentimental and pretentious obfuscation which has surrounded the novel from the start—"but the soul of humanity is lacking."

# Voyage to Everywhere

*by Sybille Bedford*

*Ship of Fools, Das Narrenschiff, Stultifera Navis:* "I took for my own this simple almost universal image of the ship of this world on its voyage to eternity. It is by no means new—it [is] very old and durable and dearly familiar...and it suits my purpose exactly. I am a passenger on that ship." Katherine Anne Porter has written a tremendous novel. It took twenty years. One might pause for an instant to imagine this. Twenty years. The courage, the discipline, the fortitude; the cost of every kind, the pressures involved in bearing what must have been at times an almost intolerable burden. And here it is at last, the legend become print: the book has been out (in the United States) for barely half a year and already something of its substance has eaten itself into the marrow of those who read it. The Great American Novel has appeared; ironically, it has turned out to be a great universal novel.

The framework is a voyage on a ship of the North German Lloyd from Veracruz to Bremerhaven in 1931, lasting twenty-seven days. The theme is not (as might be said) an icy condemnation of the human race, but a condemnation of its condition; a clinical exposition, point counterpoint, of the facts of the flesh, the quakings of the spirit, the unavailing antics and defences against the whole unalterable mesh of fear, lust, greed, decay, private demons, random malice, death and alienation. The passengers embark—"*Quand partons-nous vers le bonheur?*"—at Veracruz. And here at once in a few opening pages we have what may well endure as one of the indelible set-pieces of black literature: the gruesomeness and beauty of Mexico, and its blank indifference, the anguish of all journeys. The Mexicans of the white-linen class staring behind their iced limeades into the square, the shapeless, sweaty, pink-faced travellers trudging from stony-eyed clerk to clerk, from customs shed to office, the cy-

"Voyage to Everywhere." From Sybille Bedford's review of *Ship of Fools, Spectator* (November 16, 1962), pp. 763-64. Reprinted by permission of *Spectator*.

cle of the fish-scrap, rotting banana and small copper coin flung to
the crawling deformity, the dog, the Indian, the chained monkey
and the cat—here it is the abyss between race and race, comfortable
and poor, man and man, man and creature. The travellers reach the
ship; their anonymity dissolves, the characters emerge, their pasts,
their physiques, their worlds. There are some thirty of them, passengers of the first class, all wonderfully separate, realised, *seen,*
and there are also, as thick, as tangible, what one might call the pre-
sences, the ship's company of dapper nameless officers and fair snub-
nosed sailors, the hydra of Cuban students, the steerage passengers,
"eight hundred and twenty-six souls." The author exercises an un-
canny physical compulsion upon her readers, we are all, and not only
in her allegorical sense, passengers on that ship: as we read we are
always there; we lean against the rail, we walk that deck, we eat in
that saloon (gross Germanic soup-scoops as well as delicious things:
Miss Porter's dichotomous attitude to the food on her ship invites
a thesis), we sit in those musty cabins while the men shave and the
women let their hair down, we hear them and, above all, we see. The
lamentable shape of many of the German passengers, the youth and
slenderness of the Spanish sluts, the huge, mysteriously tormented
Swede sleeping with his feet outside the upper bunk, Herr and Frau
Professor mopping up after their dog. We see the captain's wattles
swell purple in temper and the greasy pores of the unloved Swiss
girl. We see them skip and waddle and stride towards one another
—on Katherine Anne Porter's ship the people are what they look,
and they do as they are. They sleep with each other, or try to (she is a
virtuoso of such situations), take virulent dislikes, band together,
score off, snub. A man goes overboard; there are some acts of violence (the least expected of them has a disturbing echo in one of the
author's early stories). Some ugly things occur. Every scene, every
incident, every interchange, is convincing, alive, is happening, has
happened before our eyes. When it is over, one stops (if one does
stop) and asks, how was it done? how does she do it? With words,
evidently. Miss Porter's style is elegant and precise; it is straight
without being thin, rich without the slightest trace of cloying. It is
neither colloquial nor baroque, and she never permits herself a
mannerism or an idiosyncrasy. In fact, it is a very fine style, put to
use with the greatest skill, but this style and her words have a way of
vanishing from consciousness and the page while flesh and blood
take over.

Miss Porter's contrapuntal theme of hopelessness is perhaps most originally sustained by six of her main characters, or rather by three couples. These are: the Spanish twins; the American lovers, Jenny angel and David darling; and two of the Germans, Herr Rieber and Fraulein Lizzi Spockenkieker. The Spanish twins are six years old. They are dead-end characters (a Katherine Anne Porter specialty), born purely malevolent, without a spark of anything else, and nothing whatsoever will redeem them. (We *are* made to believe this.) This little boy and girl, "as light as if their bones were hollow," hate all grown-ups, other children, animals, and they make the children in *A High Wind in Jamaica* and *The Turn of the Screw* appear rational, amenable human beings. The young American lovers, conscious creatures of good will, enact throughout one irremediable predicament: they cannot love each other in each other's presence. They meet filled with tenderness, remorse; they meet, hate and quarrel. They part, if only for a walk round deck, and once again they melt and hope. And here, too, it is made quite clear that they cannot let each other go, nor ever be at peace together. Herr Rieber is a bouncing, bumptious, genial little German, full of coyness, sentimentality and good cheer, who goes off the deep end on the subject of the master race. There is one notable passage.

> Herr Rieber and Lizzi Spokenkieker pranced on to the deck, and Lizzi screamed out.... "Oh, what do you think of this dreadful fellow? Can you guess what he just said? I was saying, "Oh, these poor people, what can be done for them?" and this monster—she gave a kind of whinny between hysteria and indignation—"he said, "I would do this for them: I would put them all in a big oven and turn on the gas." Oh,' she said weakly, doubling over with laughter, "isn't that the most original idea you ever heard?"
>
> Herr Rieber stood by smiling broadly, quite pleased with himself. ... Lizzi said, "Oh, he did not mean any harm, of course, only to fumigate them isn't that so?"
>
> "No, I did not mean fumigate," said Herr Rieber stubbornly.

The other Germans on board, who think that Herr Rieber, whom they look down on socially, goes too far, are heftily united in their feelings about German blood, their nationalism, their laments over the lost war, their contempt for America (polluted by The Negro) and their terror of and disgust with the smell of the poor, the Spanish rabble in the steerage. When there is some trouble down there, the captain, a blustering bully, behaves abominably out of sheer acquired inhumanity and funk; and there is one very nasty episode indeed, an act of anti-Semitism, not violent and rather more sinister for being aimed at the absent wife of a Christian passenger, which leaves a mark on the whole voyage.

*Ship of Fools* will be and has been called anti-German. One might as well say that the book is anti-human. The Spaniards, Americans, Mexicans and Cubans on that ship come out differently, but they do not come out any better. Two out of the limited number—four? —six?—of "decent" characters are German, Dr. Schumann and Frau Otto Schmitt. Miss Porter took some Germans of the early 1930s as she found them, but surely this choice of nationalities is subordinate and incidental to the main theme of her work? If she had chosen, she might have had her ship captained by a chauvinistic French climber or a jingoistic Englishman with the same ultimate effect.

Faults? Miss Porter believes in the repeated blow, the massed detail. The book might have been even more effective, more stunning, for less length. Bulk, whatever the quality, blunts. Also, there is perhaps rather too much insistence (deverbalised Huxleyan) on armpits, smells and fat. And we would have been *as* horrified if she had gone a little more lightly on the grotesques. Did the only Jew on board have to be such an utter wretch? did he *have* to trade in rosaries? Could we not have done without the actual hunchback on the passenger list? But this comes dangerously near to quarrelling with the artist's vision. (Being not wholly certain about Mrs. Treadwell does not. She is the one main character over whom the author seems to waver. There is something magazine-y about that lady and her inner monologues.) There is something else that might be looked at as a flaw: the novel remains static, the characters move on tramlines towards crescendos, not towards development; there is accumulation straws on camels' backs, but no choice, no crossroads, no turning-points. But this *is* quarrelling with the artist's vision, for the point is that hers is not in terms of classical tragedy or Jamesian decisions: her cards *are* already stacked, the tableau *is* the *donum*.

There are moments of transport, of otherness. When the boy and the Spanish dancer make love for the first time (the boy having about killed his uncle to get some money to pay the girl and her pimp), the key changes and one is utterly carried away, and it is young and sensuous and good. Then there are the Mexican bride and groom, the lovers who do not speak, who float, silent, hand in hand, past the more solid apparitions. But the Mexican lovers have been left on another plane, they are never substantiated and remain, too faintly, a symbol. Perhaps the high moment of the book comes when the whales are seen, three whales flashing white and silver in the sunlight, spouting tall white fountains, and the Spanish twins wave their arms in pure ecstasy, and "not one person could take his eyes from the beautiful spectacle...and their minds were cleansed of death and violence."

But the whales recede. There are no windows after all on that voyage, no wider views, no liberation. Only escapes. Wine, food and loving destroy the body. The intellectuals on board are arid pedants. Religion does not get off the ground; art remains extraneous; pity is self-pity; love the *angst*-ridden cry of self-love. There is one single italicised passage in the book, it comes towards the end, and it goes:

> What they were saying to each other was only, *"Love me, love me in spite of all! Whether or not I love you, whether I am fit to love, whether you are able to love, even if there is no such thing as love, love me!"*

They will not. Not for long; not enough. On that ship there is no help, no hope, no light, no change. *There will be no message.* The best one can do is to muster a thin form of modern stoicism, some *tenue,* behave with a little more dignity than the next person. It is better not to cry in public, not to wolf one's food, to keep one's waistline, carry one's liquor, for women to wear clothes accordant with their age; there is something to be said for the masculine passion for physical discipline, the German addiction to duty....It is not the noblest hypothesis about the voyage; it is one that has been held— and denied—by artists and laymen through centuries. *Ship of Fools* is a sustained version. Katherine Anne Porter has given us a Brueghel; we can hope, but cannot be sure, that it is less true than a Piero della Francesca.

# No Safe Harbor

## by Howard Moss

Katherine Anne Porter's *Ship of Fools* (Atlantic-Little, Brown) is the story of a voyage—a voyage that seems to take place in many dimensions. A novel of character rather than of action, it has as its main purpose a study of the German ethos shortly before Hitler's coming to power in Germany. That political fact hangs as a threat over the entire work, and the novel does not end so much as succumb to a historical truth. But it is more than a political novel. *Ship of Fools* is also a human comedy and a moral allegory. Since its author commits herself to nothing but its top layer, and yet allows for plunges into all sorts of undercurrents, it is disingenuous to read on its surface alone and dangerous to read for its depths. Miss Porter has written one of those fine but ambiguous books whose values and meanings shift the way light changes as it passes through a turning prism.

Except for the embarkation at Veracruz and a few stopovers at ports, all the events occur aboard the *Vera,* a German passenger freighter, on its twenty-seven-day journey from Mexico to Germany in the summer of 1931. There is no lack of passengers; the cast is so immense that we are provided with not one but two keys at the beginning, so that we can keep the characters clearly in mind. The passenger list includes many Germans; a remarkable company of Spanish zarzuela singers and dancers—four men and four women— equally adept at performing, thieving, pimping, and whoring; the satanic six-year-old twins of two of the dancers: and four Americans: William Denny, a know-nothing chemical engineer from Texas; Mrs. Treadwell, a divorcee in her forties, who is constantly thwarted in her attempts to disengage herself from the rest of the human race; and David Scott and Jenny Brown, two young painters who have been having an unhappy love affair for years, have never married, and quarrel endlessly. There are also a Swede, some Mexicans, a Swiss innkeeper and his family, and some Cubans. The Germans are almost uniformly disagreeable—an arrogant widow, a windbag of a professor named Hutten, a violently anti-Semitic publisher named Rieber, a drunken lawyer, an Orthodox Jew who loathes Gentiles, a dying religious healer, and a hunchback, to name just a few. Each suffers from a mortal form of despair—spiritual, emotional, or religious. At Havana, La Condesa, a Spanish noblewoman who is being deported by the Cuban government, embarks, and so do eight hundred and seventy-six migrant workers, in steerage. They are being sent back to Spain because of the collapse of the Cuban sugar market.

In the little world of the *Vera,* plying across the ocean, the passengers become involved with one another not from choice but by proximity. Because of this, not very much happens, from the viewpoint of conventional drama. Miss Porter is interested in the interplay of character and not in the strategy of plotting. Her method is panoramic—cabin to cabin, deck to writing room, bridge to bar. She has helped herself to a device useful to a natural short-story writer: she manipulates one microcosm after another of her huge cast in short, swift scenes. Observed from the outside, analyzed from within, her characters are handled episodically. Place is her organizing element, time the propelling agent of her action. The *Vera* is a Hotel Universe always in motion.

As it proceeds, small crises blossom into odious flowers and expire. There are three major events. An oilman, Herr Freytag, a stainless Aryan, is refused the captain's table once it is learned that the wife he is going back to fetch from Germany is Jewish. A wood carver in steerage jumps overboard to save a dog thrown into the sea by the twins, and is drowned. And the zarzuela company arranges a costume-party "gala" whose expressed purpose is to honor the captain but whose real motive is the fleecing of the other passengers. The characters, seeking release or support in one another, merely deepen each other's frustrations. Often these random associations end in violence—a violence always out of character and always revealing. Hansen, the Swede, who talks about a society in which the masses are not exploited, clubs the publisher with a beer bottle. The source of his immediate anger is his disappointed passion for one of the Spanish dancers. The funeral of the wood carver, the gentlest of men, becomes the occasion for a religious riot. Mrs. Treadwell, a carefully contained woman, well aware of the pointlessness and danger of meddling in other people's business, emerges from behind her bastion and beats up Denny in a drunken frenzy with the heel of a golden evening slipper.

If the relationships are not violent, they are damaging. Schumann, the ship's doctor, falling suddenly in love with the drug-addicted and possibly mad Condesa, risks his professional, spiritual, and emotional identity. The American painters hopelessly batter themselves in an affair they cannot resolve or leave alone. And the most solid of *Hausfraus*, Professor Hutten's wife, speaks up suddenly, as if against her will, to contradict her husband at the captain's table, an act doubly shameful for being public. Unable momentarily to put up with her husband's platitudes, to support a view of marriage she knows to be false, Frau Hutten, in her one moment of insight, undermines the only security she has. As character after character gives way to a compulsion he has been unaware of, it becomes evident why Miss Porter's novel is open to many interpretations. Through sheer accuracy of observation rather than the desire to demonstrate abstract ideas, she has hit upon a major theme: order vs. need, a theme observable in the interchange of everyday life and susceptible of any number of readings—political, social, religious, and psychological. Every major character is magnetized in time by the opposing forces of need and order. Mexico is the incarnation of need, Germany the representative of an order based on need. At the beginning, in Veracruz, there is a hideously crippled Mexican beggar, "dumb, half blind," who walks like an animal "following the trail of a smell." And the very last character in the book is a German boy in the ship's band, "who looked as if he had never had enough to eat in his life, nor a kind word from anybody," who "did not know what he was going to do next" and who "stared with blinded eyes." As the *Vera* puts in to Bremerhaven, he stands, "his mouth quivering while he shook the spit out of his trumpet, repeating to himself just above a whisper, '*Gruss Gott, Gruss Gott,*' as if the town were a human being, a good and dear trusted friend who had come a long way to welcome him." Aboard the *Vera,* there is, on the one hand, the captain's psychotic authoritarianism, with its absolute and rigid standards of behavior, menaced always by human complexity and squalor; on the other, the Condesa's drug addiction and compulsion to seduce young men. Both are terrifying forms of fanaticism, and they complement each other in their implicit violence.

Dr. Schumann is the mediating agent between these two kinds of fanaticism. Suffering from a weak heart, he is going back to Germany—a Germany that no longer exists—to die. He is the product of a noble Teutonic strain, the Germany of intellectual freedom, scientific dispassion, and religious piety. He is a healer equally at home in the chaos of the steerage and in the captain's stateroom. But the Condesa shatters his philosophic detachment. He goes to her cabin at night and kisses her while she is asleep; he orders six young Cuban medical students to stay away from her cabin because he is jealous. Both acts are symptoms of a progressive desperation. First he refuses to express his need openly, out of fear; then he masks it by a display of authority. He becomes, finally, a conspirator in the Condesa's addiction. Since he is not able to separate the woman from the patient, in Dr. Schumann need and order become muddled. Mrs. Treadwell, an essentially sympathetic character, is drawn into Freytag's dilemma the same way—casually, then desperately. It is she who innocently tells her anti-Semitic cabinmate that Freytag's wife is Jewish, not knowing the information is meant to be confidential. He is bitter, forgetting that he has already blurted out the fact at the captain's table in a fit of anger and pride. Mrs. Treadwell wisely points out that his secret should never have been one in the first place. This is odd wisdom; Mrs. Treadwell has a few secrets of her own.

It is from such moral complications that the texture of *Ship of Fools* evolves—a series of mishaps in which both intention and the lack of intention become disasters. The tragedy is that even the best motive is adulterated when translated into action. Need turns people into fools, order into monsters. The *Vera's* first-class passengers stroll on deck gazing down into the abysmal pit of the steerage—pure need—just as they watch in envy the frozen etiquette of the captain's table and its frieze of simulated order. Even dowdy Frau Schmitt, a timid ex-teacher who cannot bear suffering in others, finally accepts the cruelty of Freytag's dismissal from the captain's table. If she does not belong there herself, she thinks, then where does she belong? A victim, she thus becomes a party to victimization —a situation that is to receive its perfect demonstration in the world of Nazi Germany, which shadows Miss Porter's book like a bird of carrion. Through the need to belong, the whole damaging human complex of fear, pride, and greed, a governing idea emerges from *Ship of Fools* that is rooted in the Prussian mystique of "blood and iron." It is the manipulation of human needs to conform to a version of order.

The flow of events in *Ship of Fools* is based on addiction (sex, drugs, food, and drink) or obsession (envy, pride, covetousness, and the rest). Yet even the most despicable characters, such as the Jew-hating Herr Rieber, seem surprisingly innocent. It is the innocence of ignorance, not of moral goodness. The humbug and misinformation exchanged between the passengers on the *Vera* are voluminous. Each person is trapped in that tiny segment of reality he calls his own, which he thinks about, and talks about, and tries to project to a listener equally obsessed. Not knowing who they are, these marathon talkers do not know the world they are capable of generating. Love is the sacrificial lamb of their delusions, and though it is pursued without pause, it is always a semblance, never a reality. Though they are terribly in need of some human connection, their humanity itself is in question.

Only the Spanish dancers seem to escape this fate. They transform need into a kind of order by subordinating it for financial gain or sexual pleasure, without involvement. They are comically and tragically evil; they have arranged a universe of money around sex and fraud. Consciously malignant, they are outdone by the natural malice of the twins, who throw the Condesa's pearls overboard in a burst of demoniacal spirits. The pearls are a prize the Spanish dancers had planned to steal. The evil of design is defeated by natural evil—a neat point. Even in this closed, diabolical society, in which the emotions have been disciplined for profit, the irrational disturbs the arrangement of things.

At one point, Jenny Brown recalls something she saw from a bus window when she was passing through a small Indian village in Mexico:

> Half a dozen Indians, men and women, were standing together quietly in the bare spot near one of the small houses, and they were watching something very intently. As the bus rolled by, Jenny saw a man and a woman, some distance from the group, locked in a death battle. They swayed and staggered together in a strange embrace, as if they supported each other; but in the man's raised hand was a long knife, and the woman's breast and stomach were pierced. The blood ran down her body and over her thighs, her skirts were sticking to her legs with her own blood. She was beating him on the head with a jagged stone, and his features were veiled in rivulets of blood. They were silent, and their faces had taken on a saintlike patience in suffering, abstract, purified of rage and hatred in their one holy dedicated purpose to kill each other. Their flesh swayed together and clung, their left arms were

wound about each other's bodies as if in love. Their weapons were raised again, but their heads lowered little by little, until the woman's head rested upon his breast and his head was on her shoulder, and holding thus, they both struck again.

It was a mere flash of visions, but in Jenny's memory it lived in an ample eternal day illuminated by a cruel sun.

This passage could be the center from which everything in Miss Porter's novel radiates. The human relations in it are nearly all reenacted counterparts of this silent struggle. Inside and out, the battle rages—the devout against the blasphemous, the Jew against the Gentile, class against class, nation against nation. The seemingly safe bourgeois marriages—of solid Germans, of stolid Swiss—are secret hand-to-hand combats. It is no better with lovers, children, and dogs. The dog thrown into the sea by the evil twins is at least rescued by the good wood carver before he drowns. But on the human level the issues are obscure, the colors blurred; the saint is enmeshed with the devil. Struggling to get at the truth— *Vera* means "true" in Latin—the passengers in *Ship of Fools* justify its title. What truth is there for people who must lie in order to exist, Miss Porter seems to be asking. Against her insane captain and her mad Condesa, Miss Porter poses only the primitive and the remote—an enchanting Indian servant aboard ship, the appearance of three whales, a peasant woman nursing a baby. They are as affecting as a silence in nature.

Miss Porter is a moralist, but too good a writer to be one except by implication. Dogma in *Ship of Fools* is attached only to dogmatic characters. There is not an ounce of weighted sentiment in it. Its intelligence lies not in the profundity of its ideas but in the clarity of its viewpoint; we are impressed not by what Miss Porter says but by what she knows. Neither heartless nor merciful, she is tough. Her virtue is disinterestedness, her strength objectivity. Her style is free of displays of "sensitivity," musical effects, and interior decoration. Syntax is the only instrument she needs to construct an enviable prose. But the book differs from her extraordinary stories and novellas in that it lacks a particular magic she has attained so many times on a smaller scale. The missing ingredient is impulse. *Ship of Fools* was twenty years in the writing; the stories read as if they were composed at one sitting, and they have the spontaneity of a running stream. *Ship of Fools* is another kind of work—a summing up, not an overflowing—and it is devoid of one of the excitements of realistic fiction. The reader is never given that special satisfaction of the drama of design, in which the strings, having come unwound, are ultimately tied together in a knot. Miss Porter scorns patness and falseness, but by the very choice of her method she also lets go of suspense. She combines something of the intellectual strategy of Mann's *Magic Mountain* (in which the characters not only are themselves but represent ideas or human qualities) with the symbolic grandeur of *Moby Dick* (in which a predestined fate awaits the chief actors). Her goodbye to themes of Mexico and Germany (two subjects that have occupied her elsewhere) is a stunning farewell, but it lacks two components usually considered essential to masterpieces— a hero and a heroic extravagance.

*Ship of Fools* is basically about love, a human emotion that teeters helplessly between need and order. On the *Vera's* voyage there is precious little of it. The love that comes too late for the Condesa and Dr. Schumann is the most touching thing in it. But the Condesa is deranged, ill, and exiled; the dying Doctor is returning to a Germany that has vanished. The one true example of love—a pair of Mexican newlyweds—is never dwelt upon. We are left with this image of two people, hand in hand, who have hardly said a word in all the thousands that make up Miss Porter's novel. In *Ship of Fools*, every human need but one is exposed down to its nerve ends. Love alone remains silent, and abstract.

# Bound for Bremerhaven—and Eternity

## by Louis Auchincloss

Katherine Anne Porter's first novel, which she started in 1941 and completed two decades later, brings none of the disillusionment usually associated with long awaited things.

Miss Porter has selected neither her country nor her countrymen as her principal models. We know precisely the where and when of her characters for they are all passengers or crew of the North [German] Lloyd S. A. *Vera* en route from Veracruz to Bremerhaven, August 22—September 17, 1931. As the author states in a foreword, she has taken the "old and durable and dearly familiar" image of the ship of this world on its voyage to eternity. The small first class contains a motley of nationalities, prevailingly German, and in steerage are 876 Spanish workers, deported from Cuba to Spain because of the failure of the sugar market. Jammed in below deck in a fetid atmosphere of sweating flesh where seven babies are born in the course of the trip, they are presented to the reader as a mass, a device which successfully simulates the pyramid of the human condition of earth: a huge poverty-stricken base and a tiny self-conscious peak. Steerage is never insisted on in the novel; it never becomes a bore, but the reader, like the first-class passengers, even the most hard-boiled of them, is always uneasily aware that it is there.

First class, like first class anywhere, is rampant with offended vanities and frustrations. Nobody is treated in accordance with what he deems to be his dignity. Nobody is satisfied with his cabin, his cabin mates, his table or table companions. The wretched little shipboard romances are all abortive. The stout publisher of the ladies garment trade journal fails with the skinny Fraulein Lizzie, the Texan engineer with the Spanish dancer, the ship's doctor with the Condesa, the young officer with the middle-aged Mrs. Treadwell, the sixteen-year-old Swiss girl with the Cuban medical student.

"Bound for Bremerhaven—and Eternity." From Louis Auchincloss's review of *Ship of Fools, New York Herald Tribune* (April 1, 1962). Reprinted by permission of the author.

And Jenny and David, the American lovers who have been separated for the trip in different cabins, find, in the artificial barrier between them, opportunities for newer and deeper misunderstanding.

Only two major events occur on the whole trip: a German businessman is removed from the Captain's table when it is discovered that his wife (not on board) is a Jewess, and a poor old bulldog, pushed over the rail by a pair of villainous Spanish children, is rescued by a steerage passenger who is drowned in the process. It is no doubt significant that the rescuer is a woodcarver, whose knife has been confiscated, and that three great whales appear, spouting and swimming Southward, immediately after his burial at sea. Miss Porter's book is rich enough to be read on different levels and will keep the lovers of symbols happy. To me it is enough that the woodcarver is the one person on board capable of a disinterested act. If he has redeemed the ship's company by his self-sacrifice, it is not long before they need redemption again.

For Miss Porter does not moon like a modern playwright over loneliness and the tragic difficulties of communication. Her characters cannot communicate because they reject communication. They have decided in advance what is due them in the way of honor, friendship and love, and they have predefined their friends and lovers as persons who must supply these needs. They are not looking for human beings but for fantasies. Consequently, they must reject, even hate the persons who seem to offer friendship or love. But their plight is not really pitiable. Selfishness and egotism are not pitiable. They can be funny, and parts of the book are uproariously funny. But Miss Porter is never guilty of the sentimentality that masquerades as compassion. When she evokes pity, it is for the sheer horror of what she describes: the beggar at Veracruz, at the beginning of the novel, who has been so intricately maimed in preparation for his calling that he hardly resembles a human being. He does not come aboard, but a hunchback does, and we never lose sight of either.

How then does the author sustain the interest through five hundred pages dominated by a group of Germans, pedantic, sentimental, prejudiced and cruel, who are going to stamp their feet and shout themselves (hoarse for Hitler in a year's time? Because this vivid, beautifully written story is bathed in intelligence and humor. Because Miss Porter can make her reader feel how easy it would be for anyone to turn into even the most repellent of these incipient Nazis, how simply the most monstrous things can grow out of fear.

None of us is so different; we are all, as her title implies, fools—
German, Spanish, Cuban, Swiss, American fools. The Spanish dancers shrug at the anti-Semitism of the Germans, the Germans at the
thievery of the Spanish dancers. The American girl observes and in-
effectively protests. And out of our foolishness a world may be born
that is worse than the world we inherited. But it doesn't have to be.
There is no feeling in the book that the fools are doomed to be fools.
They can be what they wish—all but the maimed beggar.

There is a magnificient scene at the Captain's table after Herr
Freytag has been expelled because of the discovery of his absent
wife's Jewish origin. Until then nobody has had a thing against him;
immediately afterwards he represents a threat and his elimination
an infinitely reassuring factor. The ring is closed again; the faces
relax with sensual gratification. They exchange toasts, smack their
lips and say "Ja, ja!" "Even little Frau Schmitt, who suffered at the
very thought of the miseries of the world; who wished only to love
and to be loved by everybody; who shed tears with sick animals and
unhappy children now felt herself a part of this soothing yet
strengthening fellowship," The gas chambers are ready.

Miss Porter supplies a passenger list to which it is necessary to
make frequent references in reading her early chapters. But, as in
the case of the big Victorian novels, the effort involved in meeting
the characters pays off in the richness of illusion created. The reader
feels that he has been on board the *Vera* for the twenty-six days of
her voyage, but unlike his fellow passengers, he is reluctant to
disembark.

# Ship of Fools

## by Smith Kirkpatrick

When you read Katherine Anne Porter's novel, you will find yourself already aboard her *Ship of Fools,* not overtly, not through the usual identification with one of the characters, but through a more subtle involvement with a familiar action.

Miss Porter's ship is a real, not purely symbolic, ship traveling from Vera Cruz to Bremerhaven during the early thirties and is peopled with passengers talking and traveling in that troubled time, but as the journey aboard the *Vera,* truth, continues the passengers tend to develop more towards caricature than characterization. And this is very close to Miss Porter's point. She has no clearly identifiable protagonist or antagonist. Her subject is too large to be shown through a central character; for as the ship progresses from the "true cross" to the "broken haven" she shows us how each passenger journeys not only to Bremerhaven but through life. In so doing she shows us the common manner in which we make the voyage, and she shows us the necessarily concomitant subject of what she views life to be.

Since the reader cannot identify himself with one of Miss Porter's characters, just how does she involve his heart? She has chosen to locate the novel aboard a ship, to limit her action within the confines of a sea voyage where the characters for the most part are strangers to one another. With the ship-board opportunity for new friendships and fresh, self-appraisals it is important to look at what the passengers bring with them on their journey. As the title says, the voyagers are all fools. The nature of their foolery is what the passengers bring aboard with them, and Miss Porter reduces the foolery to the oldest mark of the fool, the one thing that all fools in all time have had in common: the mask. She shows how intricately contrived are the masks. Each man wears not one but many. He peers at his existence from behind the various masks of nationality, age, sex, creeds,

*"Ship of Fools"* by Smith Kirkpatrick. From the *Sewanee Review* (Winter 1963). Reprinted by permission of the author.

social rank, race, wealth, politics, and all the other existential distinctions made by both the elemental and civilized man.

At times the masks are as pathetically simple as that of Frau Baumgartner, who in the tropic heat is momentarily too angry with her small son to heed his pleas to remove the buckskin suit in which she has wrongly encased him. She taunts him over his inability to endure the riding costume meant for mountain coldness and even begins to enjoy her cruelty and the pleasant feeling of hurting the pride of the boy sitting on the divan "...yearning for kindness, hoping his beautiful good mother would come back soon. She vanished in the frowning scolding stranger, who blazed out at him when he least expected it, struck him on the hand, threatened him, seemed to hate him." But in the next moment she "sees him clearly" and is filled with pity and remorse and tenderness.

At other times the intricacy of the masks is nearly as confusing as it is to Denny the Texan whose bible is *Recreational Aspects of Sex as Mental Prophylaxis—A True Guide to Happiness* and whose consuming passion on the voyage is to buy, at *his* price, the wares of Pastora, a dancer in the zarzuela company. Sitting in the ship's bar Denny has an atheist on one side speaking like a bolshevik and over here a Jew, criticizing Christians and meaning Catholics. He didn't like Jews *or* Catholics and knew if he said, "I think Jews are heathens," he would be accused of persecuting Jews. He wished himself home in Brownsville "...where a man knew who was who and what was what, and niggers, crazy Swedes, Jews, greasers, bone-headed micks, polacks, wops, Guineas and damn Yankees knew their place and stayed in it."

Denny wants the mask simple and set, and Miss Porter shows the results of a mask settling into reality through Mrs. Treadwell, an American divorcée, to whom the past is so bad, as compared to a future full of love she had expected as a child, it seems something she has read in newspapers. Denny in his final determination to conquer Pastora confuses the door and drunkenly mistakes for the face of Pastora the face of "unsurpassed savagery and sensuality" which Mrs. Treadwell in drunken idleness painted on herself following the failure of the young ship's officer to arouse any feeling in her. She shoves Denny to the deck, and using her metal capped high heel beats in the face of the fallen and stuporous man with "furious pleasure" and is afterwards delighted at the sight of her "hideous wicked face" in her mirror. When worn as a reality, the mask comes close to covering insanity, which becomes a terrifying comment on all the Brownsvilles in the world.

Usually, though, the masks shift and change like the postures of a dance. Jenny and David, the American painters who have been living together but are now traveling in separate cabins, approach each other with feelings of love only to have their feelings turn suddenly into hatred and the hatred as it shows itself on their faces evokes the love again. They can no more decide their emotional destiny than they can decide their physical destination. One wants to visit Spain; the other, France. In the course of their constant argument they even swap positions but always the change is in reaction to an action or reaction in the other. And here Miss Porter takes the breath away with her absolute genius. Never, not once in the seemingly unending continuum of emotional and rational action and reaction, whether between total strangers operating behind the complicated masks of their civilized pasts or whether between selves almost submerged in old marriages, never, no matter how abrupt may be the reversal of a position or of a thought pattern, is there anything but complete belief that, yes, this is the way it would really be.

This constant change is the reason the passengers tend towards caricature. Exactly when is the passenger undergoing the final unveiling to his ultimate truth? Amparo and her pimp, Pepe, steal, swindle, and blackmail behind a flurry of costumery and poses and when at last they are left together, away from their victims, Amparo still full of the strange smells and heats of the recently departed liberal Swede, Arne Hanson, the final truth of these two seems about to be revealed. And the truth is beautifully revealed of them as pimp, whore, and lovers; but the scene ends with the revelation that both parties have long before planned, and even now are working towards, their mutual betrayals.

Perhaps the truth of the characters lies not in revealing the total man facing an action as large as life itself (perhaps no man can) but in the manner or the method with which the characters face life. If in this or that situation they wear this or that ready-made mask and in the next situation wear yet another of the thousand faces molded by the forms of civilization and elemental man, then perhaps we really are caricatures with our true selves forever unrealized. Certainly the passengers behind their masks hide from each other their love. Mrs. Treadwell says the passengers are all saying to each other,

*"Love me, love me in spite of all! Whether or not I love you, whether
I am fit to love, whether you are able to love, even if there is no such
thing as love, love me!"*

The Germanic mask of discipline and family is so stolid on the
face of Dr. Schumann, the ship's doctor, that even though he loves
the beautiful Cuban Condesa, who has forsaken herself to ether and
self-caresses, he degrades her and wants rid of her. In horror of himself he renounces all human kinship and in his own drugged sleep
the Condesa's deathlike, bodiless head danced before him still smiling but shedding tears. "Oh, Why, Why?" the head asked him not
in complaint but wonder. Tenderly he kissed it silent. This was
probably the last opportunity for love in his life.

The one unmasked act of love aboard the ship, an act nearly performed earlier by Dr. Schumann when he risked overtaxing a weak
heart by stepping forward to save a cat, was performed by a man in
steerage, a wood carver who cries like a child when his knife is
taken from him and who, when the white dog is thrown overboard
into the night sea, leaps after the white object without hesitation or
knowledge of whether it is a man or a dog and is drowned saving it.
In the lean raggedness of this "worn but perhaps young" wood
carver, who cannot but bring to mind another worker in wood, and
in his unselfish act, is an opportunity for the passengers to see
behind man's facade. But even the parent-like owners of the dog
want only to forget the wood carver's name, and they lose themselves
in the carnal interest the act has rediscovered for them.

The wood carver's burial ends with the priests turning their
backs while their Catholic flock in steerage nearly kills a taunting
atheist. The final results of the wood carver's act are that the dog is
saved and fun is had by Ric and Rac, the twin children who threw
the dog overboard in the first place.

If La Condesa can say of the Cuban students, "They are just their
parents' bad dreams," then certainly this can be said of Ric and Rac
even though their parents are in the zarzuela company and are
almost bad dreams themselves. Ric and Rac have named themselves
for two comic cartoon terriers who "made life a raging curse for
everyone near them, got their own way invariably by a wicked trick,
and always escaped without a blow." And this is Ric and Rac. They
steal, kill, destroy, and hurt not for gain but from some profound
capacity for hatred which with the capacity and need for love lurks
always behind the mask. It is almost as though this capacity for
hatred is the reason of being for the masks of civilization, and Miss

Porter is writing of civilized men. She is writing of the passengers living in the upper decks, and they are terrified of the masses of humans traveling in animal misery in steerage. All weapons are taken from the masses, even the wood carver's knife. The elemental man is too apparent. Jenny is haunted by the memory of two Mexican Indians, a man and woman locked in a swaying embrace, both covered with blood and killing each other with cutting weapons. "They were silent, and their faces had taken on a saintlike patience in suffering, abstract, purified of rage and hatred in their one holy dedicated purpose to kill each other." In her dreams she is horrified to see that this is she and David.

And no matter how tightly the passengers may be enclosed in their formalized attitudes the zarzuela company reveals how thinly surfaced they are. By subverting the masks, the whores and pimps make the passengers pay them to usurp the Captain's table, toast confusion, send the pompous Captain fleeing, and in their hatred mock the passengers by parodying them on the dance floor. The dance itself being a formalization, the parody by the whores and pimps becomes not only a parody of the individual passenger but of everything he considers civilized.

And the parody is meaningful because the passengers themselves are parodies, fools. Fools because behind all the masks and the love and the hatred is a selfishness, and the most selfish of all is the old religious zealot. His final prayer is that he be remembered for one merciful moment and be let go, given eternal darkness, let die forever—be the one man in all time released from the human condition, which must be lived to whatever its ends may be.

The novel comes to no conclusions, answers no questions; its ending is the end of the journey. But these masks are our masks; this is the way we cover our naked selves for the swift passage; this life is our lives moving steadily into eternity, the familiar action in which we are all involved. And the novel is a lament for us all, a song artistically resolved, sung by a great artist of the insoluble condition of man.

# Ship of Fools

## by Ray B. West, Jr.

The setting of *Ship of Fools* is a German vessel sailing from Veracruz, Mexico, to Bremerhaven, Germany, in 1931, thus paralleling the author's first voyage to Europe after winning a Guggenheim Foundation Fellowship. Miss Porter's first title was to have been *The Promised Land*. It was then changed to *No Safe Harbour* and was identified as such in the excerpts that began appearing in periodicals in 1944, and continued almost to the date of publication. Its final title, Miss Porter tells us in a prefatory note, was taken from a moral allegory by Sebastian Brant, *Das Narrenschiff,* published in Latin as *Stultifera Navis* in 1494. Miss Porter's *Ship of Fools* is also an allegory. It might be called "a moral allegory for our time," or, perhaps more accurately reflecting the present concerns, "an existentialist fable." The ship is called *Vera* (truth), and the most general contrast represented in its passengers and crew (who are the characters of the novel) is a familiar one from the author's short fiction: a juxtaposition of passionate, indolent, irresponsible Latins with the cold, calculating, and self-righteous Nordics. These extremes not only represent a majority of the passengers and crew, but also suggest the beginning of the voyage in Mexico and its ending in Germany. Adding the necessary complexity are the characters that fall between these extremes: an Indian nursemaid, four Americans, a family of Swiss, a Mexican political agitator, a Basque, a Swede, and six Cuban medical students on their way to France. As a voyage, events may be likened to Dante's progress in *The Divine Comedy,* not in any specific way, but in the sense that Katherine Anne Porter, in this novel, is concerned with arriving at a sense of felicity for our time in much the way that Dante was for his. *Ship of Fools* is a comedy for today in the same high sense that Dante used the term in the fourteenth century.

"*Ship of Fools.*" Excerpted from Ray B. West, Jr., *Katherine Anne Porter,* University of Minnesota. Pamphlets on American Writers, vol. 28, 32-43. Copyright © 1963 by the University of Minnesota. Reprinted by permission of the University of Minnesota Press, Minneapolis.

The word "fool," as used by Miss Porter in her title, contains a double irony. In one sense she is using it as Brant must have used it, as "God's fool," suggesting man's foolishness as compared to God's wisdom. Similarly, the foolishness of the acts committed aboard ship resemble the absurdities of human action as portrayed by modern existentialism. Whether one takes the traditional Christian view of man as fool or the modern atheistic view of man as absurd, one comes from either with a feeling that truth is being expressed, only the framework has been altered. In each case man is viewed as a pathetic creature, struggling in one instance to overcome his limitations and approach God's province, in the other to organize the actions of his life around an impossible dream. In each case, he is more to be pitied than condemned.

Appropriate to this ideological point of view, Miss Porter has chosen in *Ship of Fools* to see the action from the position of an omniscient narrator (something unusual, and considered particularly risky, in our time). The authorial eye is located mostly away from and above the characters, effaced in the modern manner, but capable upon occasion of moving into their very minds to provide insights into their often warped, sometimes tender, occasionally right ways of thinking. Necessary to this view is a strong sense of authorial responsibility, and Miss Porter gains this, one feels, by the extreme honesty and objectivity of her vision. She has, as she has been reported to have said to a friend, not "loaded the dice" against her characters. "I would not take sides," she said. "I was on everybody's side."

It might be objected that to be "on everybody's side" is to be on no side, but the attitude behind such a statement illuminates what has been constant in Katherine Anne Porter's work: a sense of understanding based on a firm belief in the imperfectibility of man, but an understanding held with compassion. Understanding without compassion might have led to bitterness, cynicism, even arrogance; compassion without understanding could easily have led to sentimentality.

The action of *Ship of Fools* is made up of three sections: Part I, Embarkation; Part II, High Sea; Part III, The Harbors. Each is prefaced with an epigram. The first is a quotation from Baudelaire: *"Quand partons-nous vers le bonheur?"* (When do you sail for happiness?); the second is from a song by Brahms: *"Kein Haus, Keine Heimat"* (No House, No Home); the third is from Saint Paul: "For here have we no continuing city..." Glenway Wescott has warned the reader not to put too much emphasis upon Miss Porter's allegorical intentions. To disregard them, however, would be more serious, particularly the implications of the section headings: man persists in setting sail for happiness, only to find himself, after all, houseless and homeless, to become aware at last that his city is doomed. It is significant that Miss Porter gives only the first clause of Paul's advice to the Hebrews. The complete verse reads: "For here have we no continuing city, but we seek one to come." To have quoted the verse entire would have been to acknowledge the hopes and consolation of orthodox Christianity. Miss Porter's consolation is of another sort, not un-Christian, but certainly secular. Like Miranda in "Pale Horse, Pale Rider," she is unable to invoke the mystery: "Oh, no, that is not the way, I must never do that, she warned herself." As with Miranda, the reality lies only in "the dazed silence that follows the ceasing of the heavy guns; noiseless houses with the shades drawn, empty streets, the dead cold light of tomorrow." Yet the recurring hope ("Now there would be time for everything"), the recurring struggle.

*Ship of Fools* is a story of forlorn hope and recurring struggle. In Part I we become acquainted with the various characters, recognize their relations to each other, necessary or personal, as groups and nationalities; we come to sense their very real and pathetic isolation. In Part II, which has more than half the book's pages, the major events occur; and this might be called The Wasteland Section *(Kein Haus, Keine Heimat)*, containing as it does the torment of the passengers in steerage, the struggle for detachment or for involvement of the passengers and ship's officers above, their regimented hates and their pathetic attempts to love. In Part III, as the ship nears its destination, the effects of the preceding events begin to tell. A bacchanalian fiesta put on by a group of Spanish dancers in honor of the captain brings out all the hidden fears, guilts, and repressions of the participants, followed by the usual remorse and readjustment in relationships.

We see the passengers of the ship *Vera* first as they assemble for boarding in the Mexican port town of Veracruz. We see them through the eyes of the townspeople, who, the author tells us, "live as initiates in local custom"; we see them from the point of view of the author, against a background of "alternate violence and lethargy"; they remain at a distance, a cosmopolitan group fleeing Mexico, or being deported, or merely departing on some private errand; we watch them undergo the many little inconveniences of leaving a foreign port, see them "emerging from the mildewed dimness of the customs sheds, blinking their eyes against the blinding sunlight," all having "the look of invalids crawling into hospital on their last legs."

The cast of characters is necessarily large. Among the passengers and crew in the upper class, the Germans appear in greatest number. They include Frau Rittersdorf, whose husband died in the war and who keeps a journal; Frau Otto Schmitt, recently widowed, accompanying her husband's remains back to the fatherland; Herr Siegfried Rieber, publisher of a ladies' garment trade magazine; Fraulein Lizzi Spockenkieker, who is said to own three ladies' dress shops; Herr Karl Glocken, a hunchback; Herr Wilhelm Freytag, who works for an oil company, is married to a Jewess, and is returning to Germany to fetch his wife and her mother back to Mexico; Herr Julius Lowenthal, a Jewish manufacturer and salesman of Catholic religious articles; and the following groups: Herr Professor Hutten, his wife, and their bulldog Bebe; Herr Karl Baumgartner, his wife, and son Hans; Herr Wilibald Graf, a dying man in a wheelchair, who is accompanied by his nephew and attendant, Johann.

The second largest group are the Spaniards and Mexicans. The Spaniards include a singing and dancing group, made up of four men and four women, along with the two children, twins, of one of the couples; and La Condesa, who is called a "déclassée noblewoman who has lived many years in Cuba," but is now being deported as a political undesirable to Tenerife. The Mexicans include the wife of an attache to the Mexican embassy in Paris, her infant child, and an Indian nurse; two Catholic priests; and a bride and groom going on a honeymoon to Spain.

Other nationals included are four Americans: William Denny, a young Texas engineer; Mary Treadwell, a forty-five-year-old divorcee; and an unmarried couple, David Scott and Jenny Brown, traveling together to Europe. There is a Swiss family, Herr Heinrich Lutz, his wife, and their adolescent daughter. There is a Swede, Arne Hansen. There is a group of six medical students from Cuba. The occupants of the steerage are almost nine hundred Spanish workmen being deported from Cuba after the failure of the Cuban sugar crop.

It is difficult to say who are the principal characters in the events of the novel. Obviously Miss Porter has attempted to give each his share in the action. Among the ship's personnel, the doctor and the captain appear most prominent. Captain Thiele is the embodiment of Teutonic authority, firm, unyielding, formal, and wrongheaded. Dr. Schumann represents, within the German *Kultur,* almost exactly the opposite. He is warm and compassionate, although somewhat impersonal; he is a devout Bavarian Catholic with a heart condition that might cause death at any moment, suffering too from guilt at his inability to do more than supply drugs for the patient for whom he would do most, La Condesa. Among the passengers, relations are established between Arne Hansen, trapped in his masculine, but sterile, lust, and Amparo, the Spanish dancer-prostitute; between Jenny Brown, the American companion of David Scott, and Wilhelm Freytag, who has a Jewish wife in Germany; between Johann, the nephew of Wilibald Graf, and Concha, another of the Spanish women, who effects Johann's sexual initiation, not without tenderness, but for a price; between William Denny, a carbuncular young American, and Pastora, a third Spanish dancer, who provide a study in awkwardness and frustration; and, finally, there is the highly comic affair between Siegfried Rieber and Lizzi Spockenkieker that ends in estrangement after weeks of teasing and attempted conquest. The one character among the voyagers who chooses isolation, as protection against personal pain and disgust, is Julius Lowenthal, the Jew. The single relationship that is evoked but rendered with slight detail is that of the Mexican newlyweds, who appear in their momentary bliss as entirely sufficient unto themselves.

The steerage passengers are seen generally only as a group, viewed from above by the first-class passengers; but from them do emerge two figures of significance to the novel. One is a Basque, known only as Echegaray, who carves wooden figures with a penknife and who is drowned when he jumps overboard to save the Huttens' bulldog, cast into the sea by the Spanish twins. The other is an unnamed political agitator who makes fun of the religious observances among the steerage passengers and is struck over the head with a wrench by one of them after he had laughed during the services for Echegaray.

The significance of these two figures, like the significance of the Mexican honeymooners, lies in the very vagueness with which the author presents them, almost without name, with only the brief and fatal accident to define the one, with only his political position and his wound to define the other. Both are, in a sense, savior figures, reminiscent of Miss Porter's use of such figures in "Flowering Judas," but presented with less insistence in the novel than in the short story. Also, an additional level of significance is added in the case of the Basque, who, if he is a crucified Christ in his plunge into the sea and dies ironically in an attempt to save an aged and repulsive bulldog, is also a "creator," whose artistry is presented as more genuine than that of the American couple in the upper class who call themselves artists. The agitator, as modern savior, is allied to La Condesa (the political exile), who, like Eugenio of "Flowering Judas," can gain peace only in the sleepy world of drugs administered by Dr. Schumann. The ship's doctor, like Laura, serves the cause of betrayal, and so is inhibited from meaningful action.

The similarity of these themes in the novel and in the short story suggests that the themes of *Ship of Fools* may not be too different from themes present in the earlier works and that the principal differences lie in the necessary richness of the longer work and in the technical excellence that integrates and unifies so diverse a body of material. We can see in the puritanical Protestantism of the German society on the ship a resemblance to the attitude of Miriam, the midwestern schoolteacher wife of the artist-turned-journalist of "That Tree," where self-righteous self-assurance appears to triumph over the more leisurely, apparently indolent, ambitions of the poet. We can see in the cheerful amorality of the Spanish dancers a resemblance to María Rosa and Juan Villegas in "María Concepción." There is a hint of María Concepción herself in the brief appearance of the Indian nurse for Señora de Ortega's infant on board the ship. The vacillations and misunderstandings of Jenny Brown and David Scott are reminiscent of the husband-wife relationship in "Rope." Ric and Rac, the Spanish twins of the novel, have no counterparts in the short stories, but they do, nevertheless, represent what Miranda reported as her grandmother's conviction in "The Old Order," that children were born in evil, thus were to a degree the embodiment of it in its most simple and direct form.

Incidents of special importance in the novel include the banishing of Herr Freytag from the captain's table because it is learned that he has married a Jew, the throwing overboard of Frau Hutten's bulldog (which resulted in the death and burial of Echegaray), the riot in the steerage that followed the funeral of the drowned Basque, the posting on the bulletin board of "truth notes" concerning the various passengers by the Cuban students, the meetings of Dr. Schumann and La Condesa, and, finally the various events preceding, during, and following the fiesta put on in honor of the captain by the Spanish dancing troupe. These would include the stopover at Santa

Cruz, where the Spaniards steal the tawdry prizes to be given away at the party; the fight between Herr Rieber and Arne Hansen; the recognition of special qualities of character by Frau Rittersdorf and Mary Treadwell; the quarrel and reconciliation of the Baumgartners; the rebellion of Johann against Herr Graf that leads to his going to Concha; the humiliating beating of William Denny; and the ironic confrontation between the proper Prussian captain and the easy-going members of the Spanish dancing group.

There is little "story," in the conventional sense, in *Ship of Fools.* Perhaps the nearest thing to it is the affair between Jenny Brown and David Scott, because the fluctuations of love and hate, or even like and dislike, are acted out during the voyage, and their relationship had a prior origin in Mexico and presumably will have a future in Europe. There is a sense, however, in which each character represents a little "story" of his own, and each thread of plot is intertwined with others to form the over-all pattern of the book. We come to know each character briefly at a moment that constitutes for most of them a particular crisis or alteration of attitude. But the individual stories are not resolved; rather, what serves for resolution resides in the remarkable ability of the author to make the total composition come alive, both in its rendering of the individual characters and in its evoking a kind of over-all theme, or meaning. Yet it is less a "meaning," in the sense of reducible paraphrase, than it is an attitude subtly conveyed.

Perhaps the nearest Katherine Anne Porter comes to expressing what the story is about is when she has Mary Treadwell interpret the effusive show of manners between Herr and Frau Baumgartner at the end of the voyage (significantly Miss Porter put the major portion of the passage in italics): "What they were saying to each other was only, *Love me, love me in spite of all! Whether or not I love you, whether I am fit to love, whether you are able to love, even if there is no such thing as love, love me!*" Where had the trouble come from? Mrs. Treadwell considers her own case: "…what had it been but the childish refusal to admit and accept on some term or other the difference between what one hoped was true and what one discovers to be the mere laws of the human condition?" *The mere laws of the human condition!* This is skepticism, and if we need a name to distinguish Miss Porter's special attitude, perhaps "skepticism" will do. The only truth available to man lies in "the human condition."

It is the human condition that is represented aboard the *Vera.*

But that condition varies from country to country and race to race; it differs even in individuals. The one thing we can know is that the dream, whether it be of race superiority or of the perfect relation between man and woman, will never be achieved. Man becomes "foolish," in that quasi-religious sense, when he pursues it; but pursue it he will, because that, too, is part of "the human condition." The novel says it better than this, because the skill of the author proved equal to the larger and more complicated intentions that the book itself embodies.

The critical reception of *Ship of Fools* when it first appeared was almost unanimously enthusiastic. What dissent occurred concerned itself with three features of the novel: the rendering of the characters, the pessimism of the theme, and what some critics considered an absence of suspense. Stanley Kauffmann, a reviewer for the *New Republic*, wrote: "The characters are well perceived and described, but we know all that Miss Porter can say about them after the third or fourth of their episodes." Granville Hicks, writing for the *Saturday Review*, said: "There is in [the novel], so far as I can see, no sense of human possibility. Although we have known her people uncommonly well, we watch unconcerned as, in the curiously muted ending, they drift away from us." The *New Yorker* review by Howard Moss complained that *Ship of Fools* was "devoid of one of the excitements of realistic fiction. The reader is never given that special satisfaction of the drama of design, in which the strings having come unwound, are ultimately tied together in a knot. Miss Porter scorns patness and falseness, but by the very choice of her method, she also lets go of suspense."

It is difficult to answer the charge of dullness or of inadequate character portrayal except by counter-assertion. One can point to the novel's tremendous popular success, but Theodore Solotaroff, writing in *Commentary*, dismisses this explanation by calling the novel the long awaited work of a beloved figure—the "Eleanor Roosevelt" of letters. In a curiously vituperative article, he characterizes *Ship of Fools* as "massive, unexciting, and saturnine." Such charges are reminiscent of the response made to another American work a century earlier, when one critic called *Moby Dick* "...trash, belonging to the worst school of Bedlam literature." Many considered Melville's novel dull, its action clogged by extraneous matter.

There is, however, a key to Miss Porter's method—a key that has long since opened and preserved the treasures of Herman Melville's masterpiece. This method is pointed out most clearly by Eric Auerbach in his critical volume *Mimesis*. Auerbach discusses a puzzling quality of epic narrative, what he calls the retarding principle and what Goethe characterized as "the retarding element appropriate to Homeric epic." Such retardation consisted in the breaking off of a dramatic incident in order to shift and explore the background character of the event. It was, Auerbach maintains, "In dire opposition to the element of suspense." Miss Porter utilizes this retarding principle in the construction of her comic epic, much as it was used by Dante in *The Divine Comedy*, for the purposes of deepening and enriching her narrative; and these are the qualities that impressed most critics of the novel.

The charge that *Ship of Fools* shows little "sense of human possibility" reminds us of early charges made against another significant American work, *The Waste Land* of T. S. Eliot. As does Eliot in his poem, Miss Porter portrays much of modern life as sterile and impotent, but she also suggests, as does Eliot, the fructifying possibilities of love. She is less extreme than Jean-Paul Sartre in her rendering of what is disgusting and absurd in human life, nearer to Albert Camus in her attitude of detached observation; superior, perhaps, to either in the over-all sense of compassion that finally pervades her work.

# The Responsibility of the Novelist

## by M. M. Liberman

The title of this essay is, I suppose, somewhat misleading, in the way that a title can be, when it seems to promise a discourse on an arguable concept. In this instance it suggests a certain premise: namely, that the question, "What does the author owe society?" is one which still lives and breathes. In fact, I think it does not. I suspect, rather, that its grave can be located somewhere between two contentions: Andre Gide's that the artist is under no moral obligation to present a useful idea, but that he is under a moral obligation to present an idea well; and Henry James's, that we are being arbitrary if we demand, to begin with, more of a novel than that it be interesting. As James uses the word *novel* here, I take it to mean any extended, largely realistic, narrative fiction, but his view is applicable as well to fiction in other forms and modes.

If a literary work is more than immediately engaging, if, for example, it stimulates the moral imagination, it is doing more than is fairly required of it as art.

Why, then, if I think it is in most respects dead, do I choose to raise the question of the writer's responsibility? The answer is that I do not choose to raise the question. The question is continually being raised for me, and because literature is my profession, it haunts my house. Thus, I am moved to invoke certain commonplaces, as above, of a sort I had supposed to be news only to sophomore undergraduates. This was the case markedly on the occasion of the publication of Katherine Anne Porter's *Ship of Fools* in 1962. Twenty years in the making, a book club selection even before it was set up in type, restlessly awaited by a faithful coterie, reviewed widely and discussed broadly almost simultaneously with its appearance on the store shelves, this book caused and still causes consternation in the world of contemporary letters to a degree which I find interesting,

"The Responsibility of the Novelist" by M. M. Liberman. From *Criticism,* 8, no. 4 (1966), 377-88. Reprinted by permission of the Wayne State University Press and the author. Copyright © 1966 by Wayne State University.

curious, and suspect. The focus of this paper will be on the critical reception of this book and I hope that the relevance of what remains of the responsibility question will issue naturally from it. Finally, I must quote at awkward length, in two instances, in order to be fair to other commentators.

The first brief waves of reviews were almost unanimous in their praise of *Ship of Fools* and then very shortly the many dissenting opinions began to appear, usually in the most respectable intellectual journals where reviewers claim to be, and often are, critics. These reviews were characterized by one of two dominant feelings: bitter resentment or acute disappointment. A remarkable instance of the former appeared in the very prestigious journal, *Commentary* (October, 1962) as it features article of the month, under the byline of one of its associate editors. That Miss Porter's book should have been originally well-received so rankled *Commentary's* staff that a lengthy rebuttal was composed, taking priority over other articles on ordinarily more-pressing subjects, such as nuclear destruction and race violence. The article progresses to a frothing vehemence in its later pages. I will quote from the opening of the piece which begins relatively calmly, as follows:

> Whatever the problems were that kept Katherine Anne Porter's *Ship of Fools* from appearing during the past twenty years, it has been leading a charmed life ever since it was published last March. In virtually a single voice, a little cracked and breathless with excitement, the reviewers announced that Miss Porter's long-awaited first novel was a "triumph," a "masterpiece," a "work of genius...a momentous work of fiction," "a phenomenal, rich, and delectable book," a "literary event of the highest magnitude...."
>
> Riding the crest of this wave of acclaim, *Ship of Fools* made its way to the top of the best-seller lists in record time and it is still there as I write in mid-September. During these four months, it has encountered virtually as little opposition in taking its place among the classics of literature as it did in taking and holding its place on the best-seller lists. A few critics...wound up by saying that *Ship of Fools* fell somewhat short of greatness, but only after taking the book's claim to greatness with respectful seriousness. Some of the solid citizens among the reviewers, like John K. Hutchens, found the novel to be dull and said so. Here and there, mainly in the hinterlands, a handful of independent spirits...suspected that the book was a failure. But who was listening?
>
> Prominent among the circumstances which have helped to make a run-away best-seller and a *success d'estime* out of this massive, unex-

citing, and saturnine novel was the aura of interest, partly sentimental and partly deserved, that Miss Porter's long struggle with it had produced. Most of the reviews begin in the same way: a distinguished American short-story writer at the age of seventy-one has finally finished her first novel after twenty years of working on it. As this point was developed, it tended to establish the dominant tone of many reviews—that of an elated witness to a unique personal triumph, almost as though this indomitable septuagenarian had not written a book, but had done something even more remarkable—like swimming the English Channel.

The *Commentary* critic goes on to charge Miss Porter with having written a novel contemptible in two decisive ways: (1) badly executed in every conceivable technical sense, particularly characterization and (2) unacceptable on moral grounds, being pessimistic and misanthropic. "But the soul of humanity is lacking," he says, quoting still another reviewer sympathetic to his own position. Why Dostoevsky, for example, is permitted to be both massive and saturnine and Miss Porter not is a question spoken to later only by implication. The critic's charge that her writing is "unexciting" is curious considering his own high emotional state in responding to the work. The charge of misanthropy is, of course, directly related to the alleged technical failure of the characterization, which he says "borders on caricature" in the way it portrays nearly every human type as loathesome and grotesque, with hardly a single redeeming feature. In considering the charge of misanthropy we are, perforce, confronted with the question of the writer's social responsibility in the moral sphere, for the attribution of misanthropy to a writer by a critic is typically a censure and is seldom merely a description of the writer's stance. The writer is usually, as in this case, denied the right to be misanthropic on the ground that it is immoral to hate and, given the writer's influential function, it is deemed irresponsible of him to clothe such a negative sentiment as hate in intellectually attractive garb. In my efforts at synthesis, I will get back to these questions. But for the moment I should like to point out that *Commentary's* view of *Ship of Fools* as depicting mankind in a hatefully distorted, therefore, untruthful, therefore, immoral way, is in fact the view of the book commonly held by the normally intelligent and reasonably well-educated reader of fiction, if my impressions are accurate.

I turn now to the other mode of reception: acute disappointment. One of the most clearly and intelligently presented of this group was

Professor Wayne Booth's critique in the *Yale Review* (Summer, 1962) from which I quote, in part, as follows:

> Katherine Anne Porter's long-awaited novel is more likely to fall afoul of one's bias for finely-constructed, concentrated plots. In this respect her own earlier fiction works against her; part of the strength of those classics, *Pale Horse, Pale Rider* and *Noon Wine*, lies in their concision, their economy, their simplicity. *There* is *my* Katherine Anne Porter, I am tempted to protest, as she offers me, now, something so different as to be almost unrecognizable—a 225,000-word novel (more words, I suppose, than in all of the rest of her works put together) with nearly fifty characters. What is worse, the manner of narration is fragmented, diluted. Her plan is to create a shipload of lost souls and to follow them, isolated moment by isolated moment, in their alienated selfishness, through the nasty, exasperating events of a twenty-seven day voyage, in 1931, from Veracruz to Bremerhaven. She deliberately avoids concentrating strongly on any one character; even the four or five that are granted some sympathy are kept firmly, almost allegorically, subordinated to the portrayal of the ship of fools ("I am a passenger on that ship," she reminds us in an opening note).
>
> Her method is sporadic, almost desultory, and her unity is based on theme and idea rather than coherence of action. We flash from group to group, scene to scene, mind to mind, seldom remaining with any group or observer for longer than three or four pages together. While the book is as a result full of crosslights and ironic juxtapositions, it has, for me, no steady center of interest except the progressively more intense exemplification of its central truth: men are pitifully, foolishly self-alienated. At the heart of man lies a radical corruption that can only occasionally, fitfully, be overcome by love. . . .
>
> Once the various groupings are established—the four isolated, self-torturing Americans, two of them lovers who hate and fear each other when they are not loving; the sixteen Germans, most of them in self-destructive family groups, and all but two of them repugnant almost beyond comedy; the depraved swarm of Spanish dancers with their two demon-children; the carefree and viciously irresponsible Cuban students; the half-mad, lost Spanish countess; the morose Swede; and so on— each group or lone traveler is taken to some sort of climactic moment, most often in the form of a bungled chance for genuine human contact. These little anti-climaxes are scattered throughout the latter fourth of the book, but for most of the characters the nadir is reached during the long "gala" evening, almost at the end of the journey. . . .
>
> Such a work, lacking, by design, a grand causal, temporal sequence, depends for complete success on the radiance of each part; the reader

must feel that every fragment as it comes provides proof of its own relevance in its illustrative power, or at least in its comic or pathetic or satiric intensity. For me only about half of the characters provide this kind of self-justification. There are many great things: moments of introspection, including some masterful dreams, from the advanced young woman and the faded beauty; moments of clear and effective observation of viciousness and folly. But too often one finds, when the tour of the passenger list is undertaken again and again, that it is too much altogether. Why, why did Miss Porter feel that she should try to get everything in?

Since a useful version of Aristotle's *Poetics* has been available to us, there have been critics who have been engaged in what has been called criticism proper, the task of determining what literature in general is, and what a given work of literature in particular is. One fundamental assumption of criticism proper is that by a more and more refined classification, according to a work's properties, all literature can be first divided into kinds and sub-kinds. Ideally, and as such a process becomes more and more discriminating and precise, and as the subdivisions become small and smaller, criticism will approach the individual work. Accordingly the proper critic assumes that all questions of evaluation, including, of course, moral evaluation, are secondary to and issue from questions of definition. Or to put yet otherwise, the proper critic asks: How can we tell what a work means, let alone whether it's good or bad, if we don't know what it is to begin with?

At this turn, I call attention to the fact that in none of my own references to *Ship of Fools* have I spoken of it as a novel. The *Commentary* editor calls it a novel and Mr. Booth calls it a novel, and in the very process of describing what it is about this alleged novel that displeases them, they go a long way toward unintentionally defining the work as something else altogether. But instead of evaluating *Ship of Fools* on the grounds of their own description of its properties, both insist on ignoring this analytical data, making two substitutions in its stead: (1) the publisher's word for it that *Ship of Fools* is a novel and (2) their own bias as to how the work would have to be written to have been acceptable as a novel. Mr. Booth is both candid and disarming in making explicit his bias for finely-constructed, concentrated plots. To entertain a preference for *Pride and Prejudice* or *The Great Gatsby* over, say, *Moby Dick* or *Finnegans Wake* is one thing and legitimate enough in its way. To insist, however, that the latter two works are inferior because their integrity does not depend on traditional plot structure would be to risk downgrading two admittedly monumental works in a very arbitrary and dubious way. Finally, to insist that every long work of prose fiction should be as much like *Pride and Prejudice* as possible is to insist that every such work be not only a novel, but a nineteenth-century one at that.

The *Commentary* critique has its own bias which is not, however, stated explicitly. It is the bias of the journal itself as much as of the critic, and is one it shares with many another respectable publication whose voice is directed at an audience it understands to have a highly developed, independent, post-Freudian, post-Marxist, humanitarian social consciousness. Neither especially visionary, nor especially doctrinaire, such a publication has, typically, nevertheless, a low tolerance for anything that smacks of the concept of original sin, having, as this concept does, a way of discouraging speculation about decisively improving the human lot. Miss Porter's book appears to take a dim view of the behavior of the race and that is enough for the intellectual journal, despite its implied claim to broad views and cultivated interests, including an interest in fiction. The aggrieved critic cannot come down from high dudgeon long enough to see that a view of literature as merely an ideological weapon is in the first place a strangely puritanical one and wildly out of place in his pages. Secondly, there are a few more commonplaces about literature which are usually lost sight of in the urgency to claim that people are not all bad and therefore can and must be portrayed in fiction as likely candidates for salvation. Most works of fiction, *as anyone should know,* are not written to accomplish anything but themselves, but some works of fiction are written to demonstrate to the innocent that there is much evil in the world. And others are written to demonstrate to the initiated, but phlegmatic, that there is more evil than even they had supposed and that, moreover, this evil is closer to home than they can comfortably imagine. In any case, since fiction is by definition artificial, the author is within his rights in appearing to overstate the case for the desired results. It is nowhere everlastingly written that literature must have a sanguine, optimistic, and uplifting effect. Is there not sometimes something salutary in a work which has the effect of inducing disgust and functioning therefore as a kind of emetic? Had the critic given Miss Porter her due as an artist he might have seen that *Ship of Fools* condemns human folly, but it never once confuses good and evil. It is one thing to be a writer who smirks at human decency and argues for human destruction (Marquis de Sade)—it is another to be a writer who winces at human limitations and pleads by her tone, her attitude towards her readers, for a pained nod of agreement.

Said Dr. Johnson to the Honourable Thomas Erskine some 200 years ago: "Why, sir, if you were to read Richardson for the story, your impatience would be so much fretted that you would hang yourself. But you must read him for the sentiment." In the case of *Ship of Fools,* this sentiment is so consistent and so pervasive as to make us wonder how anyone could have scanted or mistaken it. It is the very opposite of misanthropy in that far from taking delight in exposing human foibles, in "getting" her characters' "number," Miss Porter's narrative voice has the quality of personal suffering even as it gives testimony. It seems to say: "This is the way with the human soul, as I knew it, at its worst, in the years just prior to the Second World War. And alas for all of us that it should have been so." By way of illustration, recall the characters Ric and Rac. I select them because Miss Porter's readers of all stripes agree that these two children, scarcely out of their swaddling clothes, are probably as thoroughly objectionable as any two fictional characters in all literature in English. Twin offspring of a pimp and a prostitute, they lie, steal, torture, attempt to murder a dumb animal, cause the death of an innocent man and fornicate incestuously; they are not very convincing as ordinary real children and for a very good reason. They are not meant to be. I cite a passage from that section where, having made a fiasco of their parents' larcenous schemes, they are punished by those parents:

> Tito let go of Rac and turned his fatherly discipline upon Ric. He seized his right arm by the wrist and twisted it very slowly and steadily until the shoulder was nearly turned in its socket and Ric went to his knees with a long howl that died away in a puppy-like whimper when the terrible hold was loosed. Rac, huddled on the divan nursing her bruises, cried again with him. Then Manolo and Pepe and Tito and Pancho, and Lola and Concha and Pastora and Amparo, every face masking badly a sullen fright, went away together to go over every step of this dismaying turn of affairs; with a few words and nods, they decided it would be best to drink coffee in the bar, to appear as usual at dinner, and to hold a rehearsal on deck afterwards. They were all on edge and ready to fly at each other's throats. On her way out, Lola paused long enough to seize Rac by the hair and shake her head until she was silenced, afraid to cry. When they were gone, Ric and Rac crawled into the upper berth looking for safety; they lay there half naked, entangled like some afflicted, misbegotten little monster in a cave, exhausted, mindless, soon asleep.

For 357 pages a case has been carefully built for the twins' monstrous natures. The reader has been induced to loathe the very sound of their names. Suddenly the same reader finds himself an eye witness to the degree of punishment he has privately imagined their deserving. But even as they are being terribly chastised they demonstrate an admirable recalcitrance and suddenly it is the adult world which appears villainous, monstrous and cruel. Finally, in the imagery of our last view of them, they are not demons altogether, or even primarily, but in their nakedness, which we see first, they are also merely infants and this is what does—or should—break the reader's heart. The reader is meant to sympathize, finally, with these hideous children, but more than that, his moral responses have been directed to himself. He has been led to ask himself: Who am I that I should have for so long despised these children, however demonic they are. Am I, then, any better than their parents?

When I contend that Ric and Rac are not meant to be taken as real children. I am agreeing for the moment with the *Commentary* critic who spoke of Miss Porter's method of characterization as caricature, as if to speak of this method so, were, *ipso facto*, to condemn it, as if realism were the only possible fictional mode and the only category into which a long fiction can be cast. But if *Ship of Fools* is not a novel, what would a novel be? I rely on the recent study by Sheldon Sacks, *Fiction and the Shape of Belief,* to define it as follows: a novel would be an action organized so that it introduces characters about whose fates the reader is made to care, in unstable relationships, which are then further complicated, until the complication is finally resolved, by the removal of the represented instability. This plainly is not *Ship of Fools*. Our most human feelings go out to Ric and Rac, but we cannot care further about them precisely *not* because we are made to hate them, but because they are clearly doomed to perpetual dehumanization by the adult world which spawned and nurtured them. In the same image in which Miss Porter represents them as helpless infants, she also declares them "mindless." The generally unstable relationships which define the roles of most of the other characters in the book remain unstable to the very end and are not so much resolved as they are revealed. The resolution of the manifold conflicts in the work is part of the encompassing action of the work, that which the reader can logically suppose will happen after the story closes. The Germans will march against Poland and turn Europe into a concentration camp. The others will, until it is too late, look the other way. This is a fact of history which overrides in importance the fact that no one on the ship can possibly come to good.

Nor is *Ship of Fools* a satire which is organized so that it ridicules objects external to the fictional world created in it. Rather, it is, I believe, a kind of modern apologue, a work organized as a fictional example of the truth of a formulable statement or a series of such statements. As such it owes more than its title to the didactic Christian verses of Sebastian Brant, whose *Das Narrenschiff, The Ship of Fools*, was published sometime between 1497 and 1548. Brant's work was very influential and no one thinks of it as misanthropic when he reads:

> The whole world lives in darksome night,
> In blinded sinfulness persisting,
> While every street sees fools existing
> Who know but folly, to their shame,
> Yet will not own to folly's name.
> Hence I have pondered how a ship
> Of fools I'd suitably equip—
> A galley, brig, bark, skiff, or float,
> A carack, scow, dredge, racing-boat,
> A sled, cart, barrow, carryall—
> One vessel would be far too small
> To carry all the fools I know.
> Some persons have no way to go
> And like the bees they come a-skimming,
> While many to the ship are swimming,
> Each one wants to be the first.
> A mighty throng with folly curst,
> Whose pictures I have given here.
> They who at writings like a sneer
> Or are with reading not afflicted
> May see themselves herewith depicted
> And thus discover who they are.
> Their faults, to whom they're similar.
> For fools a mirror shall it be,
> Where each his counterfeit may see.

As an apologue Miss Porter's work has more in common with Johnson's *Rasselas* than with *Gone with the Wind*. As an apologue it not only has the right, it has the function by its nature to "caricature" its actors, to be "saturnine," to have a large cast, to be "fragmented" in its narration and above all, to quote Mr. Booth again, to achieve "unity based on theme and idea rather than coherence of action…

[to have] no steady center of interest except the progressively more intense exemplification of its central truth. ..."

In addition to calling attention to its formal properties for evaluating Miss Porter's book not as a novel but as something else, one ought to stand back a bit to see how the work fits a reasonable definition of the novel historically, that is, according to traditional and conventional themes and types of action. Recall that though the English word novel, to designate a kind of fiction, is derived from the Italian *novella,* meaning "a little new thing," this is not the word used in most European countries. That word is, significantly, *roman.* One forgets that a work of fiction, set in our own time, and thus bringing us knowledge of our own time, that is, news, is not, however a novel by that fact alone, but may be a literary form as yet undefined and, therefore, unnamed. For, in addition to bringing us news, the novel, if it is such on historical principles, must pay its respects to its forebears in more than a nominal way. It must do more than bear tales and look like the *Brothers Karamazov.* It must, I suspect, as a *roman,* be in some specific ways romantic.

We understand that the novel is the modern counterpart of various earlier forms of extended narrative. The first of these, the epic, was succeeded in the middle ages by the *romance* written at first like the epic, in verse, and later in prose as well. The romance told of the adventures of royalty and the nobility, introduced a heroine and made love a central theme. It relocated the supernatural realm from the court of Zeus to fairyland. The gods were replaced by magical spells and enchantments. When magical spells and enchantments were replaced, in the precursors of contemporary fiction, by the happy accident, the writer took unto himself a traditional given and the romantic tradition continued in the novel. When Henry James arranged for his heroine, Isabel Archer, to inherit a substantial sum of money from a relative who didn't know her, this was very Olympian of him; at any rate it was a piece of modern magic, legitimately granted to the novelist. Realist though he was, James recognized that the romantic element gets the novel going, frees the hero or heroine from those confinements of everyday life which make moral adventure undramatic. When in the most arbitrary way James makes Isabel an heiress he launches her on a quest for self-realization. He gives her her chance. Now in this connection, I quote again from *Ship of Fools:*

> While he [Freytag] shaved he riffled through his ties and selected one, thinking that people on voyage mostly went on behaving as if they

were on dry land, and there is simply not room for it on a ship. Every smallest act shows up more clearly and looks worse, because it has lost its background. The train of events leading up to and explaining it is not there; you can't refer it back and set it in its proper size and place.

When Miss Porter, who could have put her cast of characters anywhere she wanted, elected to put them aboard ship, she made as if to free them, in the manner of a romance, for a moral quest; that is, they are ostensibly liberated, as if by magic, precisely because they *are* aboard ship—liberated from the conventions of family background, domestic responsibility, national custom, and race consciousness. Theoretically, they can now emerge triumphant at the end of the journey, over duplicity, cruelty, selfishness and bigotry. But they do not.

Freedom they are incapable of utilizing for humane ends. Freedom Miss Porter can grant them, but since they are men of our time, they cannot, in her view, accept it responsibly. That is, they cannot make good use of their lucky accident because their freedom is only nominal. On the one hand, history has caught up with them; on the other hand, psychology has stripped their spiritual and emotional lives of all mystery. In Miss Porter's world the past is merely the genesis of neurosis (there is no point in pretending we've never heard of Freud) and the future, quite simply, is the destruction of Isabel Archer's Europe of infinite possibilities (there is no point in pretending we've never heard of Neville Chamberlain). *Ship of Fools* argues that romantic literary conventions do not work in the modern world, and emerges as even more remote from the idea of the novel than a study of its formal properties alone would suggest. One can see it finally as anti-novel.

In her 1940 introduction to *Flowering Judas,* Miss Porter says that she spent most of her "energies" and "spirit" in an effort to understand "the logic of this majestic and terrible failure of man in the Western world." This is the dominant theme of *Ship of Fools* as it is of all her writing. Nearly every character in the work is a staggering example of an aspect of this failure. And here is the only passage in the work emphasized by italics:

> What they were saying to each other was only, *Love me, love me in spite of all! Whether or not I love you, whether I am fit to love, whether you are able to love, even if there is no such thing as love, love me!*

# Chronology of Important Dates

1890        Born May 15, Indian Creek, Texas, daughter of Harrison and Mary Alice Jones Porter. Of old American stock. Jonathan Boone, Daniel's brother, a great-great-grandfather.

1892        Mother dies. Family moves to Kyle, Texas, and guardianship of grandmother Catherine Anne Porter. Time divided between house in town and farm. Books of literary value available from early age.

1901        Grandmother dies. End of Old Order, and of remnant of Kentucky prosperity.

1901-17    Farm sold. Moves to San Antonio for short period. Attends several convent schools in South, though family apparently Methodist. Eloped from convent school, probably in New Orleans, age sixteen. Name of husband not available. Divorced at nineteen. Newspaper work and bit parts in movies in Chicago (1911). Returns to Texas to support self as entertainer. Possible attack of tuberculosis.

1917        On *The Critic*, weekly newspaper in Fort Worth.

1918-19    *Rocky Mountain News* in Denver; love affair as background of "Pale Horse, Pale Rider." Dangerously ill of influenza. Death of lover.

1920        New York; hack writing, ghosting.

1920        Studies art in Mexico.

1921-22    Period in Mexico; writing for a trade journal and at her own fiction ("María Concepción"). Acting in Fort Worth Little Theatre. Return to Mexico; preparation of Mexican art for the United States. Publication of "María Concepción" in *Century Magazine*—first appearance (and last for some years) in large national magazine.

1925        "Rope" appears in second *American Caravan* (hard-cover annual of the "new" writing).

1927        "He" in *New Masses*.

1929        "The Jilting of Grandmother Weatherall" in *transition* (Paris); life in New York, work on biography of Cotton Mather and general book reviewing.

1930*    Publication of *Flowering Judas*, first book.

1931     Guggenheim Fellowship; returns to Mexico; friendship and bitter quarrel with Hart Crane. Voyage from Mexico to Europe provides background for *Ship of Fools*.

1933     Marriage (ending in divorce) with Eugene Pressley of foreign service. *Katherine Anne Porter's French Song Book*—collector and translator.

1935     Expanded version of *Flowering Judas*.

1937     Book-of-Month-Club Award, $2500.

1938     Married Albert Russell Erskine of Louisiana State University and *Southern Review;* lived in Baton Rouge. Divorced 1942.

1939     Volume *Pale Horse, Pale Rider* appears.

1940     First annual Gold Medal for Literature, from Societies of Libraries of New York.

1942     Translation (with introduction) of *The Itching Parrot* by Fernández de Lizárdi.

1943     Elected to National Institute of Arts and Letters.

1944     *Leaning Tower and Other Stories.*

1949-62  Lecturer at various universities, including Stanford University, University of Michigan, University of Chicago, University of Liege, University of Virginia. Honorary doctorates from various institutions.

1950-52  Vice President of National Institute of Arts and Letters.

1952     *The Days Before* (essays); Emerson-Thoreau Award, American Academy of Arts and Sciences.

1960-62  Ford Foundation Grant.

1962     *Ship of Fools* published with stunning success.

1967     Elected to the American Academy of Arts and Letters; receives the Gold Medal for Fiction.

1965     *Collected Stories.*

1966     National Book Award for Fiction; Pulitzer Prize for Fiction.

1970     *Collected Essays.*

1977     *The Never-Ending Wrong* (personal reminiscence of the Sacco-Vanzetti case).

         Lives in College Park, Maryland.

---

*After this publication the dates of individual stories are not entered.

## Notes on the Editor and Contributors

ROBERT PENN WARREN, born in Guthrie, Kentucky, in 1905. Educated at Vanderbilt University, University of California, Yale Graduate School, Oxford. Has taught at various universities, including Louisiana State University and Yale. Now professor of English, emeritus, at Yale. Has published ten novels, twelve volumes of poetry, and various critical works. Member of American Academy and Institute of Arts and Letters, American Academy of Arts and Sciences, a Chancellor of Academy of American Poets. He is the recipient of various awards and honorary degrees.

LOUIS STANTON AUCHINCLOSS, born in Lawrence, New York, in 1917. Educated at Groton, Yale, University of Virginia (law). Partner in firm of Hawkins, Delafield, and Wood, New York City. A number of novels, among the best known being *A Law for the Lion, The Great World and Timothy Colt,* and *The Embezzler.* A member of the American Academy and National Institute of Arts and Letters.

SYBILLE BEDFORD, an Englishwoman, born in Germany, in 1911, and educated privately. Among her numerous works are *A Journey to Don Otavio, The Best We Can Do,* and more recently, *Aldous Huxley, a Biography.* She is an expert on wines.

CLEANTH BROOKS, born in Murray, Kentucky, in 1906. Educated McTyre School, Vanderbilt University, Tulane University, Oxford (Rhodes Scholar, B.A., B. Litt. Various honorary degrees. Founder and an editor of the *Southern Review.* Gray Professor of English, Emeritus, Yale University. Cultural Attache, American Embassy, London, and a Senior Fellow of the National Endowment for the Humanities. Member of the American Academy and National Institute of Arts and letters and of the American Academy of Arts and Sciences. Numerous books and scholarly works, and text books, including *Modern Poetry and the Tradition, The Well Wrought Urn, Understanding Poetry* (with R. P. Warren), *Literary Criticism: A Short History* (with W. K. Wimsatt), *William Faulkner: The Yoknapatawpha Country, A Snapping Joy* and *William Faulkner: Toward Yoknapatawpha and Beyond.*

GEORGE CORE, born in 1939, educated at Vanderbilt University and the University of North Carolina. Editor of the *Sewanee Review.* He has contributed to various magazines including the *New Republic,* and has edited four books. Forthcoming is the *Literalist of the Imagination.*

SMITH KIRKPATRICK, born in Roseville, Arkansas, for many years a member of the English Department of the University of Florida. Recipient for the *Sewanee Review* Fellowship and a fellowship from the National Endowment for the Arts. Author of a novel and numerous articles.

M. M. LIBERMAN, born in New York City in 1921, is Professor of English at Grinnell College. His books include *A Preface to Literary Analysis, The Practice of Criticism,* and *Katherine Anne Porter's Fiction.*

HOWARD MOSS, a New Yorker, born in 1922, was educated at the University of Wisconsin, Columbia, and Harvard. He is the author of a number of distinguished volumes of poetry, and recipient of the National Book Award. He is the poetry editor of the *New Yorker,* and a member of the Academy and National Institute of Arts and Letters.

VICTOR SAWDON PRITCHETT, born in Ipswich, Suffolk, was educated at Alleyn's School. He is director of the *New Statesmen* of London and has held various academic posts in America. Among his numerous books are *The Living Novel, Collected Short Stories, London Perceived, A Cab at the Door, Blind Love* (stories), and *Balzac.* He has served as President of the English P.E.N. Club and as President of the International P.E. N. Club; is an honorary member of the American Academy and Institute of Arts and Letters and of the American Academy of Arts and Sciences, commander of the Order of the British Empire, and recipient of The Royal Society Literary Award.

KATHERINE ANNE PORTER: See Chronology in this volume.

MARK SCHORER, born in Sauk City, Wisconsin, in 1908. Educated University of Wisconsin, and Harvard (Ph.D.) Taught at various universities, including Harvard, and died in 1977 as Professor of English emeritus at the University of California, at Berkeley. He had served as a fellow of the Center of Advanced Study in Behavioral Sciences, a Bollingen Fellow, a Senior Fellow of the National Endowment for the Humanities. Among his numerous scholarly and critical words are *William Blake: The Politics of Vision, Sinclair Lewis, an American Life, The World We Imagine,* and *D. H. Lawrence.*

EDWARD G. SCHWARTZ: No data available.

THEODORE SOLOTAROFF, born in Elizabeth, New Jersey, in 1928; received his B.A. with honors from the University of Chicago in 1956, where he also did graduate work and taught. He has served as associate editor of *Commentary,* Editor of *Book Week (Herald Tribune)* and editor of the *New American Review.* Contributions to various magazines are now collected under the title *The Red Hot Vacuum.* He has edited a posthumous volume of essays by Isaac Rosenfeld.

EUDORA WELTY, born in Jackson, Mississippi in 1909, attended the Mississippi State College for Women, and did work at Wisconsin and Columbia.

She began her career as a writer with a collection of stories, *A Curtain of Green*, which gave ample promise of the quality of work to come. Her last books are *Losing Battles* and *The Optomist's Daughter*. She has received the Pulitzer Prize for fiction, The Gold Medal for the Novel, and the Gold Medal for Fiction from the National Institute of Arts and Letters, and the Creative Arts Medal for Fiction of Brandeis University. She is a member of the American Academy and Institute of Arts and Letters.

GLENWAY WESCOTT, born in 1901 in Kewaskum, Wisconsin, was educated at the University of Chicago, after which he lived a number of years abroad. Best known as the author of *The Apple of the Eye, The Grandmothers,* and *The Pilgrim Hawk,* he has written other works of fiction as well as poetry and criticism. He is a member of the American Academy and Institute of Arts and Letters, and is a winner of the Harper's Prize.

RAY B. WEST, JR., born in 1908, has taught at various universities, and received a Fulbright Fellowship and a Rockefeller Scholarship. He is the author of *The Art of Modern Fiction* and *Katherine Anne Porter* (in the University of Minnesota Pamphlets on American Writers Series) and has contributed stories and criticism to various magazines. He has edited the *Rocky Mountain Review* and the *Western Review.*

EDMOND WILSON, born in Red Bank, New Jersey, in 1895. Though occasionally practicing most literary forms, his great fame was based on his critical and historical work. Best known works probably *Axel's Castle, To the Finland Station, Patriotic Gore, The Dead Sea Scrolls.* He had been a practicing journalist at various times, on the editorial staff of *Vanity Fair* and the *New Republic,* and a staff reviewer for the *New Yorker.* Died 1972.

# Selected Bibliography

Emmons, Winfred S. *Katherine Anne Porter; The Regional Stories....* (Austin, Tex., Steck-Vaughn, 1967). Southwest Writers Series, 6.

Hardy, John Edward. *Katherine Anne Porter.* (New York: Frederick Ungar, 1973). Modern Literature Monographs.

Hartley, Lodwick Charles and Core, George, editors. *Katherine Anne Porter; a Critical Symposium.* (Athens: University of Georgia Press, 1969).

Hendrick, George. *Katherine Anne Porter.* (New York: Twayne Publishers, 1965). Twayne's United States Author Series, 90.

Kiernan, Robert F. *Katherine Anne Porter and Carson McCullers: A Reference Guide....* (Boston: G. K. Hall, 1976). Reference Guides in Literature, 9.

Krishnamurthi, M. G. *Katherine Anne Porter: A Study.* (Mysore: Rao and Raghaven, 1971).

Liberman, Myron M. *Katherine Anne Porter's Fiction....* (Detroit: Wayne State University Press, 1971).

Mooney, Harry John. *The Fiction and Criticism of Katherine Anne Porter* (Pittsburgh: University of Pittsburgh Press, 1957). Critical Essays in English and American Literature, 2.

——(Pittsburgh: University of Pittsburgh Press, 1962). Revised edition.

Nance, William L. *Katherine Anne Porter and the Art of Rejection.* (Chapel Hill: University of North Carolina Press, 1964).

Schwartz, Edward. *Katherine Anne Porter: A Critical Bibliography. Introduction by Robert Penn Warren.* (New York: New York Public Library, 1953). Reprinted from the *Bulletin of the New York Public Library* of May 1953.

Smith, William Jay. *A Rose for Katherine Anne Porter.* Drawings by Robert Dunn. (New York: Albondocani Press, 1970). Albondocani Press Publication, 9. A poem. 180 copies.

Waldrip, Louise and Bauer, Shirley Ann. *A Bibliography of the Works of Katherine Anne Porter, and a Bibliography of the Criticism of the Works of Katherine Anne Porter.* (Metuchen, N.J.: Scarecrow Press, 1969).

West, Ray Benedict. *Katherine Anne Porter.* (Minneapolis: University of Minnesota Press, 1963). Pamphlets on American Writers, 28.